Praise for

Clear Leadership

"In a time when everyone knows they need to 'get different' in their interactions and in the workplace, Bushe has given us a road map with plenty of examples."

Frederick A. Miller, CEO, The Kaleel Jamison Consulting Group, Inc.; coauthor, *The Inclusion Breakthrough* and *Be BIG: Step Up, Step Out, Be Bold*

"A wise teacher, Bushe first takes us by the hand and patiently leads us deep into the mush that constitutes so much of the noncommunication of organizational life. Then, after we have recognized ourselves as the creators of that mush, he gives us the knowledge and practical tools we can use to break through the mush and create the clarity essential to effective leadership."

Barry Oshry, president, Power & Systems Inc.; author, *Seeing Systems: Unlocking the Mysteries of Organizational Life*

"*Clear Leadership* is a thoughtful and thought-pr⸀   ⸀k explaining how to untangle the hidden mush and brus⸀   ⸀, your team's, and your organization's effectiveness. I⸀   ⸀n of theory and practice with extensive examp⸀   excellent resource for anyone who wan⸀   ⸀g with others at work and at home."

Robert J. Marshak, author, *C⸀*

"*Clear Leadership* provides new co⸀   ⸀o the thinking on leadership. The skill sets are not just for leaders,⸀   ⸀or everyone engaged in partnering with others to accomplish something; and in today's world, leading learning is just as important as leading performing."

David W. Jamieson, PhD, president, The Jamieson Consulting Group, Inc.; adjunct professor of management, Pepperdine University; adjunct professor, American University/NTL Institute MSOD Program

"Rarely does one find a business model with as much impact on human behavior in the work of transforming relationships and organizations as the 'experience cube.' This masterful and ingenious creation of Gervase Bushe has without reservation been our model of choice in dealing with executives and their aversion to having difficult and authentic conversations. I am in awe with the feedback our company receives after introducing the 'experience cube' to organizations and their leadership teams."

Greg W. Nichvalodoff, president, Inscape Consulting Group Inc.

"Bushe offers lessons for handling the most pressing problem for knowledge-based organizations—organizational mush. He goes beyond the question of what is taking place in troublesome partnerships and looks into the essential question of how to be a competent partner and collaborator. Brilliant and utterly useful. In Scandinavia, many of our most committed and skillful leaders within business, civil service, and politics apply the theory and practice of clear leadership."

Anders Risling, PhD, licensed psychologist; founder, Provins fem

clear leadership

clear leadership

sustaining real collaboration
and partnership at work

REVISED EDITION

Gervase R. Bushe

Davies-Black
an imprint of Nicholas Brealey Publishing
BOSTON • LONDON

Paperback edition first published by Davies-Black, an imprint of Nicholas Brealey Publishing, in 2010. Original hardcover edition first published in 2009.

20 Park Plaza, Suite 610
Boston, MA 02116, USA
Tel: + 617-523-3801
Fax: + 617-523-3708

3-5 Spafield Street, Clerkenwell
London, EC1R 4QB, UK
Tel: +44-(0)-207-239-0360
Fax: +44-(0)-207-239-0370

www.nicholasbrealey.com

Special discounts on bulk quantities are available to corporations, professional associations, and other organizations. For details, contact us at 888-273-2539.

ISBN: 978-0-89106-382-7

Printed in the United States of America.
17 16 15   7 8 9 10

Library of Congress Cataloging-in-Publication Data

Bushe, Gervase R.
   Clear leadership : sustaining real collaboration and partnership at work / Gervase R. Bushe.
—Rev. ed.
        p. cm.
   Rev. ed. of: Clear leadership : how outstanding leaders make themselves understood, cut through the mush, and help everyone get real at work. 2001.
   Includes bibliographical references and index.
   ISBN: 978-0-89106-227-1 (paperback)
   1. Leadership.   2. Communication in management.   3. Labor productivity.   4. Industrial management.   I. Title.
   HD57.7.B874 2008
   658.4'092—dc22   2008023917

REVISED EDITION
First printing 2009

Contents

Preface to the Revised Edition

In the first edition of *Clear Leadership*, I wrote about clear leaders as the kind of leaders required in empowered organizations. It has been ten years since I wrote that book, and my thinking has evolved. I now think of clear leadership as a set of skills that is indispensable to collaborative organizing. In this revised edition, I present clear leadership as a model of the skills required to lead organizational learning, clearing out interpersonal mush and sustaining collaboration, in the midst of work.

The clear leadership model is premised on the idea that collaborative organizing rests on people's willingness to be in partnership with those they interact with at work. Partnership is a relationship in which people feel equally responsible for the success of their joint project or process. The clear leadership model addresses two problems of collaborative organizing:

- We each create our own experience, although we think others create it.

- We are sense-making beings and make up stories about others so that we can fill in the gaps of what we know about their experience.

The interpersonal mush that results becomes toxic over time, and partnerships fail. Collaborative organizations revert to a command-and-control approach in order to get things done in spite of the mush.

Clear leadership proposes that the willingness and ability to clear out the mush determine the level of satisfaction with and the longevity of any partnership. Clearing out the mush requires learning from our collective experience. Clear leadership assumes that teams and organizations need to perform and learn simultaneously, and rather than being about how to lead performing, clear leadership is about how to lead learning.

Where there is unequal authority among the people in the partnership, the depth of clarity is limited by what the leader is willing to talk about. Through their actions more than their words, leaders set the level of mush that will or won't plague the system, so clear leadership is a valuable set of leadership skills. But it isn't just a set of skills for leaders—it's a set of skills for anyone who wants to be an effective partner.

Like the first book, this edition is organized around the four Selves. Each Self chapter has been revised. The biggest change is the chapter on the Curious Self. This is what first motivated me to rewrite the book. There is now substantially more material on parking reactions, and I've added two new elements: make it appealing and confront for insight. The chapter on the Appreciative Self has been revised significantly to look at the skills as used in partnership. The chapters on the Aware Self and the Descriptive Self have been updated with new stories and revised models. There is a lot more material on learning conversations and creating cultures of clarity, which are now discussed in two separate chapters. The chapters on interpersonal mush and self-differentiation and the four elements of experience have been updated, but there are no big changes.

The last two chapters in the first edition of the book are gone. The chapter on creating agreement no longer fits within the focus of this book, and the material in the chapter on barriers has been updated and placed as appropriate in different chapters. Included are a new conclusion, a new glossary, and a new appendix on the findings of research into clear leadership.

Acknowledgments

In the first edition of the book, I acknowledged the people in my past who have most influenced my understanding of human interaction and organizations. Here I want to acknowledge the people who have contributed most to my learning about clear leadership since that book was written. First I want to thank Terrie Conway, Barb Smith, Ann Ovstaas, and Sue Isles, who were at the Center for Excellence in Learning at the Vancouver Island Health Authority shortly after the first edition was published. They partnered with me to bring the material to life in a variety of ways and provided an excellent test bed and research site for studying clear leadership processes.

I also want to thank Gabi Cuff and Helen Lingham, who, through the Fraser Health Authority, initiated an incredible experiment in creating a culture of clarity in an organization responsible for all aspects of health in a population of millions. That work and the related studies we've done there have contributed perhaps the most to the revised understandings of the clear leadership model contained in this book. I also want to thank my partners in Europe, Provins Fem (The Fifth Province), and in Australia-Asia, nCompassHR, who have provided additional opportunities to build on and refine the concepts of clear leadership.

Finally, and most importantly, I want to thank my wife, Carmen Farrell, who spent many an evening listening as I read the first drafts of this book, offering useful feedback, and who more recently protected the space I needed to rewrite it. Carmen continues to be the person I learn the most from when it comes to self-differentiation and appreciation, and I am blessed to have her in my life.

Gervase Bushe
North Vancouver, Canada
October 2008

About the Author

Gervase Bushe (pronounced *Jervis Bush*) is a professor of leadership and organizational change in the Segal Graduate School of Business at Simon Fraser University in Vancouver, British Columbia, Canada. He is an award-winning author in the field of organizational change and development and regularly gives talks to corporate and public audiences around the world.

Bushe is president of Clear Learning Ltd., a company that develops leadership training and licenses others worldwide to teach his leadership models and skills. He has an extensive background in the design and delivery of highly experiential management training programs that significantly improve a manager's ability to lead people and facilitate change. He has trained managers and consultants on four continents.

He is also president of Discovery & Design Inc., and a partner in the Big Rapids Group, consulting firms whose past clients include Business Objects, the Canadian government, General Motors, and Shell Oil. He has worked with companies to redesign their structures, change their cultures, improve their customer satisfaction, and increase their profitability.

Bushe lives in the rain forest of North Vancouver, is the father of two young children, and likes to play the guitar and eat good food. You can find out more about him and his work at www.gervasebushe.ca.

Introduction

All over the world we are witnessing a revolution in organizing. Just as the industrial revolution created its new form of organization (bureaucracy), the information revolution is creating its own new form of organization. We are moving from command and control to collaboration, from organizing based on a few leaders telling everyone what to do to dispersed leadership, with managers, professionals, and teams authorized to make their own decisions. In the 1980s and 1990s, I was involved in designing these new organizational structures—team-based manufacturing, cross-functional teams, de-layered and networked organizations, and so on. The combination of information technology and new forms of organizing has resulted in an explosion of innovation in how we structure organizations, all intended to increase people's capacity to collaborate, to harness the intelligence, knowledge, and commitment of everyone in the system. Yet, few of these innovations have lived up to their promise. Studies of innovative work systems show that most of them revert back to command and control within a few years.

In the 1990s, I became fascinated with why that happens—why are we unable to sustain collaborative organizations? Almost all the leaders I meet in the public and private sectors want to create collaborative work systems. Almost all the professionals, managers, and employees I meet want to work in collaborative work systems. It's not a motivation problem. I've come to believe that the problem is caused by the out-moded definitions of leadership, teamwork, and people skills we are using. Our images of how to manage people and teams are still rooted in the past. We've created amazing new organizational forms, but we're try-ing to run them the same old way. The core of the problem, as I see it, is captured in the following story. It's a story about a branch of a company run by a man who prides himself on being a collaborative leader. All the managers who work there want to work in a collaborative organiza-tion. Many of them think that things in this organization are pretty good. See if it's at all familiar to you.

In their weekly managers' meeting, Lynette, a new manager in the customer service group, describes her unit's poor performance results and what she intends to do to improve them. As she talks, other managers listen politely, and a few (always the same ones) ask a few questions "for clarification." At the end of Lynette's presentation, the boss thanks her and says he looks forward to reviewing the results of her plans in another month, and the meeting moves on. But many things have not been said. More than one manager at the meeting does not really agree with Lynette's analysis of the problems but says nothing about it. Some say nothing because they want to avoid embarrassing Lynette, and others don't want to be seen as quarrel-some. Doug wonders if Lynette is competent and really understands the situation. Marlene believes Lynette knows perfectly well what is going on but has chosen not to talk about the whole story in order to protect people in her department. Bruce thinks Lynette is trying to protect herself by covering up the real problems in her unit. Sondra thinks Lynette is well-intentioned and her employees are taking advan-tage of her. Others have different thoughts and opinions, which they keep to themselves.

After the meeting, some of the managers get together in smaller gath-erings, over coffee or lunch, and the conversation turns to what they think is really going on in Lynette's department, what Lynette is really going to do about it, and her reasons for what she is and isn't saying. Different opinions are examined and discussed, and in future interac-tions with Lynette, people look for tips and clues that support or refute their opinions about her real thoughts and feelings. In time, these managers come to develop firm opinions about Lynette's motivations and competence. Of course, none of this is ever discussed or checked out with Lynette. Over the next few months, various images of Lynette, her strengths and weaknesses, her motivations, and her agenda develop among the smaller groups, and these come to guide interactions with Lynette.

Lynette is fully aware of what is going on in her department and has some excellent ideas about what to do about it. But due to the perceptions of her boss she developed before she became his subordinate, she believes it is not a good idea to be completely truthful, especially since some of his behaviors are part of the problem. She is a little surprised by the lack of cooperation she is receiving from her peers. They don't say anything in meetings, but she notices the lack of follow-through on things she thought they had agreed to do. She attributes this to people being too busy and overworked, unaware that her co-workers are actually concerned about the accuracy of her analysis of the problems and the motivations behind her plans. "Why waste energy and resources on a doomed effort?" is the thinking behind much of the noncooperation.

In particular, Lynette distrusts Bruce, whose cooperation she really needs. She sees him as unwilling to deal honestly, always covering his butt. She had heard that Bruce doesn't like women in management, and she found her initial interactions with him awkward. He seemed uptight and never looked at her directly. She hasn't talked about this with Bruce, of course. Instead, when his behavior got to be too much, she talked to Marlene, who helped her vent and strategize how to work around Bruce.

Bruce, in turn, distrusts Lynette, who never deals with him directly and always seems to be trying to go around him in ways that discredit him. The only explanation he has for her behavior is that she is trying to make him look bad, either so he'll be blamed for her problems or so she can take his job. He thinks Marlene, whom he finds a pain in the neck, is just that way because of her personality.

Unable to get others to put some real effort and energy into turning around her department, Lynette finds it difficult to implement her plans and get results, and this further reinforces the opinions of those who suspect she isn't really competent. In desperation, at another meeting, she brings up the lack of concrete support from other departments. A certain nervous tension fills the room, and her boss, a "team player," moves quickly to smooth things over. Lynette's complaint is not examined in much detail, and all the managers profess their willingness to be more supportive. While Lynette's co-workers are well-intentioned, their behaviors, and the beliefs behind them, don't really change. An endless cycle of lunchtime conversations, unexamined assumptions, and avoidance of issues results in continued mediocre results, which everyone assumes to be pretty much normal.

Interpersonal Mush

I believe this story is all too representative of what takes place in the average organization. Interactions between people are based on stories they've made up about each other that they haven't checked out directly with the other person. I call this condition "interpersonal mush," and I am convinced that collaboration is not sustainable in interpersonal mush. In this book, I explain where interpersonal mush comes from and what it does to destroy the potential for collaboration between people. I describe the skills that are required to clear out the mush and create interpersonal clarity. Through numerous anecdotes and examples, I show why interpersonal clarity is essential for sustaining collaboration and how to make it happen.

Partnership with Others

In this book, I argue that the key to leading and working in collaborative work systems is your ability to create and sustain partnership with others. Partnership is a relationship between two or more people who are jointly committed to the success of whatever process or project they are engaged in.[1] Collaborative teams and organizations require people to be in partnership. And for the most part, people want to be in partnership with their bosses, subordinates, colleagues, customers, and suppliers. They want to be working with others who are committed to their mutual success. People always enter a partnership—whether a business partnership, a new team-based organization, or a marriage—believing that it will be great. All too often, however, the partnership breaks down in acrimony and hard feelings. This is a book on how to keep that from happening. But first, to lay some groundwork for what comes later, I need to talk a bit about organization theory, psychology, and philosophy.

```
PARTNERSHIP IS . . .
A relationship between two or more people who are
jointly committed to the success of whatever process
or project they are engaged in.
```

What About Organization Theory?

The information age first began to disrupt our old forms of organizing when the speed of technological innovation got too fast. Command-and-control structures are the most profitable way to organize if you can figure out the one best way to do something and then run that sucker for all it's worth. The problem is that things keep changing so fast that effective organizations need to be able to change and adapt—at increasing speeds. Command-and-control structures are not very good at that. The only way they can manage learning and adaptation is to spend lots of time and money on things that aren't directly related to producing—things like research and development, creating coordination teams and positions, sending people away from work to training and meetings, and so on. Organizations face a paradox because the things that support learning and innovation seem to do so at the expense of efficiency and performance. Everyone recognizes that in order to keep performing in the long run, you have to be learning, but in the short run, learning and performing seem to work against each other. Think for a moment what it's like to learn any skill. When you first start learning, you aren't performing very well. As your learning curve goes up, your performance improves, but at the point at which you are performing well, you aren't learning much anymore.

By the 1970s, we had two different kinds of organizing structures: those that were efficient (but not innovative) and those that were innovative (but not efficient). What seemed to work was to use efficient structures in stable businesses and innovative structures in unstable business environments. That was fine for a while, but the problem now is that all business environments are unstable. Everyone needs to be adapting and changing, yet organizations still need to be efficient to be successful—they need to produce more products and services at a lower cost than their competitors do or they will go out of business. How can we be efficient when the world is changing so fast?

The holy grail of organization design in the twenty-first century is work systems that can be efficient and innovative at the same time, ones that learn and perform simultaneously. This book is an attempt to answer one part of that puzzle. It's about how to create teams and organizations in which people can learn from their collective experience while they are working. Clear leadership is about how to lead learning in the midst of performing. Virtually all the books written on leadership in the past one hundred years are about how to lead performing. How do you get a group of people to accomplish some objective? That's half the problem, and we have a lot of answers to that problem. But the other half of the problem is, how do we learn from our collective experience so that we can keep improving our processes of organizing? Before we can answer that question, we need to acknowledge some things about human experience.

The Psychology of Experience

The clear leadership model is based on two mental processes that make it difficult for us to learn from our collective experience. These are the nature of experience and sense making.

We Create Our Own Experience

Ask five different people what happened at any event and you will get five different answers. Some will be more alike and some will be more different, but the point here is that everyone is having a unique experience. I was once talking to an executive team about these ideas and saying that the problem with learning from our collective experience is that everyone is having a different experience. Coincidentally, one executive excused himself to leave the room while we talked, and the conversation turned to the recent establishment of a weekly "state of the union" meeting. One of the managers said that the meetings were uninspiring and probably not a good idea. The manager who had left returned, and the leader said, "Let's check that different experience thing. Murray, what do you think about the new weekly meetings?" Murray said, "Fantastic! They're really turning people on." We all fell off our chairs laughing. But there it is.

I believe the most basic truth about humans is that we are constantly generating a stream of percepts, the building blocks of experience. We do this when we are awake and when we are asleep. We do this with or without sensory stimulation. From a position of the most extreme scientific doubt, we can never be sure that what we perceive is real (have you seen the movie *The Matrix*?), but we can be sure that we perceive. There is strong evidence that our perceptions are shaped by what is going on both outside us and inside us. But even without anything going on outside us, we will continue to generate perceptions. The sensory deprivation tank, where a person floats on water in a completely dark and soundless chamber, proved that. If you stay in a sensory deprivation tank long enough, you will start to create experiences that you can't distinguish from what we normally think of as reality. We call these experiences "hallucinations."

Percept generation is a constant, ceaseless process unless you have spent many years and a great deal of effort learning to quiet the mind. Few people have. As a result, it is almost always valid to assume that you and others are constantly creating a stream of percepts. In this book, I call this stream of percepts, and your internal reaction to those percepts, your "experience." Even as you are reading this sentence, you are having an experience. Your experience is made up of the percepts you are generating and your reactions to those percepts. Your experience comes from the inside out.

The perceptions you are generating are part of your experience, and so are the reactions you are having to those perceptions. These are the thoughts, ideas, judgments, feelings, bodily sensations, wants, and desires you are having as you read this. For example, somebody might be thinking, "This is obvious; I already know this." Another might be thinking, "This is an interesting way of putting these ideas." Someone might be feeling frustrated by how "academic" it is and wondering if the book is worth reading any further. Others might be excited to find me putting words to things they've had a sense of before. The possible reactions to the varying perceptions of readers like you are extensive, maybe even infinite. That's how it is with human experience.

Note that my way of talking about human experience is different from another common way of using the word: as a description of what happened to you in the past. From the point of view of clear leadership, experience is not what you've done in the past or the things you put on your résumé. Experience is not what happens to you but the reactions you create out of what happens to you moment by moment.[2] And so a fundamental assumption is that you, I, and everyone else all create our own experience.

If you can believe that everyone reading this book is having a personally unique experience, then I pose a question to you: Who is having the right experience? In a collaborative or partnership-based organization, the answer is "everyone." But you see this makes the issue of how we learn from our collective experience a lot more complicated than just reflecting together on what happened before. I think most of what goes on when people try to sort out problems of collaborating are attempts to figure out who is having the right experience. I'm convinced that these are unproductive conversations and reduce people's interest in trying to learn from their collective experience. I also think this is one of the reasons why experiments in highly collaborative organizing revert to command and control. In the command-and-control organization, it's clear who is having the correct experience—the boss. So we can all line up behind that.

Sense Making

Sense making is the second key mental process that lies at the root of the problems Lynette and her co-workers face. As human beings, we appear to have a deep need to make sense of ourselves and of others. When we make sense, we explain our experiences within a framework that gives consistency and meaning to what we perceive. There are many aspects to this that I will take up in the next chapter, but let me point out here the key thing for being in partnership. When we try to make sense of other people's behavior, we almost always make up a story about it. That's what Lynette's peers were doing with her. They were making up stories about her "real" thoughts, feelings, and intentions.

How much of a story is pure fantasy or is based on some reality depends on two things: the quality of a person's observation and the willingness of those being observed to describe their experience. Neither of these behaviors is well developed in organizations at the beginning of the twenty-first century. Skills of human observation depend first and foremost on self-observation and self-awareness, and these are not taught in schools or in many families. The skill of describing our experience to others is also not taught in schools or in many families and is more often frowned upon. As a consequence, most interpersonal encounters, especially those in work organizations, are best described as people having different experiences while making up stories about what is going on in everyone else's mind, stories that are never checked out.

These stories then become the input for further episodes of sense making, shaping future perceptions and experiences that build on and reinforce one another, further making us certain that what we believe we see is the truth, and we almost never check that out with the people we are making up the truth about. Executives make up a story about workers, and workers make up a story about executives. Managers in one department make up stories about managers in another department. People who work together every day make up stories about one another. On and on it goes, so organizations are composed of multiple, competing fantasies of what is going on and why, stories that are rarely discussed openly and almost never examined in a way that could prove or disprove them.

In order to build organizations where partnership flourishes, we have to work with, rather than against, these two human processes. People are not going to stop creating their own experience, and they are not going to stop trying to make sense of one another. The problem is that we don't acknowledge these processes and make them visible. They aren't things we talk about. Until we talk about them, we can't manage them. Clear leadership is a set of skills that will enable you to make these processes visible, make it possible to discuss them in ways that build partnership, and lead to continuous improvement in your relationships, teams, and organizations.

What Is True?

The skills of clear leadership reflect a set of philosophical assumptions about people and society that are different from what most of us grew up with. Throughout this book I use the phrase "telling the truth of your experience." It's an awkward phrase but the best I've been able to come up with for talking about a kind of truth that is different from "the truth."

Objective and Subjective Truth

Recent philosophers assume that there is more than one kind of truth.[3] I bring this up because one of the reasons for the lack of clarity in organizations is the tendency to try to assess everything against the standards of objective truth. When it comes to managing and working with people, most of the truths we are dealing with are not objective. That is probably why people who are well trained in matters of objective truth, like engineers and accountants, are often viewed as having poor people skills. I don't think it is an innate deficiency, just a lack of understanding and training in what the truth of experience is and how to go about thinking about it, talking about it, and learning from it.

Even as children, we learn the difference between objective and subjective truth. On the one hand, objective truth is truth that can be measured and validated independent of your percepts or mine. This is the truth of science and technology. Subjective truth, on the other hand, is based entirely on what is going on in each individual. For example, there is an objective truth to how much you get paid at work. What you think, feel, and want regarding how much you get paid is a subjective truth. Objective truth is based on our ability to objectively measure whatever we are talking about. When someone says what he thinks, feels, or wants, how do you know if it is true? Subjective truth has to do with the quality of a person's awareness and the authenticity with which she expresses it. When I talk about the truth of your experience, I'm referring to subjective truth. While modern society has made great strides in developing ways of assessing and validating objective truths, we are still novices at assessing and validating subjective truths. Yet subjective truth is an essential part of working with people, and its importance is amplified in collaborative work systems. One of the challenges of clearing out the mush, learning from collective experience, and sustaining partnerships is to get clear about your subjective truth and the subjective truths of the people you work with. It is impossible if we try to treat subjective truths in the same way we treat objective truths.

Intersubjective Truth

There is a third kind of truth, intersubjective truth. This consists of things that are true because you and I agree they are. So much of what is true in organizations is intersubjective truth. What is success? What is quality? Is

Bob a good boss? What is an adequate return on investment? The correct answers to questions like these in any organization are intersubjective truths. Intersubjective truths are the essence of social reality, and they are always co-created. All the people involved contribute to creating, maintaining, and changing the reality or truths they face at work. Again, we don't have very developed methods of assessing and validating, or even thinking about, this kind of truth. Building collaboration among people, however, is a lot about intersubjective truth, and the skills in this book are very concerned with understanding, creating, and changing intersubjective truths.

The Skills of Clear Leadership

Even though this book is about leadership, I want to be clear that these skills are useful for all persons, regardless of their position, who work in any organization that is based on principles of teamwork, personal initiative, and partnership. All people, regardless of role, provide leadership when they do something that helps a group or organization achieve its goals or increase its effectiveness. Anytime someone helps the members of a group increase their clarity, learn from experience, and improve their ways of working together, that person is providing leadership. You can provide leadership whatever your position in an organization. I will show you how managers and professionals use these skills to gain clarity and build partnerships among people who work together. The skills of clear leadership are

- Self-awareness
- Descriptiveness
- Curiosity
- Appreciation

In this book, I want to describe what mastery of these skills looks like. When you master something, you embody it. When a virtuoso guitarist plays music and a great fencer fences, they don't think about what they are doing: something in them takes over. The skill itself takes over. Similarly, to master the skills in this book, a person must be able to embody them— to allow them, in a sense, to take over. In chapters 5 through 8, I describe in detail the nature of the Aware Self, the Descriptive Self, the Curious Self, and the Appreciative Self.

The Aware Self knows, moment to moment, what she is thinking, feeling, observing, and wanting. She understands the processes she uses to create her experience. She is clear about how much of her experience is based on facts and how much is her sense making.

The Descriptive Self is able to help other people empathize with him. He can describe all the facets of his experience clearly. He is able to describe difficult, confrontational aspects of his experience in a way that doesn't make others defensive but elicits a willingness to listen and understand.

The Curious Self is a master at uncovering other people's experience. She is able to observe, question, and probe until she fully understands, as much as is humanly possible, what her partners are thinking, feeling, and wanting, often increasing the other's awareness in the process.

The Appreciative Self works through imagination and conversation to amplify the best in people and processes. He builds partnership and a willingness to learn collectively from experience by seeing the normal human virtues in every person and bringing those out in interaction.

I will show you how to integrate these skills to create learning conversations in which people clear out the mush, learn from their collective experience, and build partnerships that really do lead to superior organizational performance.

The Attribute of Self-Differentiation

Clear leadership isn't just skills and techniques. The personal attribute that underlies a person's ability to use clear leadership and create an atmosphere that supports others in using these skills is her level of self-differentiation. A person acts in a differentiated way when she is able to be separate from and simultaneously connected to other people. This means that her experience is not simply in reaction to other people. Her thoughts and feelings cannot be hijacked by other people. She doesn't attain this state of certainty and clarity by isolating herself from others, however. A differentiated person wants to know what other people think and feel but does not take responsibility for their experience or demand that they have different thoughts and feelings. Most of us can learn to be more differentiated in our interactions at work. Most managers are too separate from their employees and disconnected from their employees' experience, or they are overly connected, so their own experience becomes wrapped up in that of their employees. In chapter 3, I describe these issues in much greater detail.

The Issue of Authority

Authority is an important thread that is woven throughout this book. Contrary to popular images and poorly reasoned books on the subject, collaborative work systems do not decrease or eliminate authority even if they do flatten hierarchies and reduce command and control. Authority and hierarchy are two separate things. Authority is the power to make and enforce decisions. Collaborative organizations create much more authority than command-and-control systems do because authority is dispersed widely in collaborative organizations. More people are authorized to make decisions and take actions that obligate others in the organization to make complementary decisions and take complementary actions. That is one of the reasons why you need many people using the skills of clear leadership for these organizations to work well. But collaborative organizations still require some hierarchy for focus and direction. Hierarchy, because of the uneven power it creates, gets in the way of people telling their truths to one another. The many ways in which managerial authority is a two-edged sword, both supporting and blocking clear leadership, are discussed in various parts of this book.

A Clear Leadership Example

Here is a condensed version (the actual episode lasted more than thirty minutes) of a true story that exemplifies a group of managers learning from their collective experience. Their leader, Pierre, is using clear leadership skills with a subordinate, Stan, who is also using the skills of clear leadership. It is an example of a group working in a culture of clarity.

It has been four months since the president, Pierre, declared his and the board's intention to change the organization's sole emphasis on Product A, which has been its focus for the past ten years, and introduce a new product, B. As he sits in a meeting of his executive committee, Pierre is worried that Stan, the vice president of the unit responsible for Product A, is resisting this change. He was very unhappy with Stan's performance at yesterday's board meeting, where Stan seemed confused and not in line with the new strategy. Pierre was also concerned by the very negative reaction some board members voiced about Stan after Stan left the room. He values Stan, who has been an outstanding performer for many years, but realizes that he really doesn't know what Stan thinks about the change in strategy. As the discussion turns to the new strategy, Pierre shows leadership in telling the truth of his experience.

Pierre: *Stan, the board meeting yesterday created confusion for me, and I want to get clear with you about where each of us stands on the Product B strategy. I raise this here because it affects all of us, and we all need to be clear on what each of us thinks about this. So let me begin. I was concerned by your apparent confusion yesterday, as I thought we had discussed the new product strategy fully and were all in complete agreement. It raises some doubt in my mind about whether you really support the Product B strategy, and, frankly, I'm starting to be concerned that you might resist it because you're afraid it will take resources away from Product A. I want you to be clear about where you stand on this, and I want us to find a way for you to feel fully behind both products, A and B.*

Stan, who is visibly disturbed by Pierre's remarks, asks questions to get more clarity about Pierre's perceptions before reacting to what he has heard.

Stan: *Could you tell me what, exactly, I did that caused you concern at the meeting?*

Pierre: *A number of times when you were fielding questions, you made statements that are contrary to the strategy the board has endorsed. For example, when Brian asked about the marketing strategy, you talked about building on the brand recognition of Product A even though we've decided it's better to keep the two products distinct in our clients' eyes.*

Stan: *Anything else?*

Pierre: *Well, yes. Your response to Marilyn about product launch and what you said to Herschel about expected cost of capital were not what we had agreed to.*

Stan: *Just so I'm clear, Pierre, can you tell me what you think I said and what we've agreed to?*

Pierre describes what he heard Stan say at the meeting and what he thinks was wrong with it.

Stan: *OK, I think I'm clear on what you're unhappy about, but before I respond to what you've just said, Pierre, I want to check if there are any other reasons why you think I might not be fully behind the change.*

Pierre: *Well, since you asked, I was taken aback a week or so ago by a conversation I had with Barbara* [one of Stan's direct reports], *who seemed to have some pretty confused fears about what effect this change is going to have on your department. Then I noticed a similar set of thoughts coming from Kevin* [another of Stan's managers]. *It got me wondering just how much of that is coming from you.*

Stan: *Were they talking about having to shift people to the new business unit?* [Pierre nods.] *Yeah, I know what you're talking about. Anything else causing you to wonder where I'm at?*

Pierre: *No, that's about it.*

Stan: *OK, well, let me start by saying I'm somewhat surprised by all this. I had no idea that things went sideways at the board meeting, so I guess I'm glad you are telling me about it, and I do want you to know that I'm fully behind Product B. Let me deal with the meeting issues first. With Herschel, I think I just must not have gotten my thoughts out clearly because I agree with what you're saying about our financing and how much debt we're willing to take on. But I have to tell you that I am confused about our marketing strategy and launch plans, because I thought we had decided to build on the brand recognition and tie-in with Product A.*

Pierre: *No, no—that was decided at least a month ago.*

Robert: *I have to tell you, Pierre, I'm with Stan on that one. I thought the opposite as well.*

Susan: *I didn't know a decision had been made.*

Pierre: *I don't understand this. We talked about this issue for weeks, and then at the last meeting, the board's strategy committee made the decision to keep the two products separate and distinct in our sales campaign.*

Robert: *Well, I remember the discussions, but I thought we were all leaning toward product tie-in. I don't remember hearing that the strat committee had made a decision.*

Errol: *I knew about it from the meeting you had with the marketing group, Pierre, but I don't know if it ever came up here.*

Pierre: *Oh heck, I thought I had announced that at our last meeting.*

At this point, Pierre tells the group about the decision the board's strategy committee had made and the rationale behind it. A discussion ensues, and it becomes clear that this is the first time the group has heard and talked about this decision.

Stan: *To finish off with the issues you were bringing up, Pierre, it's true that people in my unit are afraid they're going to lose resources to Product B. I don't think it's going to be nearly as drastic as some people fear, but obviously some resources are going to have to be redirected, and we haven't really decided yet on what this is going to be. Frankly, I think the sooner we decide, the better, because the uncertainty is starting to fuel a lot of speculation, and since I don't really know what is going to happen, there's not a lot I can tell folks to calm them down. But you need to understand that, as far as I'm concerned, bringing on Product B is absolutely essential to the future health of our company, and I am 100 percent behind it.*

Pierre: *I'm glad to hear that, Stan, but why are your people not on the bus, too?*

Stan: *Oh, I don't think anyone questions the wisdom of moving into the Product B space, Pierre. It's just that no one's sure what the ramifications for Product A will be, and that's creating a lot of rumors and unfounded gossip. Last week someone asked me if we were closing down the Product A unit.*

Pierre: *That's ridiculous! Product A is the core of this company. Isn't that obvious?*

Stan: *I think it is to us, but there does seem to be some confusion in the ranks.*

Errol: *I'm having a similar experience, Stan. A couple of days ago, I overheard a conversation in the cafeteria, where some people were guessing how the Product A unit was going to be reorganized.*

Stan: *I think the buzz coming from below is causing some of the concerns you are hearing from my managers, Pierre.*

Pierre: *Are any of the rest of you picking this up?*

The group launches into a discussion about the effects the organization's culture, with ten years of sole focus on Product A, is having on implementing the new strategy. Some of this is news to Pierre, and together the group develops a picture of a pattern of misperceptions and groundless fears that are surfacing in the organization. Everyone affirms that Product A is still the backbone of the company and that a new emphasis on Product B should not mean a decrease in support for Product A.

Pierre: *We'd better do something to clear up the confusion we've created. I think Colette's team on resourcing Product B is just about finished. I'll ask her to speed up, and we can use their report to make some clear announcements throughout the company that will end all the uncertainties about who is going to be working where. Susan, can you get the communications people geared up for this? I want to make it a priority. We don't need a lot of unfounded fears and rumors getting in the way of moving Product B to market quickly and effectively.*

I'm sure glad we had this conversation, though I'm a little sorry it started because of my misgivings about you, Stan. I see that I'm somewhat responsible for what happened at the board yesterday, so I guess I owe you an apology.

Stan: *Thanks, Pierre, but I have to take some responsibility for not having checked out my facts before the presentation. I wonder if we can huddle before board meetings in the future, just to make sure I have my ducks in line.*

Pierre: *I think that would be a good idea.*

And the group moves on to deal with other items on the agenda.

Sound like fantasyland? If it does, you have spent too much of your working life in the interpersonal mush of organizations where leaders do not create a culture of clarity. You may not be able to see it yet, but by the end of this book you will recognize the set of critical skills the people in this story are using to create this interaction. Here you see an organizational learning conversation in action. I believe it is the basis for any sustained high performance in organizations that want their employees and managers to feel committed, take the initiative, negotiate agreements together, and coordinate their actions with one another. That is what this book is about.

Some months before the event I've described took place, this was a typical organization where people didn't talk about their perceptions and concerns openly, face-saving and backroom conversations were the order of the day, and people often didn't know what others thought of them and didn't treat one another as trustworthy individuals. As it turned out, virtually all the people in this organization were decent, trustworthy, and yearning to work in an organization that didn't stress them out. It was not their lack of integrity or intention that made their system the way it was. It was simply a lack of the basic skills that you will learn about in this book. Once they had those, and authorities were willing to create a culture of clarity in which telling the truth of one's experience was valued, the result was a place where people could talk easily and honestly about what was really on their minds and so make sane and sensible decisions that they could follow through on.

Clear leadership is about creating clarity in every interaction and every group you are a part of. It requires understanding the nature of experience and the reasons for the difficulty involved in getting people to tell the truth of their experience to one another. So let's turn first to one of the key assumptions required for building cultures of clarity—that we are sense-making beings—and examine the critical implications of that understanding for the kinds of organizations we create.

1

Where Interpersonal Mush Comes From and What It Does to Organizations

The content may be different, but the process described in the story below goes on in organizations every day, all over the world. It seems to be a process beyond culture, something that is true of all human beings. In this book I call it "sense making." Sense making is making up a story about other people's experience (what they are thinking, feeling, and/or wanting) to fill in the gaps in our knowledge. Read the following scenario and see if it is at all familiar to you. Bill, the general manager, is widely considered one of the most collaborative executives in this organization, and he has a team that by all conventional measures works well together.

Bill, the general manager for the eastern division, entered the room where his direct reports had been waiting ten minutes for their weekly meeting to begin. They knew he had been on the phone to headquarters on the West Coast and paid close attention to his appearance as he entered. Rumors had been circulating about impending budget cuts, and given the losses over the past three quarters, none in the room would be surprised if they happened. Bill briskly apologized for being late and launched into the first item on the agenda, a report on a project in one of the departments. The meeting continued to follow the agenda, and once all items were finished, Bill immediately left the room and returned to his office.

After the meeting, people met in twos and threes, sometimes including others who had not been at the meeting, to compare perceptions. Shirley thought Bill seemed flushed and angry when he entered the room. Jason didn't notice the anger but agreed that Bill had been a little more curt than usual and seemed eager to leave the meeting and get back to something. They discussed how unusual it was for Bill to leave so quickly and not stick around to chat for a while. They concluded that the phone call from the West Coast must have been bad news and wondered why Bill wasn't willing to share it with them. Shirley said, "It's just not like Bill to leave us all up in the air like that."

Meanwhile, Roger and Fernando were gathered around Kimberly's cubicle, where she was telling them she had heard from a colleague on the West Coast that another division had gotten a sizable cut in its operating budget. Fernando and Roger thought that Bill wasn't "acting normal" in the meeting and figured that he had been told they would be facing cuts as well. They wondered why he didn't say anything about it in the meeting, and all three tossed around theories ranging from the idea that he had been told not to say anything until there was a company-wide announcement to the thought that he was going to be firing someone in the room and wanted to wait until he could tell that person privately before announcing it. Roger mentioned that he was already prepared to take 20 percent out of his department's budget, and Fernando said he'd better start planning for that as well. They parted agreeing to let one another know if they heard anything new.

In another part of the building, Jennifer was telling Margaret about the last time she had seen Bill "so upset," in a previous job when Bill's boss had closed down a project that Bill felt was close to success and hadn't been given the opportunity to prove itself. "But you know," Jennifer went on, "Bill is a company man, and he closed it down without ever publicly grumbling about it. At least I never heard him say anything about it." Margaret agreed that Bill never lost his cool; it was something they admired about him.

Do you recognize the process in this story? We are all sense-making beings, that is, we will work at trying to make sense of people who are important to us until we are satisfied. We are all detectives in the interpersonal mush, building hypotheses and theories, looking for clues, fit-ting the pieces together until we have a satisfactory answer to the mystery of why someone did or said something. Then we stop until the next mystery comes along that needs to be solved. It appears that we don't do it only when we're trying to make sense of others. We even do it to ourselves. There is evidence to show that we make up stories about ourselves so that we can make sense of what we see ourselves doing,[1] but in this book, I'll focus only on how we do that with other people.

In the story above, Bill's direct reports are trying to make sense of his behavior at the meeting. Notice a few common characteristics of sense-making processes. One is that Bill's actions are being placed in a larger context: the knowledge that the division has been losing money and the rumor of impending budget cuts. In order for us to make sense of something, it has to fit with what we already believe to be true, the bigger picture. Another characteristic is that what Bill doesn't say or do is given just as much scrutiny as what he does say and do. Nonverbal actions are given meaning. Notice that people are making up fantasies about Bill's experience, about what is going on in his head. One thinks he's angry; another thinks he was eager to leave the room. Also, people are trying to understand him within the general picture they have of him ("Bill is a company man"). For us to be satisfied with our sense making, current stories have to fit with past sense making. A third characteristic is that people are talking to others for the purpose of trying to make sense of Bill. We rarely go to the person we are trying to make sense of to check out our stories— we turn to third parties. That is especially true when we don't feel good about the behavior we are trying to make sense of, and that is what fuels much of the interpersonal mush in organizations. When the event we are trying to understand is new or different, it's as though some part of us knows that we are on thin ice in trying to make sense of others, so we seek out someone else to help us. Sometimes this isn't even a person in the organization—a spouse or close friend will do.

The sense-making process is over when we have a story that we treat as "the truth." We no longer treat the story as a possible scenario but accept it as what happened, and we align our future perceptions and actions based on these "facts" unless new information surfaces that forces us to revise our story. If the new information is vague and ambiguous, however, it can easily be ignored or distorted to fit.

Are you curious about what was going on with Bill in the story above?

As it turns out, Bill was preoccupied with an important phone call he had received from his boss. The senior VP had just told him that he agreed with the argument Bill had been making for months, that divisional losses were due to his division being underresourced, especially in sales and marketing. Because cuts were being made in other parts of the company, Bill's boss did not see how the division's budget could be increased at this time, but he was prepared to fight to ensure that its budget was not cut if Bill could put together a convincing business plan and find a way to transfer his existing budget into sales. If revenues improved, the VP said he would work to increase the budget in the future. He also advised Bill not to say anything about it because it was far from a sure thing, and with cuts going on elsewhere in the company, others might try to work against them if rumors started circulating.

In this case, people were way off in the stories they were making up, but the accuracy of our stories doesn't matter—what matters is recognizing that this process is endemic to human relations. It cannot be stopped. So in work relationships, we have two choices: tell them what is going on in us or let people make up stories about what is going on in us. If you don't tell them, they make it up. Those are your only options.

What could Bill do, having been told not to mention the substance of the phone call? Well, what did Bill do? Like most people, he thought that if he said nothing, then people wouldn't think there was anything going on. Wrong. People who work closely together day in and day out are picking up all kinds of cues all the time (and making them up, too). Those with authority are the most closely watched for clues about what is really going on. Bill had no idea of the impact he was having on the people in the meeting. At work, people will notice any incongruity in the boss and use it as fodder for new rounds of in-depth sense making. Bill had a number of choices for how to influence the sense making that was bound to follow after such an important phone call, but these were pretty much out of his awareness. In this book, I argue that the best strategy is almost always to be a Descriptive Self, that is, to tell the truth of your in-the-moment experience. Let me give you an example of what Bill could have said.

Bill: *I just had an important call from my boss. I am not at liberty to tell you what it was about, and that troubles me, because I'd like us all to be honest and up front with each other, but I also understand his concern and agreed to stay silent. There may or may not be some good news for us in the near future. I want you to know the call was not bad news. I'm excited and a little distracted, but I think that is all I can say, and it's important right now that we don't start any rumors, so, please, just hang on and let's continue with our meeting as planned.*

If Bill had said something like this, he would have been letting the people he works with see what was going on in him at that moment without violating any agreement he had made with his boss. He would be describing his here-and-now experience, so people would not be forced to make it up. Any stories they made up afterward would likely be more accurate, making the interpersonal climate clearer and less mushy. Would saying this stop people from sense making? Probably not. They might still meet in small groups after the meeting to fantasize about what the good news could be. But it would stop a rush of negative, fearful fantasies that had managers spending their time thinking about how to chop 20 percent off their budgets and all the fallout from that being passed down through the division.

More important, however, is the effect of being a Descriptive Self day in and day out. It's not about the one-time hit of telling the truth of your experience but about the long-term impact on an organization when people tell the truth of their experience. When they do this, they are building a culture of clarity. If Bill had built a culture of clarity, his subordinates would have felt comfortable asking him directly about what was going on and talking about their fears so that they would have his direct input into the stories they settled on as "the truth." Any one of them would have felt comfortable saying something like, "Bill, I know you were on a call to headquarters and you seem a little distracted. Naturally, I'm wondering if that was bad news about our budget." But such an inquiry doesn't often happen in an organization characterized by interpersonal mush. People don't ask each other directly what is going on, so a lot of energy goes into sense making. In a climate of interpersonal clarity instead of mush, people would be more willing to suspend their sense making, believing that they would get a satisfactory explanation from Bill as soon as possible, because they have had that experience in the past.

Do people have to know what is going on in the boss's head? No, not if the boss just wants people to do what they're told. Working at gaining and maintaining interpersonal clarity isn't necessary if you just want people to follow instructions or deliver on whatever has been negotiated and agreed to. But it is essential to partnership—to relationships in which people are working together, all taking responsibility for the success of what they are working on. Collaboration and partnership require people to be internally committed, and that calls for a certain level of equality and give-and-take. For subordinates, the easiest move in the world is to give responsibility for success to the boss and sit back and just do what they're told. That move is so easy that any boss who wants to be in partnership with the people who work for him has to struggle against it and work consistently at spreading responsibility throughout the system.

Telling the truth of our experience is really quite simple, but it's so rare in organizations that some businesspeople at first react to my message as if I were from Mars. To them, interpersonal mush is a normal way of life, and anything else is a utopian dream. So let's pause for a moment and consider why most relationships at work exist in interpersonal mush.

Why We Live in Interpersonal Mush

First, a technical definition: the term *interpersonal mush* describes an interaction that's based on stories people have made up about one another and have not checked out. You generally don't find out if your sense making is accurate unless you ask. Most people do not describe what is going on in themselves unless they are asked. It doesn't seem like a natural thing to do. This tendency does not necessarily come from malicious intentions, fear, distrust, or any other negative source. It is just that we haven't been taught to describe our experience. Some people are even taught not to do so; they've been told that describing their experience makes them seem too self-centered. Most of us have never even thought that it might be useful or important to describe our experience to others. We have few role models of Descriptive Selves, and even when we are around those who do use clear leadership skills successfully, it's not immediately obvious what they are doing. I remember one very bright engineer in my executive MBA class who, at first, said I was nuts to tell her to be a Descriptive Self at work. A few weeks later, she came to class flush with the realization, which she had come to during a regular meeting at work, that the three most influential engineers in her organization were also the most Descriptive Selves at work.

Growing Up

We learn most about how to act around other people in the first group we belong to, our family of origin. In our families, we were children and our parents were adults. As such, there was a huge imbalance in experience, knowledge, and power. There are lots of things that might go on in adults' lives that they would not want to describe to their children (e.g., spousal problems, work fears). The problem with saying nothing is that children make up stories about what is going on and why they are excluded.

As children get older, they develop their own reasons not to tell their parents everything that is going on in their lives, so the parents make up stories about their children's lives. In most families, parents and children come, to some extent, to make up what is going on in each other's minds. Even the least dysfunctional family develops a level of interpersonal mush that children learn is the normal way to interact with others.

Then we hit adolescence, when normal developmental processes make us desperately want to fit in and belong. Most of us learn that it is not OK to have a different experience from our peers—that we are expected to have similar thoughts, feelings, and wants if we want to fit in. Then there is the double whammy of sexual relations, in which there is so much vulnerability. We learn to look for clues, get information from third parties, but never ever approach the object of our interest head-on—too scary. High school is a perfect training ground for living in interpersonal mush; it's where we learn how to keep up appearances and repress renegade thoughts, feelings, and wants. We learn how to operate in a world where it really isn't safe to be fully open and different, and we don't expect others to be open and different with us either. The successful people are those who have learned how to operate effectively in interpersonal mush, even how to use it to their advantage in their normal, well-intentioned attempts to do well, be liked, and achieve in the world.

Hierarchy and Authority

In organizations, a third force makes interpersonal mush so prevalent: hierarchy. Having a hierarchy means that some people have authority over others. There is a difference between too much authority and just the right amount. In order to organize a group of people effectively, we need to create the right amount of authority, that is, clarity about who is responsible for what and who has final decision-making power over what. One problem with a lot of large organizations is that the structure of hierarchy is haphazard, poorly designed, and more of a barrier to effective organizing than a support. It would take us too far afield to go into this topic, which is covered well elsewhere.[2] But even when hierarchy is well designed, it creates interpersonal mush because of the reactions to authority most of us develop in our families, schools, and religious institutions. Basically, most of us learn to duck and take cover around authority. We learn to try and figure out what the authorities want us to say or do, and then we say or do that when they are around. We learn to keep to ourselves the thoughts and feelings that we believe might make authorities angry, upset, or less than pleased with us. As a result, interpersonal mush is greatest in situations of unequal power, especially where one person or group feels dominated or oppressed by another.

A basic rule of thumb—and any manager who doesn't realize this is wandering around in the dark—is that information becomes distorted on its way up in hierarchies. Less and less of the real story makes its way up the hierarchy as people put positive spins on things, censor unpopular views, hide less-than-favorable results, and so on. A funny description of this process, using coarse but common language, has been passed on to me by different students over the years. It's called "The Plan" (see box). I don't know who originally wrote it. To me, it is not only a description of how hierarchy creates interpersonal mush but also a template of the kind of story people lower down in hierarchies tend to create about people higher up in hierarchies. No one knows if a process like this really takes place, but for many workers and middle managers, it is a story they are all too likely to believe.

People who have authority have power over us. The more power we perceive them to have, the more our survival and prosperity appear to depend on them. What they do, think, feel, and want affects us. So they are the most likely targets of our sense making and the people we are least

---

THE PLAN

In the beginning was the plan
and then came the assumptions.
and the assumptions were without form,
and the plan was completely without substance.
and darkness fell upon the faces of the workers.
And they spake unto their supervisors, saying:
"The plan is a crock of shit and it stinketh."

And the supervisors went unto their department heads, and said:
"It is a pail of dung, and none may abide the odor thereof."

And the department heads went unto their group managers,
and said unto them: "It is a container of excrement,
and it is very strong, such that none may abide it."

And the group managers went unto their general manager,
and said unto him: "It is a vessel of fertilizer, and
none may abide its strength."

And the general manager went before the vice presidents,
and said: "It promoteth growth and it is very powerful."

And the vice presidents went to the CEO and said unto him:
"This powerful new plan will actively promote the growth of
this company and all its business units."

And the CEO looked upon the plan, and saw that it was good,
and the plan became policy.

---

likely to go to when we are trying to figure out why they said or did something. We don't bother trying to make sense of people and actions that aren't significant to us. But our boss, our boss's boss, the president—these people can do things that do matter to us. So we talk to others to make sense of what we see and hear. A lot of the stories that are made up in organizations are attempts to make sense of what authorities are up to. Authorities are the object of a full and rich fantasy life among organizational participants. That cannot be stopped. If there weren't a lot of fantasies being woven around them, it would mean they were insignificant.

Even in a world of good intentions, it's easy to create interpersonal mush. In fact, good intentions often create the mush in the first place. Abe doesn't want to hurt June's feelings, so he doesn't tell her some of his truth. Sheryl doesn't want to cause unnecessary concern, so she doesn't tell her truth. Rhana doesn't want to disrupt the meeting, so she doesn't ask a question to get clear about Jack. Of course, when we seek to protect others, we are also often protecting ourselves, but that doesn't diminish the irony of one of the most debilitating realities of human association coming not from dysfunctional people or bad intentions but from normal folks muddling through life doing what they learned to do in their families of origin and schools. It is also true that there are some unsafe social situations, work environments, and business relations in which it is not a good idea to be a Descriptive Self, but these are not prevalent and do not account for the pervasiveness of interpersonal mush.

Why Is Interpersonal Mush "One of the Most Debilitating Realities of Human Association"?

Interpersonal mush is the cause of most of the people messes we find ourselves in. If you watch situation or romantic comedies on TV or in movies, you will notice that they usually involve people getting into some kind of interpersonal mix-up based on misperceptions. If you follow the story line, the misperceptions always begin with some critical moment when people did not tell the truth of their experience. If they had, there would have been no mess or mix-up to try and resolve. TV and movie comedies are not that serious, but our work lives and family lives are. When the interactions in these lives are based on misperceptions, inaccuracies, and mix-ups, the results can be a lot less than funny. Our sense making has long-term consequences, and when our stories are inaccurate, we end up living in a make-believe world. And as I'll explain below, our make-believe worlds are usually not rose-colored: they are often less pretty than the real one.

We See What We Believe

Part of what makes a new story satisfactory is that it fits with what we already believe to be the truth, that is, our past acts of sense making. This has two effects. One is that we tend to make up explanations and rationales for others' actions that fit with ones we've made up in the past. You can see that happening with Bill's subordinates in the story at the beginning of this chapter. The second effect is that we tend to see and hear things that fit with our previous stories and miss things that don't fit. Our beliefs distort our perceptions. Most people recognize that this happens but don't notice when they themselves are doing it. As a consequence, we live in a world of our own construction, fairly unaware of what's accurate and what's inaccurate. Both effects make it hard to see what is not already in our sense-making repertoire.

Because we have to make sense of those we are trying to collaborate with, we cannot avoid being put in the position of having to fill the gaps in our knowledge about what is going on inside them. It is inevitable that we will try to make sense of them, and if we don't check that out, we'll be operating in interpersonal mush. Sense making in an environment of interpersonal mush might be neutral if we were as likely to err on the side of the positive as on the negative. I mean, isn't it possible that the story I make up about you has you being more courageous, more concerned, more honest, more trustworthy than you really are? Couldn't my story be inaccurate in that way? Well, it could and it can. Sometimes we do make up stories that put people on pedestals. But that isn't normally what happens.

Our Stories Tend to Be More Negative Than Positive

It is an unfortunate truth that the stories we make up, and the stories that get made up about us, tend to be more unfavorable than the reality. In a vacuum of information, people tend to assume the worst, and this is particularly true in work organizations. The result of interpersonal mush is that what we believe about the organizations we work in, and the people we work with, is often worse than the reality. Executives are seen as more heartless and cruel than they really are. Organizations are seen as more political and unbending than they are. Co-workers are seen as more insensitive and uncaring than they are. Subordinates are seen as lazier and more careless than they are.

I would go so far as to say that the greater the interpersonal mush, the more negative the stories that go around. A vicious cycle is created in which we become less willing to tell the truth of our experience because it is too dangerous, thus increasing the interpersonal mush, which is what makes it seem dangerous in the first place. Interpersonal mush drives out our ability to see the basic humanity in one another—the loving, caring people who are just trying their best to do what they feel is rightfully expected of them by others.

One reason we fantasize the worst is the natural impulse to be cautious in the face of uncertainty. It's a way of preparing ourselves for the worst-case scenario. This defensive stance is amplified when a person is feeling insecure. Interpersonal mush teaches us that being negative is more realistic, so we take that belief with us into ambiguous situations. Environments of interpersonal mush feed off our fears and increase our sense of threat. But these are not what start the mush in the first place. There are a couple of reasons for this normal, human way of sense making, which psychologists uncovered during the twentieth century. Let me describe them to you.

The Fundamental Attribution Error

Psychologists have found that when we make up a story about another person's behavior, the first thing most of us do is look for external causes or sufficient justification for the behavior. For example, if I see you standing by a car at the side of the road with the hood up, I probably will assume that you are having car problems. You may be standing there for a totally different reason; it may not even be your car. But seeing you next to a car with its hood up gives me sufficient justification to believe that your behavior is caused by car problems. I have created a story that satisfies me and my sense-making ends. Now, if I can't find an external reason for your behavior, then I will assume that the cause is internal (e.g., your character, values, motivation, personality). The fundamental attribution error is the common tendency to assume that the cause of someone's behavior is internal when it is really external.

This typically plays out in partnerships in the following way. When I mess up (such as missing a deadline), I can almost always show you how it was caused by the situation I am in. When I see you mess up, however, I assume it is because you have some kind of defect (you have no sense of time, you're overemotional, you lack some skill or knowledge, and so on). Just about everything we do is shaped to some extent by the situation we perceive ourselves to be in. Research has shown that situational factors are far better predictors of behavior than personality or other internal factors. But when we make up stories, we work only with the facts we have. If we don't understand the situation the other person is in, then it can't be included in our stories. To create a satisfactory story with sufficient justification, we make up internal justification.

It is even more complex than that, because what really counts is not the objective situation people are in but the situation they perceive themselves to be in. Remember, ten people in the same objective situation will be having ten different experiences, and therefore their experiences will actually be of ten different situations.

Projection

Another reason why the stories we make up are often more unfavorable than the reality has to do with where we get the raw material for our stories. The theory of projection is used to explain some things that psychologists have observed about perception. Basically, it says that we see outside ourselves what is inside ourselves. To some extent, we are projecting ourselves onto the world around us all the time. For example, when I'm happy, the world seems like a happier place; when I'm depressed, the world seems like a more miserable place.

One of the reasons we project all the time is that it is almost impossible to perceive things that we don't have inside ourselves. Most of us know what it is like to learn a word that we had never seen before and then start seeing it all over the place. This happens because until we learn that something exists, it is almost impossible for us to see it (I'll see it when I believe it). In chapter 5, I describe what I call "mental maps," products of past learning that shape what we experience in the future. When it comes to interacting with people, we tend to see what is on our maps and miss what isn't. This is why being able to work well with people requires a deep knowledge of ourselves: the more we can understand all the different parts of ourselves, the more complicated our maps become, and the more we can see in other people while at the same time recognizing the difference between what is us and what is them.

We use one type of projection, defensive projection, to defend ourselves from becoming aware of parts of ourselves we don't want to be aware of. All cultures socialize people by telling them that certain qualities are good, positive, and acceptable and other traits are bad, negative, and unacceptable. We learn and are encouraged to deny and repress these "bad" qualities, but they exist within us nonetheless. Numerous studies show that people who are most psychologically healthy in the sense of feeling happy, being optimistic, having a desire to achieve and accomplish in the world, and so on have an inflated, overly positive, and illusory view of themselves and the world. People who are successful and confident tend to forget their failures while exaggerating their successes in their memories and to ignore their negative actions while focusing on their positive social values.[3] It appears that people who have the most accurate and realistic view of themselves can also be depressed and fatalistic. So it is not at all unusual for people to repress and deny parts of themselves they see as small, bad, inferior, or weak. The people who succeed in business and organizations are the most likely to do this. So what happens to these repressed parts? They become the raw material that we use in stories to explain other people's failures and less-than-perfect actions.

The theory is that part of me wants me to see all of me, the bad as well as the good, but another part prevents me from seeing it. When I am pushing myself to see something about myself, I can avoid it by letting the image slip past me and land on you. By using split-off material in my sense making, I get to kill two birds with one stone: create a satisfying story about you and defend myself against dealing with parts of me I don't like. In organizations, people make up judgments about other people by taking their own negative motivations and projecting them onto others.

Here's a hypothetical example: Say you are my colleague and I notice that you're shirking your work—you're sitting at your desk surfing the Web or buying something personal online. I see the behavior and label it "shirking," and now I have a story about you, one that is going to reduce my desire to be in partnership with you. Anyone could plainly see that you are shirking your work, and who wants to be in partnership with a shirker? But what I wouldn't know is that you have been staying up very late for the last three nights, working to meet a deadline, which you have met, and now you are catching up on some personal business. Of course, I didn't know that, so I had to fill in the gaps of your experience to make sense of what I saw, but why did I choose "shirking"? It's probably because when I'm surfing the Web on company time, that's what I'm doing—but I would never label myself a shirker. Heck no, I'm a hardworking, committed team player. It helps me not see the part of me that shirks when I see it in you. I don't want to see my own procrastination, so I see you as a procrastinator. I'll come back to this problem of projection in chapter 7.

If you are going to use the skills of clear leadership effectively, you have to acknowledge these normal tendencies of human sense making and acknowledge that you are likely to be projecting and making attribution errors. You need to be constantly open to the possibility that your stories are inaccurate. You can't stop yourself from sense making; you have to do it. So your only other option is to get people to tell you the truth of their experience. The Curious Self tries to understand how the world looks from other people's perspectives, getting clear about their experiences and not making up what is going on in their heads. Managers build a culture of clarity by helping people get clear about one another. Most importantly, leaders who want to build collaborative work systems tell others what is going on in themselves so that there are fewer attribution errors and less projection is placed on them. By doing this, they lead by going first: modeling how to create a culture of interpersonal clarity and making it safer for others to be clear as well.

It is true that personal characteristics also contribute to the amount of interpersonal mush going on. It's not just a product of socialization at home and in the family. Clear leadership requires clear psychological boundaries, and in managers a lack of these boundaries makes it almost impossible to get rid of interpersonal mush and create interpersonal clarity in organizations. But that issue takes us away from focusing on sense making, interpersonal mush, and interpersonal clarity in organizations, so we'll save it for a later chapter.

What Is the Effect of Interpersonal Mush on Organizations?

Interpersonal mush is sustained by an organizational culture that does not expect or support people in being Descriptive Selves and by managers who do not work at creating interpersonal clarity in the workplace. Interpersonal mush is endemic to most organizations, large and small. As a result, many organizations are much less than they could be and collaboration cannot take firm root. We assume that teams and committees will waste time and be laborious, that bureaucracy will put up barriers to innovations, that people are unmotivated and will resist change. That's just the way it is, isn't it?

I know it doesn't have to be that way, because I've seen many instances of things being different—work groups, departments, divisions, and whole companies where the mediocrity we call "normal organization" is far surpassed by an environment of high motivation, real synergy, rapid innovation, and mastery of change. I have come to the conclusion that the one common factor in every such example I have seen is the lack of inter-personal mush and the presence of leaders who are learners and can lead learning. Remember the story of Lynette in the introduction? When she brought up the lack of support she was experiencing from others, that was the crucial moment for her boss to switch from leading performing to leading learning. He needed to engage everyone in that room, including himself, in a process of describing the truth of their experience so they could learn from their collective experience and change the pattern that was getting in the way of their success. It's not the structure, technology, market, product, or service that makes the difference. It's interpersonal clarity. Before I talk about how people create interpersonal clarity, I want to make sure you are convinced that interpersonal mush is at the core of so much organizational dysfunction, and I'd like you to imagine what an environment might be like if, instead of hiding our experience from each other, we told each other the truth of it. Let's start with the more obvious consequences and then move on to the subtler issues.

Fragmentation Increases and Subcultures Form

In an environment of interpersonal mush, people seek out others they can sense-make with. These are the people they turn to when they are con-fused, to share stories and talk over what they really think and feel about the actions of others. They tend to form fairly stable cliques that develop a common set of perceptions about others. The team, division, or orga-nization becomes fragmented into these subcultures. It is difficult to get real collaboration about anything because people in the different subcul-tures are operating out of different sets of assumptions. The people in each subculture reinforce the perceptions of the others in their group, so it becomes difficult to get any of them to see a different point of view. This pattern can escalate to a situation in which the members of each subgroup think they have truth and goodness on their side and other groups are wrongheaded or evil. Intergroup conflict increases the fragmentation, the isolation, and, therefore, the amount of inaccurate fantasy in each group's stories about the other groups. There are real, reasonable reasons for people and groups to have conflicts in organizations—I would even say that it is healthy. But it is unhealthy when conflicts are based on misperceptions and inaccurate stories that groups are making up about one another.

An Environment of Distrust and Failed Expectations Develops

In an environment of interpersonal mush, we aren't clear on what others are experiencing, the reasons for what they are doing or saying. This ambiguity and uncertainty creates a certain amount of anxiety. It's not safe, though we can't be exactly sure why (yet, when pushed, we can make up some good stories about why it's not safe).

In a lot of organizations, especially smaller and younger ones, there is a kind of benign interpersonal mush that means we don't distrust people, we just try to be "sensitive" to people's feelings and cautious about what we say. For many, this is as good as it gets at work. We don't expect our co-workers or leaders to do anything malicious, but we would feel vulnerable if we told them what we really think or really want. We keep parts of our experience to ourselves and don't expect others to tell us the whole truth of their experience.

Then there is the less benign form of interpersonal mush, in which we are unhappy about our work relationships and don't trust them. Unfortunately, the normal human tendencies described earlier inevitably lead environments of benign interpersonal mush to become less benign over time. The stories that get made up are more and more negative. This is what causes many partnerships to fail. No matter how excited or hopeful we were when we started the partnership, unless we regularly clear out the mush, it grows and becomes more and more toxic until the partnership falls apart. In my clinical research, I estimate that about four out of five conflicts in organizations are due entirely to interpersonal mush. Clear out the mush, and the conflict goes away. Let me give you an example.

I had been working with the executive team of Far North Enterprises for about two years when I arrived for a couple of days of team building and strategic planning. The isolation and size of the small Alaskan community in which the company was located meant that these executives not only worked together but were neighbors, had many friends in common, and were highly visible in the community. I enjoyed their easy camaraderie and had developed personal relationships with most of them. I had not seen the team for six months, and the day before the two-day retreat I met with all the executives separately to talk about how they were and what they wanted from the two days. I was shocked by what I heard. The VP of HR was in tears, describing months of broken promises, increasing distrust, and deep sadness at interactions taking place between her and three other members of the executive team. The CFO was angry and hurt by things he was sure were taking place behind his back, and he was actively looking for a new job "down south." The COO was sad that people were being so emotional about things and that the quality of relationships had decreased substantially, but he didn't see what could be done about it, attributing the problems to personality characteristics of different people. The CEO was aware that something wasn't right but had no idea how bad things were. Each executive who spoke to me about his or her anger or sadness explicitly forbade me to raise any of this during the retreat, certain that it would only makes things worse.

The first day of the retreat was flat and uninspiring. In desperation I gave the executives an overnight assignment, asking them to think of all the things they appreciated about each member of the team, and said that we would discuss it first thing the next day. The next morning, the VP of HR blurted out, "I can't do this! I was up all night thinking about how much I don't appreciate any of you!" Right after that, team members began fessing up, checking out a long series of inaccurate stories they had made up about one another, and admitting the things they had done because of those stories. It had all started months earlier when the VP of HR had been mistakenly left off a list of invitees to an important event. After two hours of talking, the sense of relief was palpable, and executives in the group began laughing at themselves over what had taken place. Partnership had been restored.

When interpersonal mush is rampant, people become more and more cynical as they attribute worse and worse motives to their leaders and coworkers. Organizations become places of distrust. People assume that other people, not their own stories, are the causes of the problems they experience, so they think that there is nothing they can do and that talking about it will just make it worse. Interpersonal mush creates a spiral of distrust, and actions based on that distrust will further fuel the distrust. Eventually, this creates the reality that was initially just a story someone made up to explain someone else's behavior.

People, Especially Leaders, Can't See the Consequences of Their Actions

Here's another tendency of human thinking that psychologists have unearthed. When I judge myself, I do so based on the intentions I have. I decide whether my motivations are good or bad before I decide whether what I did was good or bad. But when I judge you, I do it on the basis of the effect you have on me. Unless I ask, I don't know what your intentions were.

In a relationship of interpersonal mush, I don't ask. I make it up, and I do so based on how your actions landed on me. In an environment of interpersonal mush, I'm not likely to even tell you the effect you are having on me. In the world of interpersonal mush, victory goes to those who maintain a cool and calm appearance, who never seem ruffled or anxious. You could be making me irritated, confused, or hurt, but it's not likely I'll want to let you see that, especially if you have authority over me. As a consequence, you may not have a clue about the effect you are having on me. And, of course, the story I will make up about you will not be a pleasant one.

Let me give you an example from one of my undergraduate classes.

In this course, student teams were given a series of tasks that earned them points, which eventually made up part of each student's grade for the course. One of the early tasks was for each team to make a presentation on a topic, with points for the quality of the presentation itself. One group selected a young man from China to present its results. This student had been in North America less than a year, and his English was almost unintelligible. I gave the group a very low mark, trying to make the point that teams need to utilize their resources effectively. Choosing this person to do the presentation was poor resource utilization. Many students in the class were embarrassed for the poor guy and angry at me for my decision. Outside class, students began to discuss my "racist" decision. Someone had heard that I was involved in a men's support group, and in the interpersonal mush, this was quickly turned into a white supremacist men's group. Soon there were concerns that I was sexually harassing women in the class. For weeks, the atmosphere in the class degraded, while students built on and embellished an active fantasy life. As the authority, I heard about none of this until one student cautiously approached me to ask if I really did belong to a white supremacist group. Fortunately, I could and did bring this matter out into the open, which provided a great learning experience for the students about what happens in interpersonal mush.

In this case, the structure and content of the class made working the issues very appropriate. Few leaders, especially in work organizations, have this luxury. Instead, negative reactions and perceptions grow into a poisonous work environment that has no basis in reality. From the perspective of organizational effectiveness, perhaps the most damaging result is that those with authority and responsibility for making good decisions get the least accurate feedback. If the organization has a culture of negativity toward authority, the leaders become isolated and cannot get good information about the effect they are having on the people they lead. As a result, they become unable to lead in any meaningful way.

An Active "Organizational Unconscious" Is Created

In organizations characterized by interpersonal mush, two separate worlds develop. Imagine organizations for a moment by using the metaphor of the human mind. In our mind, we talk to ourselves, and there can be many different voices—or perspectives—saying things, making judgments, urging different courses of action, offering opinions. We are very aware of some of this. That's the conscious mind. It tends to be the rational, logical part of the mind, the part we focus our awareness on. Just below that are parts of the mind we are less aware of. This is the level of daydreams, where we talk to ourselves and make up stories that we can't quite remember a few minutes later. At this level of the mind, other, less rational parts urge us to do one thing instead of another, interpret things one way instead of another, suggest certain courses of action and ignore others. That's the subconscious mind, which psychologists say is a very powerful determinant of what we do. Contained here are what psychologists call "scripts" and "schemas," and some therapies, such as neuro-linguistic programming and rational-emotive therapy, operate mainly on this subconscious level of the mind. The idea is that we are talking to ourselves all the time, but we don't pay attention to all of it. Some is outside our awareness, but that doesn't mean it doesn't affect us. In fact, the effects can be very powerful because we're not aware of them.

It's the difference between the rational, logical part of me (I call it the "New Year's resolution" part of me) that says "Gotta lose ten pounds. Gotta get to the gym more." Meanwhile, at the breakfast meeting, the inner dialogue is saying, "Don't the doughnuts look good?" In the tug-of-war between the rational mind and the inner dialogue, who wins? Usually the doughnuts.

The same thing happens in organizations that are full of interpersonal mush—there is a conscious, rational part of the organization, and there is a subconscious inner dialogue that has powerful effects on the organization. The conscious, rational part is made up of the things that are said between people in official forums of organizational business, at events like committee and departmental meetings, workshops and off-site retreats, and strategic planning sessions. All employees who are in attendance can discuss what is said, and in that sense the organization as an entity is consciously aware of it. Before and after these events, however, people talk about other things in smaller groups or in confidential conversations. This is the organization's inner dialogue. These conversations are full of interpretations, judgments, feelings, and preferences about the discussions and decisions made in official forums, which people are not comfortable bringing up in the larger group. To the extent that these are not discussable in any official forum of organizational business, they are outside the organization's awareness. They are like the inner dialogue of the human mind that operates at a subconscious level, and they have a powerful effect on organizational actions.

Since the organizational inner dialogue is about things that people don't feel comfortable saying out loud except to a small circle of intimates, it indicates that people don't fully agree with or support what is going on in the conscious part of the organization. Yet they are making sense of it in the subconscious, inner-dialogue part of the organization! Because it is not discussable in the official forums of organizational business, it can't really be dealt with in normal business operations. In effect, interpersonal mush creates a subconscious part of the organizational mind that powerfully affects how people experience the organization and therefore act at work. And this subconscious part tends to be at odds with the conscious part—that's why it exists in the first place.

Poor Implementation and Follow-Through Result

The presence of this inner dialogue explains why some apparently good, well-supported plans and actions are not followed through on or are poorly implemented. I stumbled across this idea when I started wondering why many of the great plans and ideas came out of the workshops and retreats I facilitated were implemented poorly or not at all. What about all those strategic plans that are forgotten within a few months? I am still amazed by how willing people are to appear to be supporting managerial decisions or actions that they really have grave misgivings about. In interpersonal mush, there are rules or norms that people have to follow if they want to belong. Generally, these involve certain thoughts that are OK and other thoughts that aren't, certain feelings that are OK and others that aren't. Successful managers learn that they have to frame their plans and actions according to the thoughts, feelings, and wants that are OK. One result can be that groups agree to things that no one individual actually wants.

I'm aware of one managerial group that planned layoffs for seven months without following through on them. The discrepancy between the managers' words and actions was becoming so great that they were starting to really fall apart. With the help of a consultant, they finally told the truth of their experience to one another and discovered that everyone hated the decision they had made. All of them felt unhappy about what they were proposing to do, particularly the plan for carrying out the layoffs. They did not like the way it would have made them feel about themselves, but it had not been OK to talk about that in this group. In this organization, decisions were supposed to be impersonal, based on the organization's needs and not personal needs. It is not altogether uncommon for organizations to make the personal needs of managers and employees undiscussable or discussable only when it serves the organization. Of course, that increases the interpersonal mush and ensures spotty implementation of poorly supported decisions. In this case, once the managers told one another their real experience, they were able to make plans and decisions they were willing and able to act on decisively. So one rule of thumb I've developed over the years is that if the inner dialogue of an organization does not support the plans and decisions of the organization's rational processes, they aren't implemented well.

People Are Unable to Learn Together from Experience

Under conditions of interpersonal mush, people can't learn together from their experience because they are not describing their experience. People are not getting accurate information about the effect they are having on others. Different subgroups have no idea what stories other subgroups are making up about them. Important thoughts, feelings, and intentions are not talked about openly, so people make up fantasies about one another. Without real information, learning cannot take place.

This is a book about organizational learning and leading learning in organizations, so let me be clear what I mean by it. *Organizational learning* is a term that has come into popular usage, and, as typically happens with new management fads, its meaning has been watered down until it can mean just about anything. Since organizational learning is a concept, you cannot prove that one model is more valid than another. Rather, you can ask which model is more useful, provides a new and more powerful lens, and leads to insight and action. I believe that the approach to organizational learning in this book is a practical and doable method for increasing organizational effectiveness and renewal. I believe it is essential for sustaining partnerships and collaborative work systems.

What is an organization? An organization is not its tasks or goals; an organization *has* tasks and goals. An organization is not its people; an organization *has* people who come and go. An organization is not its products, markets, or technologies. Rather, an organization is found in its processes of organizing—in the repetitive patterns of how people relate to one another, gather and interpret information, solve problems, make decisions, manage conflict, and implement change while accomplishing the organization's purpose. In other words, organizations exist in the patterns of relationships among people. These relationships take place in the context of particular goal and task demands, though the relationships have meaning and life beyond the organization's formal tasks and goals. An organization is found in the patterns of organizing that are formed and repeated over time.

I define *learning* as the outcome of an inquiry that produces knowledge and leads to change. All three components (inquiry, knowledge, and change) have to be present for an episode of organizational learning to take place. Knowledge that doesn't come from inquiry is revelation, not learning. Knowledge that does not lead to change might be called "conceptual learning," but without practical results, it's not organizational learning.

Organizational learning takes place within the relationships that make up the organization. From this point of view, learning is a social, not an individual, phenomenon. Organizational learning happens when two or more people inquire into their patterns of organizing (how they work together) and produce knowledge that leads to a change in their patterns of interaction. It is the change in patterned relations that makes learning organizational and not simply individual.

You can have technological learning, in which the organization implements new technologies. You can have skill development, when people learn new techniques. But organizational learning means that a change in the organization, that is, in the patterns of organizing, has taken place. The patterns of organizing are "how things really get done around here." It's the way your department typically interacts with other departments. It's the way you typically deal with that fellow in purchasing. It's how you and your boss deal with new tasks. All the typical ways in which you and others in the organization interact while doing the business of the organization are what I mean by the term *patterns of organizing* or *patterns of interaction*. Unless these change, the organization doesn't really change. Perhaps you have gone through a major restructuring, and after the dust settled, people said that nothing had really changed. Nothing really changed because the patterns of interaction didn't change.

Under conditions of interpersonal mush, organizational learning simply isn't possible. There isn't any inquiry into our various experiences, and, at best, learning is about things, like technology or markets or products. It is useful learning, but it's not organizational learning.

Problem Patterns Never Go Away

With interpersonal mush, the patterns of organizing don't change unless something happens in the group's or organization's environment that forces a change. The problem patterns—the typical interactions that make us less effective, demotivate us, and reduce our capacity to understand the real issues—never go away. The same boring meetings go on and on. The same petty conflicts never get resolved. The same round of mindless budget cuts happens each fall. The same lackluster performance becomes not only tolerated but expected.

Attempts to change these problem patterns through such methods as team-building workshops, survey feedback, managerial training, strategic planning, and process reengineering have little or no effect on the problem patterns if they do not create more interpersonal clarity. Rational discussions in which people make lists of good intentions, create organizational visions, and write values statements soon disappear, swallowed up in the interpersonal mush.

People need to make sense of problem patterns as much as anything else. Because interpersonal mush seems normal, they don't blame it for these problems. Sometimes people make up stories about how it's "the system" that needs to change. More often we make sense of problem patterns by blaming individuals—the fundamental attribution error. In most problem patterns, it is clear to us that the other person is the problem. It's because he or she has bad intentions, is incompetent, doesn't listen, is on a power trip, whatever. So we figure nothing can be done about it except to get rid of or work around the person. The last thing we'd think of doing is talking about our here-and-now experience with that person. But as it turns out, that is the only real solution, because the problem pattern is as much a function of the interpersonal mush as of anything else.

This is one reason why the ideas in this book are simple and powerful. They're simple because no matter what is getting in the way of collaborative work relationships, there is one solution that almost always makes it better: increase the interpersonal clarity. That won't solve technical, product, or market problems, but it will lead to solutions to organizational problems. They're powerful because every time two or more people inquire into their in-the-moment experience of a problem pattern, they develop new knowledge about the pattern that leads to change. The only way this will not happen is if they stop short of following through on the inquiry before everyone is totally clear.

Interpersonal Mush Makes Us Victims, Not Masters, of Change

An organization with interpersonal mush has fragmented subgroups that are telling different stories about one another, leaders who can't see the effects of their actions on the people they are leading, an inner dialogue that is in opposition to plans and decisions that have been announced and apparently agreed to, poor implementation and follow-through, and an inability to learn together from experience. No wonder people seem to be unable to sustain collaboration even when they want to. And no wonder change seems so hard to plan and implement. Resistance to change seems endemic to organizational life, and real changes in problem patterns seem to occur only in a crisis—only when the environment of the group or organization has changed so much that its current patterns of organizing can no longer sustain it.

Many of the transformational changes organizations have undergone in the past two decades were forced on them by the environment. People don't feel they are in control of what is happening, and that includes the people at the very top. So many of the changes they make seem forced on them by the market and competitors, and so few of the change programs that cost companies millions of dollars seem to return much change at all. I know of one large progressive company where no executive is willing to champion any change program because in the past two decades every change program, from quality circles to process reengineering, is remembered as a failure. Yet, at the same time, this company has totally transformed itself from a sleepy, bureaucratic, inward-focused firm to an innovative, dynamic, market-focused global competitor. But the people in this company feel like victims, not masters, of change, and fear of the future is greater than at any time in the past twenty years.

Even the new collaborative organizing processes that have made clear leadership indispensable (e.g., breaking down tall hierarchies, using teams, breaking down functional departments, reducing centralized control and allowing more local autonomy, minimizing bureaucracy, getting rid of rules and making people interact and negotiate, focusing on results and not procedures) have been forced on organizations. Little was actually planned by any company.[4] Piecemeal adaptations to threats from competitors, new technology, new products, and new processes have accumulated over time, willy-nilly, in most of today's organizations. Only in retrospect can companies point to triumphs of planned change. Unless a company has a healthy dose of interpersonal clarity, the problems of interpersonal mush doom from the start any large-scale planned change effort that requires collaboration with employees.

People Get Stress Disorders

Most of the focus to this point has been on the negative impact of inter-personal mush on organizational effectiveness, but I would be remiss if I didn't point out the negative impact it has on people in the workplace. Over the past twenty-five years, the number of employees on sick leave in Western companies for various kinds of stress and emotional disorders, ranging from depression to chronic fatigue syndrome, has increased dramatically. It is almost an epidemic. I think the negative interpersonal mush people live in day after day at work is a contributing cause. Sure, there are other causes, such as too much work with too few resources, reduced job security, and incessant competition, but interpersonal mush makes it all that much worse. When my daily experience is of secrecy and gossip, when it isn't safe to tell the truth of my experience, when I am constantly having to hunt for clues to fuel my sense making, after a while I burn out. If I'm lucky, I get out and do something else. But if I feel trapped by mortgage payments and the children's education and a myriad of other obligations and responsibilities, that is a hard place to be.

Why is this situation having such an impact now? Because the de-structuring and reengineering that has been going on in Western organizations for the past two decades has created environments where interpersonal mush is more toxic. One of the great advantages to bureaucratic organization is that there is a rule for everything and a center of responsibility for everything. If you and I have a conflict, there is someone else who can resolve it for us. If you want something from me, we only have to look in the rule book to see if you should get it. It may not be effective, and it may set up barriers to innovation, but it does create a work environment where things move more slowly and with less uncertainty. When we take the rules away and tell employees to figure out the best way to do things locally, we have created a great deal more uncertainty. I no longer have the rule book to put between you and me. I have to deal with you not just as a role but as a real human being. In the world of interpersonal mush, this is a very stressful development.

Let me give a concrete example. In the good old bureaucracy, if an employee asked to leave work early to watch a child's sporting competition, his supervisor simply had to find out what the policy was and enforce it. There was nothing personal about it. The interaction between the supervisor and the employee was completely bound by their respective roles. If the supervisor said no, the employee might not have liked it, might even have made up a story about the supervisor, but everyone understood the bigger picture, that this interaction was embedded in a larger, impersonal system.

Now take the same request in a partnership-based organization where the hierarchy has been flattened and the rule book thrown out. It is a whole different experience. The supervisor has to make the decision, and the employee is bound to experience it as personal. The supervisor has to trade off a whole host of issues—this employee's morale, the needs of the organization, what is happening on that particular day, the precedent this will set for other employees, and on and on. It is much more stressful for the supervisor. In an environment of interpersonal mush, these stresses are not talked about. The supervisor is unlikely to ask for more information to gauge the importance of this request. The employee may not think his personal life is any of the supervisor's business anyway. The supervisor is likely to give her decision without describing to the employee her experience in making that decision or finding out about the impact of her decision on him. Feeling awkward about saying no, she may just send a curt e-mail. The employee gets to fantasize all sorts of things from this e-mail. Maybe he makes up a story that the supervisor is cold and uncaring. Or that he is out of favor and on the way out. Who knows? What I do know is that the daily grind of interpersonal mush in supposedly empowered organizations, where people need to but are not willing to describe and discuss their patterns of organizing, drives just about everyone crazy.

Summary

We are sense-making beings. Nothing you or I can do will change that. As sense-making beings, we are compelled to make sense of people and events that are important in our lives. We do this by making up a story about what is going on inside them, which lets us fill in the gaps of what we think we know. Those stories then become our reality, and future sense making is based on them. When we don't check out those stories, our interactions are filled with interpersonal mush. Over time, the mush becomes toxic, as the stories get worse and worse. If we work in a place where we don't have to rely on the quality of our relationships to get work done, the organization can continue to operate in the mush. But if we are hoping to be in partnership with others, to be mutually committed to the success of what we are doing together, the mush becomes a major impediment, and eventually the partnership will break down.

Sense making doesn't occur just around big decisions or events, or when people are acting mysteriously or not saying much. Most of us are sense making in every interaction and conversation we have. As Jennifer listens to her co-worker discuss the new product plan, she makes up a story about how much he really knows about what he is saying, what his purpose is in talking, how he feels about the plan, and what he wants from her. She does this without even noticing that she is doing it—it is as natural as breathing. We can't really stop ourselves from doing this. The best we can do is notice when we are doing it, assume that our stories are usually wrong in some way, and check them out before we act as if they are real.

Because people tend to assume the worst, the stories we make up about one another and the organizations in which we work tend to be more negative than positive. And because future acts of sense making are based on past acts of sense making, those stories create negative spirals that lead to organizations full of cynicism and distrust. People are afraid to tell their managers what they really think, so managers get less and less accurate feedback and ultimately can't see the effects of their actions on others. An organizational inner dialogue is created in which people's real thoughts, feelings, and wants are discussed in ways that make them unmanageable. As a result, decisions that people apparently agree to are poorly implemented, and resistance to change seems endemic. With the increasing breakdown of impersonal, bureaucratic rules and regulations, which allowed people to deal with one another as roles instead of as people, the necessity of negotiating agreements and managing conflict among peers makes interpersonal mush a highly stressful environment to work in.

The antidote to interpersonal mush is interpersonal clarity. Gaining interpersonal clarity requires a kind of conversation very different from the kind most of us are used to having, so let's take a look next at the kinds of conversations that allow people to learn from their collective experience, clear out the mush, and sustain partnership.

2

Introduction to the Organizational Learning Conversation

In this chapter, I will give you a brief introduction to the process that is required to escape from interpersonal mush and create interpersonal clarity. *Interpersonal clarity* describes an interaction in which people know what their own experience is, what another person's experience is, and the difference between the two. I call the process required to achieve interpersonal clarity a "learning conversation." When this happens between people who work in the same organization, organizational learning takes place. Taking the time every so often to have a learning conversation and clear out the mush is essential to sustaining partnership. My hope is that this chapter will give you a clear idea of interpersonal clarity and why it is so critical to partnership-based teams and organizations.

As I described in chapter 1, the model of organizational learning in this book revolves around two or more people inquiring into their experience and generating new knowledge that leads to a change in their patterns of organizing. Patterns of organizing are the typical interactions we have at work, the way we and others go about identifying and solving problems, dealing with conflicts, making decisions, assessing performance, serving customers, managing stakeholders, communicating up and down the hierarchy, budgeting, and so on. When these patterns are unproductive and/or unsatisfying, we tend to view them as manifestations of conflict. We have a "problem" with so-and-so. If we were to talk about it with that person, we think it would just create more conflict, so we most often don't. And the possibility of partnership dwindles away.

A Learning Conversation in Action

The purpose of a learning conversation is to talk about the things that are getting in the way of our being fully in partnership—things about you that stop me from bringing all my energy and commitment to the success of whatever process or project we are engaged in—and, we hope, to get past them. When we are successful, we get rid of whatever is causing our interactions to be unproductive or de-motivating. I've found that close to 80 percent of the problems or conflicts that destroy partnership among people and groups are actually created by the mush, and once the mush is cleared out, the conflict goes away. Let me give you a concrete example of a learning conversation.

I was running a weeklong training program for thirty-five managers to teach them the skills described in this book while working on real organizational issues. There was a staff of six trainers. Because of the flexibility of this course, we met frequently to discuss what was happening and what to do next. On the evening of the third night, one staff member, Bruce, voiced his desire to spend most of next day working with the small group he was leading. The rest of the staff thought that other, large-group activities were more appropriate. At this point, I noticed that Bruce did not participate much as we developed a plan for the next day. On the morning of the fourth day, I announced the day's schedule to the assembled participants. From the back of the room, Bruce called out, "What? What's the plan?" I reiterated it. He said, "That's the plan?! When did that plan get decided?" I was starting to feel a little annoyed but tried not to show it as I said, "Last night at dinner." He turned away, walked toward the back of the room, and muttered loudly, "Hmmm... I wonder where I was when that plan was decided."

Later that day, the entire group of managers was involved in a very tense and emotional discussion as people were finally telling the truth of their experience with some recent changes that had taken place in the organization. I was leading this segment of the workshop and had some clear goals for increasing interpersonal clarity. One manager,

Heather, brought up some issues that were important to her but that I considered tangential to the larger purpose of the session. She had finished talking and another person was about to speak when Bruce stepped in and said, "I want to hear more from Heather." I responded by saying, "I think what Heather has to say is important, but it is not focused on the issue we are dealing with here, and I'm concerned that we only have so much time." Bruce said, "Yeah, well, I still want to hear more from Heather." I looked at him pointedly, raised my voice, and yelled "No." Bruce looked startled, turned on his heel, and walked back to his seat.

It was obvious to everyone in the room that Bruce and I had just had a conflict. A few hours later, we met to have a learning conversation about it. By this time, I had gotten myself worked up over Bruce acting out because he hadn't gotten his way. I thought his behavior that morning had been completely uncalled for and was feeling pretty self-righteous, especially because, in my mind, Bruce is more rigid than I am about not letting others interfere in a session he is leading. Here is how that went.

Bruce: *I need to talk about what happened this afternoon. I have to tell you that I did not like how you talked to me, and I'm still angry about it.*

Gervase: *Yeah, well, I didn't like how I acted either, but obviously I was angry and that came out.*

Bruce: *Yeah, I've been wondering if something started going on before that incident.*

Gervase: *Of course! After what you did this morning, I was pretty upset.*

Bruce: *This morning? What did I do this morning?*

I started to tell him the story I had made up about his behavior first thing that morning. In my mind, he still wanted to spend time in his small group and was resisting the design the rest of us had agreed on. When he turned and muttered the way he did, I thought he was complaining that his views were not being considered. I did not like him acting this way in front of participants after the decision had been made.

Bruce listened calmly to all of this and asked some questions to get clear about my experience. As I talked more about it, I realized that I had started getting upset with him the night before. My story, which I hadn't been fully aware of, was that he stopped participating in the design conversation because he didn't get his way. By the next morning, I was already seeing him as petulant, and that affected how I experienced his behavior. Then I thought he was attacking my leadership, so by the time of the afternoon incident, I was primed to experience his actions as attacks on my authority. My outburst was as much in response to my thinking that he was being very inappropriate in managing his petulance as from feeling attacked.

Bruce asked me questions until he and I both thought that he was clear about what I had observed, thought, felt, and wanted, and then he told me his experience. He had not been aware that he was not participating the night before but now realized that he had been preoccupied by some bad news he'd received when he'd called home before dinner. He did not care that we did not meet in the small groups—it had been his preference but not a strong preference. That morning, he really had not remembered the design conversation from the night before, and his loud mutter as he turned his back was mockery aimed at himself, not me. At that moment, he had felt guilty about not tuning in to the design for the day and was mentally attacking himself, not me, for having zoned out. So, completely unaware of the experience I was having, he was pretty shocked when I yelled *"No"* that afternoon.

After we got completely clear about each other's experience, Bruce said that he sometimes has this effect on people—they feel he is challenging their leadership. He wasn't conscious of wanting to challenge other people's leadership and wanted to learn more about how he creates that impression. Bruce owned that he has a part in this pattern that is still outside his awareness and said that he is learning more about it. I owned that the problem started for me during the planning meeting at dinner but that I hadn't been paying attention to it and it had gotten out of hand. I realized that I should have checked the story I was making up about Bruce—that he was withdrawing because he didn't get his way—instead of letting it fester just on the edge of my awareness (something I do too often). I also owned that when I don't get my way, I sometimes withdraw and act petulant and that I had projected this onto Bruce.

I asked Bruce how he felt about my leadership, and he assured me that he was perfectly satisfied with the way I was running the workshop. He asked me how I felt about his participation, and I assured him that, except for that meeting, I was very pleased with his contributions. We did not have any more problems for the rest of the time we worked with that organization. In fact, Bruce is one of my favorite consultants to work with.

That learning conversation lasted about twenty minutes. As you can see, once I began describing my experience, I got clearer about my experience of Bruce. When he understood my experience, Bruce was able to describe his own experience and show me where my sense making was way off. Once we got clear about each other's experience, the conflict went away. Like so many organizational problems, the real issues were that he and I were operating from completely different perceptions and that I had inaccurate assumptions about him. Notice that we spent no time discussing whether Heather should have been given more airtime. That would have been irrelevant to understanding the underlying conflict that was developing between Bruce and me. If we had simply focused on that and gotten into a debate about who was right, probably nothing useful would have resulted. Yet how many attempts to resolve conflict at work revolve around the right way to do things and lead to little or no change?

Imagine if we worked together every day but did not have a learning conversation about this incident. Can you imagine the stories Bruce and I would continue to make up about each other, the amount of conflict we'd experience, the reduction in our ability to work effectively together, and, ultimately, the less and less we'd like going to work because we'd each have to deal with "that jerk"? What chance would we have of being in partnership? Does that go on between people who have to work together in organizations everywhere, every day? Of course it does, and amazingly, organizations have been able to continue to pump out products, service clients, and make money in spite of it.

As I described in the introduction, command-and-control organizations can function adequately in this state of affairs. But partnership-based organizations can't. They rely on people working together to get things done. They can stumble along, surviving in the interpersonal mush as long as conflicts don't escalate to the point of breakdown and/or their competitors are not creating cultures of clarity. But they never achieve anything close to their potential unless people have learning conversations, when needed, to clear out the mush and rebuild partnership.

Learning Conversations Versus Normal Conversations

There are a number of reasons why normal conversations at work rarely result in interpersonal clarity and a change in problem patterns. A learning conversation helps overcome at least three obstacles.

- Part of the problem, as I describe in chapter 5, is a lack of awareness of our own experience. If we don't know what our experience is, we and others can't learn from it. So, in a learning conversation, part of what happens is that we become more aware of what our own experience actually is.

- Part of the problem is sense making. We think the stories we are making up about the other person are accurate, or close enough, and that talking about it won't help and instead will probably make things worse. During a learning conversation, we get much more accurate information about the other person's experience. Since the stories we make up tend to be worse than the reality, finding out what was actually going on in the other person's head almost always results in each person feeling relieved and better about the other.

- Another part of the problem is that we don't see our own part in the pattern. In any problem pattern, it is always clear how the other person is the problem. If only that person would change, act differently, be motivated differently, and so on, the problem would go away. Think of people in your work life who are part of a problem pattern with you, and you can probably quickly identify something they could change that would fix the problem. But here's the thing: If I talked to them, they could probably also identify a problem pattern and point out something *you* could change that would make the problem go away. We can't be engaged in a pattern of interaction without being a part of the pattern. So part of what happens in a learning conversation is that we uncover our part in creating the problem.

Much of the tendency to avoid discussion of problem patterns comes from the belief that talking about the conflicts we have with others won't accomplish anything productive. When people at work talk about problems with organizing and what is needed to fix them, two things tend to happen that do make these discussions unproductive. First, the discussions often take place without key people who are part of the problem pattern. These people are usually considered the problem people, and the discussion focuses on how to change them. Partnership with the problem people can't be rebuilt if they are not part of the conversation. Second, if a problem person is present, the anxiety (feelings of embarrassment or guilt) created by the discussion causes people to look for quick resolutions. This leads them to talk about only the surface manifestations of the problems, the most visible behaviors and the most visible effects on performance. Lasting changes for these patterns are rarely found without a deeper exploration of the underlying experiences.

Something different has to happen before people can have a productive discussion about problem patterns at work, a discussion that will lead to clarity and the possibility of change and improvement in the pattern. A different kind of conversation needs to take place, and the people who are part of the problem pattern must be part of it. Participants should enter into these conversations with an attitude of inquiry and with the assumption that everyone is having a different experience and other people can't know about it without asking and listening.

Conversations that allow us to learn from our collective experience begin with people describing and listening to each person's experience of each other, and the problem pattern, without trying to intellectually define the problem or fix it. People describe their experience until all members of the group know what their own experience is, what the other person's experience is, and the difference between the two. Most of the time, when people reach interpersonal clarity, the conflict goes away, just as it did with Bruce and me in the story.

The Skills of Learning Conversations

Another reason we don't have learning conversations is that they require a lot of skill to do well and consistently. That's what the next part of this book is about—the attitudes and skills you need to be able to lead learning and create a culture of clarity in your teams and organizations. To give you a taste of what's to come, I'm going to return to the story I told at the end of this book's introduction. You'll recall that the story involves an executive team, led by the company's president, Pierre, who is concerned about the performance of a vice president, Stan, at the board meeting the day before. Pierre is worried that Stan, who is responsible for Product A, is not behind the change in strategy and the introduction of a new product, B. The team members use the skills of clear leadership to create a culture of clarity and learn from their collective experience. This time, I'm going to describe some of the skills and techniques they are using in the column on the right.

Skills and Techniques of a Learning Conversation

Conversation	Skills and Techniques
Pierre: *Stan, the board meeting yesterday created confusion for me, and I want to get clear with you about where each of us stands on the Product B strategy. I raise this here because it affects all of us, and we all need to be clear on what each of us thinks about this. So let me begin. I was concerned by your apparent confusion yesterday since I thought we had discussed the new product strategy fully and were all in complete agreement. It raises some doubt in my mind as to whether you really support the Product B strategy, and, frankly, I'm starting to be concerned that you might resist it because you're afraid it will take resources away from Product A. I want you to be clear about where you stand on this, and I want us to find a way for you to feel fully behind both products, A and B.*	Notice that Pierre does not lead with the judgments he has made about Stan's performance or his sense making. Instead, he describes his observations, feelings, and wants and puts his sense making (doubts about Stan's support for Product B) into a context that leaves him open to hearing something different—he is describing his experience in a way that invites the other person to describe his as well.
Stan, who is visibly disturbed by Pierre's remarks, asks questions to get more clarity about Pierre's perceptions before reacting to what he has heard. Stan: *Could you tell me what, exactly, I did that caused you concern at the meeting?* Pierre: *A number of times when you were fielding questions, you made statements that are contrary to the strategy the board has endorsed. For example, when Brian asked about the mar-*	Notice that Stan does not respond to or try to change Pierre's experience before he fully understands it. Doing this requires strong personal boundaries. Stan does not take responsibility for Pierre's experience and then get bent out of shape because Pierre is not having the experience

keting strategy, you talked about building on the brand recognition of Product A even though we've decided it's better to keep the two products distinct in our clients' eyes.

Stan: *Anything else?*

Pierre: *Well, yes, your response to Marilyn about product launch and what you said to Herschel about expected cost of capital were not what we had agreed to.*

Stan: *Just so I'm clear, Pierre, can you tell me what you think I said and what we've agreed to?*

Pierre describes what he heard Stan say at the meeting and what he thinks was wrong with it.

Stan: *OK, I think I'm clear on what you're unhappy about, but before I react to what you've just said, Pierre, I want to check if there are any other reasons why you think I might not be fully behind the change.*

Pierre: *Well, since you asked, I was also taken aback a week or so ago by a conversation I had with Barbara* [one of Stan's direct reports], *who seemed to have some pretty confused fears about what effect this change is going to have on your department. Then I noticed a similar set of thoughts coming from Kevin* [another of Stan's managers]. *It got me wondering just how much of that is coming from you.*

Stan: *Were they talking about having to shift people to the new business unit?* [Pierre nods.] *Yeah, I know what you're talking about. Anything else causing you to wonder where I'm at?*

Pierre: *No, that's about it.*

Stan: *OK, well, let me start by saying I'm somewhat surprised by all this. I had no idea that things went sideways at the board meeting, so I guess I'm glad you're telling me about it, and I*

Stan would prefer.

By first exploring Pierre's experience, Stan uncovers more information (about conversations with Stan's subordinates) that might not have come up if they had talked about only the board meeting. This helps him understand Pierre's sense making and provides crucial information for the whole group. Notice also that by trying to understand Pierre's experience, issues that are ultimately more important surface. This would not have happened if the issue had been framed as a problem to be solved, for example, how to get Stan to do better at board meetings.

Stan begins by describing his here-and-now experience—thoughts, feelings, and wants—so that others

Skills and Techniques of a Learning Conversation cont'd

Conversation	Skills and Techniques
do want you to know that I'm fully behind Product B.' Let me deal with the meeting issues first. With Herschel, I think I just must not have gotten my thoughts out clearly because I agree with what you're saying about our financing and how much debt we're willing to take on. But I have to tell you that I am confused about our marketing strategy and launch plans, because I thought we had decided to build on the brand recognition and tie-in with Product A.	will be able to sense-make more accurately about this interaction. Then he responds to what Pierre has just said and describes his own thoughts and feelings.
Pierre: *No, no—that was decided at least a month ago.* Robert: *I have to tell you, Pierre, I'm with Stan on that one. I thought the opposite as well.* Susan: *I didn't know a decision had been made.* Pierre: *I don't understand this. We talked about this issue for weeks, and then at the last meeting, the board's strategy committee made the decision to keep the two products separate and distinct in our sales campaign.* Robert: *Well, I remember the discussions, but I thought we were all leaning toward product tie-in. I don't remember hearing that the strat committee had made a decision.* Errol: *I knew about it from the meeting you had with the marketing group, Pierre, but I don't know if it ever came up here.* Pierre: *Oh heck, I thought I had announced that at our last meeting.* Pierre tells the group about the decision the board's strategy committee had made and the rationale behind it. A discussion ensues, and it becomes clear that this is the first time the group has heard and talked about this decision.	Here we see one big reason why it is so useful for individuals to have learning conversations in front of their teams. Many people prefer to have these conversations in private, if at all. But real partnership-based teams and organizational learning require a willingness to have these kinds of conversations out in the open, where the variety of experiences can be surfaced and integrated. It takes a higher degree of self-differentiation (described in the next chapter) for Stan to be able to remain calm and listen when such a potentially embarrassing interaction begins.

Stan: *To finish off with the issues you were bringing up, Pierre, it's true that people in my unit are afraid they're going to lose resources to Product B. I don't think it's going to be nearly as drastic as some people fear, but obviously some resources are going to be redirected, and we haven't really decided yet on what this is going to be. Frankly, I think the sooner we decide, the better, because the uncertainty is fueling a lot of speculation, and since I don't really know what is going to happen, there's not a lot I can tell folks to calm them down. But you need to understand that, as far as I'm concerned, bringing on Product B is absolutely essential to the future health of our company, and I am 100 percent behind it.*

Pierre: *I'm glad to hear that, Stan, but why are your people not on the bus, too?*

Stan: *Oh, I don't think anyone questions the wisdom of moving into the Product B space, Pierre. It's just that no one's sure what the ramifications for Product A will be, and that's creating a lot of rumors and unfounded gossip. Last week someone asked me if we were closing down the Product A unit.*

Pierre: *That's ridiculous! Product A is the core of this company. Isn't that obvious?*

Stan: *I think it is to us, but apparently there is some confusion in the ranks.*

Errol: *I'm having a similar experience, Stan. A couple of days ago, I overheard a conversation in the cafeteria, where some people were guessing about how the Product A unit was going to be reorganized.*

Stan: *I think the buzz coming from below is causing some of the concerns you are hearing from my managers, Pierre.*

Pierre: *Are any of the rest of you picking this up?*

Having gotten interpersonal clarity about their experiences of the Product B strategy, Pierre and Stan can now explore the real issues underlying those experiences. Here we see a leader, Pierre, willing to hear and explore experiences that are different from his own and, in that process, creating a space where real partnership can flourish.

Imagine what might have happened if they had not had this conversation. Pierre would have developed doubts about Stan's commitment and probably continued to gather ever more data to support his fears. He would have thought the team was on board with the marketing strategy, not realizing there had been no discussion of it. And perhaps most important, the group would not have developed a common understanding of the unfounded fears and rumors swirling through the organization and could not have taken action to ameliorate it.

Skills and Techniques of a Learning Conversation cont'd

Conversation	Skills and Techniques
The group launches into a discussion about the effects the organization's culture, with its ten years of focus on Product A, is having on implementing the new strategy. Some of this is news to Pierre, and together the group develops a picture of a pattern of misperceptions and groundless fears that are surfacing in the organization. Everyone affirms that Product A is still the backbone of the company and that a new emphasis on Product B should not have to mean a decrease in support for Product A. Pierre: *We'd better do something to clear up the confusion we've created. I think Colette's team on resourcing Product B is just about finished. I'll ask her to speed up, and we can use their report to make some clear announcements throughout the company that will end the uncertainties about who is going to be working where. Susan, can you get the communications people geared up for this? I want to make it a priority. We don't need a lot of unfounded fears and rumors getting in the way of moving Product B to market quickly and effectively.*	It is through their willingness to be clear with each other about their experience that they can truly support the success of the process (introducing new Product B) they are jointly engaged in, which is what collaboration and partnership are all about.
Pierre: *I'm sure glad we had this conversation, though I'm a little sorry it started because of my misgivings about you, Stan. I see that I'm somewhat responsible for what happened at the board yesterday, so I guess I owe you an apology.* Stan: *Thanks, Pierre, but I have to take some responsibility for not having checked out my facts before the presentation. I wonder if we can huddle before board meetings in the future, just to make sure I have my ducks in line.* Pierre: *I think that would be a good idea.*	The learning conversation comes to a close with Stan and Pierre describing what they have learned about how they each created this experience for themselves and making agreements on how they want to interact in the future.

Summary

Leaders like Pierre are effective because they create cultures of interpersonal clarity. If you want the people you work with to be in partnership with you, you have to assume that your stories are just that, stories, and be able to recognize the difference between what you know and what you are making up. You have to assume that everyone is having a different experience and that theirs will be different from yours. You have to be willing to test your stories and find out if they're inaccurate. You have to lead by being descriptive of your own experience and curious about other people's experience, and you have to ask those with whom you want to be in partnership to do the same. This sounds simple, and, as you will learn in the following chapters, most of the skills required are simple. But it is not easy. It isn't easy because it requires clear, strong personal boundaries. Creating clarity with others relies on your ability to be a calming presence—to not get anxious when people have experiences that are different from yours. Creating a culture of clarity relies on the personal character and actions of the people with authority. Leaders are able to create cultures of clarity only when they have clear psychological boundaries, a state called "self-differentiation." So let's turn now to understanding why people perpetuate interpersonal mush and what is required to effectively use the skills of clear leadership.

3

Understanding the Foundations of
Clear Leadership
Self-Differentiation

As human beings, we face a dilemma. We want two things that seem to be opposite or mutually exclusive. On the one hand, we value our individuality, our ability to be self-defined, to find and walk our own path. On the other hand, we value belonging, having others who care about us, both for the intimacy and for the sense of community. Looked at from the flip side, we fear the isolation and loneliness that too much separation from others could bring, but at the same time, we fear the demands for conformity and the feeling of being stifled by others' expectations that comes with close relationships.

This set of contradictory pulls, what I think of as the paradox of individuality versus belonging, is at the heart of much of the unproductive behavior in organizations. It is the source of two key anxieties that affect people's behavior. One is separation anxiety, the fear of being isolated and alone. The other is intimacy anxiety, the fear of being too close and suffocated. These are, for the most part, deeply unconscious and primitive anxieties. By "primitive," I mean they start at birth, maybe even before. By "unconscious," I mean that we can be anxious and act on that anxiety without being aware of what is motivating our actions. I'll talk more about this in the next chapter.

Separation anxiety is that tug to give in when you see the disappoint-ment in someone else's eyes. It's the part of you that is willing to let go of rationally determined goals and plans when it appears that others will dis-approve or feel hurt or reject you. Intimacy anxiety is that desire to push away when you feel crowded and closed in. It's the part of you that stops listening to others, gets annoyed, and wants to take action without any more input from those whose cooperation you need. The push and pull of these two basic, normal human anxieties lead us to adopt strategies that help relieve the anxiety but get in the way of interpersonal clarity. I will refer to them here as "fusion" and "disconnection."[1]

Think of a continuum of interpersonal behavior. At one extreme is too much closeness—where I lose myself in others, where my thoughts and feelings and desires are just reactions to what others say and do. This is a state of fusion, described in more detail below. At the other extreme is too much separation, where I have no awareness of others, no sense of what others think, feel, or want, and no curiosity about them. My actions take only my own thoughts and needs into account. This is a state of dis-connection.

Neither end of this continuum is healthy for people, groups, or orga-nizations. Let me give you some examples:

The manager who hides out may be motivated by his separation anxi-ety. If he lets people get too close to him, he finds it hard to say no without feeling anxious. He fears that asking others what they want will make it too difficult to pursue his vision, so he avoids them. As a result, he loses track of what is actually happening in his organization and undermines his ability to manage effectively for the purpose of achieving his vision.

The manager who tries to be all things to all people may be acting out of her separation anxiety, too. She also has a hard time saying no but has given up on self-definition and seeks mainly to belong. As a result, she cannot provide a guiding vision for the people who work for her and therefore cannot create anything new.

The manager who demands a high level of formality and shuns any display of emotion, by herself or others, may be gripped by intimacy anxiety. Contact with people is physically draining, and she needs to maintain as much distance as possible to be able to interact with others. As a result, she really does not understand the feelings and motivations of the people who work for her.

The manager who is constantly joking and zinging others, who seems friendly but never gets into serious interpersonal discussions, may also be motivated by his intimacy anxiety. Here as well, contact with others is avoided, but in a way that appears informal. This is usually even more confusing to people, especially after they find their attempts to make real contact are rebuffed. As a result, this manager is unable to develop much loyalty or real team spirit and is unaware that people feel attacked by his jokes.

As you can see, the same underlying anxiety can result in totally different behaviors. In each case, unconscious anxiety creates problems for real partnership and organizational success.

Successful partnerships require people to balance these extremes through self-differentiation. When I am differentiated, I am both separate from and connected to you at the same time. My experience is not simply a reaction to you. I have clear boundaries that let me know what my own experience is, separate from yours. At the same time, I am curious about you and want to find out what is going on in you. I am able to stay in connection with you while not losing myself. I am not pushed around by either intimacy anxiety or separation anxiety.

This, I believe, is the key personal difference in people who are able to lead learning in teams and organizations: they are able to stay differentiated in their work interactions. Clear leaders are able to be clear about performance expectations and stay true to their vision while listening to and seeking to understand the fears and objections of the people who will have to carry out that vision. They are willing to listen until they understand and can demonstrate that understanding but are not willing to have their agenda emotionally hijacked by others. Because of this, they do not get anxious in the face of interpersonal clarity. They welcome it. When managers don't welcome interpersonal clarity, they usually act in fused or disconnected ways and so perpetuate the interpersonal mush that is already going on. Let's get a fuller understanding of these two states before returning to a deeper appreciation of differentiation.

Fusion—Demanding That Others Manage My Anxiety

Recall that experience is the moment-to-moment stream of observations, thoughts, feelings, and desires we are having. When I am fused, one or both of the following is happening: I make you responsible for my experience, or I hold myself responsible for your experience. If you accept one of the premises of clear leadership, that each of us creates our own experience, then you can see the folly of this. But most of us have been trained in one way or another to hold others responsible for our experience ("you make me feel…") and to couch what we say and do in terms that will ensure that the other has the "right" or a "good" experience.

When I hold you responsible for my experience, I give you messages, implicit and explicit, about what experiences are OK for you to talk about. If I argue with you when you have different thoughts from me—different opinions and perceptions—you learn to keep your thoughts to yourself. When I get upset with you because of what you are asking for, you learn to be careful about what you ask for and how you ask for it. When I tell you that what you are saying is making me feel bad, you learn to not say those things. I am telling you which experiences are OK to talk about and which ones aren't. Why? So you can manage my anxiety for me. Fusion is an anxiety management strategy.

Let's say you work for me, and you start to tell me that the plan we are executing is not going to work. I start to get anxious, and instead of listening to your concerns and delving more deeply into where they are coming from, I argue with you about why you are wrong and why the plan will work. Or maybe, instead of arguing, I give you a pep talk about how it will all work out if we stay the course, and ask you to get on board. In either case, I am trying to get you to have a different experience about the plan so I won't feel anxious. Rather than taking responsibility for creating my own experience (the anxiety), I'm implicitly making you responsible for my experience. You have to change so I won't feel anxious.

What's it like to have a partner who makes you responsible for his experience? Are you willing to tell him the truth of your experience? What happens to the thoughts, feelings, and wants you have learned not to say to him? They go into the mush, of course.

When I hold myself responsible for your experience, I also give you messages, implicit or explicit, about how you should be so that I will feel

OK. For example, it's not OK for you to be scared about what I'm doing; I have to take your fear away. When I am fused with you, and hold myself responsible for your experience, I have to spend time getting you to agree that it's OK for me to go out and do that risky thing I really want to do. If you won't let go of your fear, then I won't do it. And I'll resent you. And I'll have less desire to be in partnership with you.

Again, holding myself responsible for your experience is a way of managing my anxiety. In some ways, I am fused with my wife, and when she is angry, I get anxious (separation anxiety). I notice that I become more tentative in my actions; I look for ways to calm her down. At that moment, her needs take priority over mine. What's going on is this: I don't want my wife to feel angry because then I don't feel OK. It doesn't matter what she is angry about. Her anger comes up, and my separation anxiety quickly follows. So I try to stop her from having the experience of anger. If she is angry with me, I try to mollify her. If she is angry with someone else, I try to get her to see that she needn't feel angry. Eventually she learns that if she is feeling angry and just wants to express it, talk to someone about it, she had better do it with someone other than me. She learns to hide this experience from me, and as a result, I develop a less-than-accurate view of her real experience. Over time, our partnership takes a hit if she can't talk about any anger that is interfering with the success of our mutual objectives.

This is one way that fusion causes interpersonal mush. If I am having an experience that, in your fusion, causes you to be reactive to me (act upset, worried, defensive, hurt), I get the message that having that experience is not OK or that I had better not tell you about it. You may just give me a look, you may withdraw or scold me or try to fix my problem, give me a pep talk or tell me why I shouldn't be having that experience, whatever. I get the clear message that my experience is not acceptable to you. So I learn to keep it to myself, to hide it from you. And we are on the road to interpersonal mush.

If I weren't fused with my wife, I would notice that she was angry but not react to it. My experience in that moment would not be determined by her. I would see that she was having a particular experience, and I might be curious about it. What I wouldn't do is take on responsibility for her feelings—as though I make her feel this or that, as though I have the power to create her experience. The truth is that it is very hard for me to not feel some fusion with my wife. In intimate and family relations, it may be impossible for us not to be fused with others. But I have found that no matter how fused people are, they can learn to be much less so in their work relationships.

What's it like to work with people who become reactive when you tell them what you really think about their ideas, tasks, objectives, decisions, and so on? Most people learn to not talk about things that make others reactive. A person who is fused with people she wants to collaborate with will train her partners to express only certain kinds of thoughts and feelings. The partners learn that when they say things that are out of bounds, the person gets anxious and life becomes uncomfortable. Maybe she gets angry, emotional, critical, argumentative, hurt, concerned, or condescending or tries to fix her partners' attitude. There are a lot of ways to shut people down. So partners learn to hide the truth of their experience when it doesn't fall into what is acceptable to the other person. The partnerships are slowly diminished and never live up to their potential.

Fusion, of course, is a continuum that ranges from extreme, pathological forms (in which a person literally can't tell the difference between herself and the object of her fusion) to the everyday reactivity of people being upset that another person is not having the experience they want them to have. I believe it is most useful to think of fusion not so much as a characteristic of a person as a description of an interaction. I act fused in some interactions and not in others. I'm not aware I am doing it when I'm doing it, and that is an important distinction. Fusion is a reactive process, not one we participate in consciously or by choice. Caring is different. If I make a conscious decision to care about you and act accordingly, that's not fusion. When I care, I can act differently if I choose. When I'm fused, I'm compelled to act the way I'm acting.

People who act in fused ways with their partners encourage and perpetuate interpersonal mush. Here are some examples:

Sheera learned that if she disclosed her sadness over some of the decisions they were making about layoffs, Brian would castigate her for being unprofessional. In this case, Brian's fusion caused him to unconsciously feel responsible for Sheera's sadness and then become annoyed at her for "making him" feel bad.

Paul learned that if he tried talking to Lars about his doubts regarding his ability to do the job, Lars would belittle his doubts and tell Paul why he had no reason to feel unsure of his competence. In this case, Lars's fusion caused him to feel his own fears of inadequacy, which he quickly tried to squelch through "fixing" Paul.

Sue-yee learned that if she expressed her excitement about something at work, Bernice would quickly respond with ridicule and cynicism. In this case, Bernice's fusion caused her to feel pain over her own lost excitement, which was kindled whenever Sue-yee got excited.

Odile discovered that Al would snap at her every time she talked about things she'd like to physically change in her work environment. In this case, Al's fusion led him to feel responsible for getting Odile what she wanted, and since he couldn't, he felt frustrated.

But fusion doesn't happen only with other people. It can happen with things and ideas as well. We are fused whenever we confuse ourselves with something that is not ourselves. Notice what's happening in these examples:

Robert found that whenever he tried to plan the department's move to the new building with Juanita, she became withdrawn and unresponsive. In this case, Juanita was fused with her office and felt physically ill at the thought of having to move.

Hussein learned that whenever he brought up hard questions about Rick's marketing strategy, Rick would attack him in some way. In this case, Rick was fused with his strategy and heard Hussein's questions as personal attacks.

Stories like these are a dime a dozen. They permeate organizational life. In each case, people learned to keep a part of their experience hidden from another person. One instance on its own is probably a tolerable state of affairs. But when they are all added up, work becomes a place where we find ourselves continually censoring what we say and do so that we don't have to deal with the consequences of other people's fusion. And, as described in chapter 1, the long-term consequences for team performance and organizational effectiveness are staggering.

Maybe the most debilitating thing about other people's fusion is that we don't want to check our stories out because we're afraid of the fused, anxiety-driven response we'll get from the other person. If I think something is getting in the way of our partnership, I may be afraid that if I raise issues I have with you, I might get your defensiveness instead of your interest, and that could make my working relationship with you even worse. Maybe you'll get angry or emotional. Maybe you'll look as if you are listening and interested but actually be quite angry and express that feeling to another person when I'm not around. Over time, our ability to be in partnership will diminish until it no longer exists.

Marv and Holly were members of a team of about eight people responsible for investigations and enforcement of certain laws. It was potentially dangerous work and required a healthy level of trust and mutual respect between team members. When I was called in, the team had identified a "men versus women" issue among its members. As we worked to get clear about what was going on, it turned out there was not one issue at all—in fact, just about everyone had a different set of issues. But these had all gone under the label "men versus women," as this had been a useful way for the women in the team to talk to one another about problems they were having with some of the men although it wasn't leading to any real clarity. Once they all told the truth of their experience of the "men versus women" issue, the real complexity of all the conflicts they hadn't dealt with became apparent. The one that looked like it would be the most difficult to resolve involved Holly and Marv.

Team members did most of their work independently, but they were required to pair up when needed for safety reasons. Holly and Marv had been on the team for more than five years but had not worked together for at least two years. Holly thought Marv was avoiding working with her but had been afraid to confront him about it. When she did try to broach the issue with him, he would get aggressive and angry, and she would quickly back off. For his part, Marv had avoided working with Holly for reasons she had no inkling of. He had come to the conclusion that Holly's personality was the problem, and there was nothing he could do to change that.

When Marv owned up to not wanting to partner with Holly, he began by saying that he found Holly "an embarrassment." Holly had a very difficult time listening to him after that. As his story came out, she interrupted with tangential issues and rambled on until no one, including Holly herself, knew what her point was. She pointed out flaws in Marv's behavior that had nothing to do with what he was talking about. At that moment, Holly's experience was fused with what Marv was saying, and it was making her very anxious. She lost all curiosity about his experience and began reacting in a way that normally would have brought the conversation to a grinding halt.

With some coaching, Holly was able to stop her reactions and listen to Marv until she understood him. She found out that when she had been paired with him more than two years ago, he had found her behavior inappropriate and dangerous. After tracking down and apprehending a suspect who was considered highly dangerous, Holly had flirted with him! She had done this in front of members of another police agency, which had made Marv even angrier, as it reduced the appearance of professionalism for the whole team. Marv had decided that Holly was more interested in her romantic life than in the team's work and in general was not serious about the job.

Once he had been heard, it was time for Marv to listen. Holly told him that she had flirted with the suspect so that she could find out where he had stashed his gun, which, she reminded Marv, she had been able to do. She pointed out that in dealing with detainees, the women had to use different strategies; they couldn't rely on the men's tactics of intimidation and force to gain compliance. Marv was visibly affected by what was clearly a completely different way of understanding Holly's behavior, but he was not yet convinced. "How about those really long coffee and lunch breaks you're always taking?" he demanded—to him, another sign that Holly didn't take the job seriously. Holly agreed that, yes, she did sometimes take extra time at breaks, but there were a few things he didn't know about. First, he wouldn't know that she was always in the office at least an hour before starting time. Second, she kept a record of her long breaks and subtracted the extra time from her vacation days. Marv was stunned; subtracting breaks from vacation days seemed beyond the call of duty to him.

At that point, Marv and Holly had gotten far enough past their fusion with the other person's stories and were able to pull apart all the stories they had made up about each other over the past two years. They agreed to try starting over in their working relationship.

What usually happens with the Marvs and Hollys of the world is that each requires the other to act in a way that doesn't surface uncomfortable feelings. Marv didn't like how he felt when Holly tried to broach the subject of their not working together, so he acted aggressively enough to get her to back off. Holly didn't feel good when Marv called her an embarrassment and tried to get him to take it back. Her reactivity didn't allow her to listen and understand what Marv meant by that, so she kept trying to find some way to get Marv to shut up, perhaps apologize. If she had continued doing that, nothing between them would have changed.

One consequence of fusion is that people might not really want to know the truth of another person's experience if it falls outside their comfort zone. If I am fused with you, there is a part of me that is going to avoid asking you about your real thoughts and feelings because I am afraid that I won't like what I'll hear. But I can't stop myself from sense making about your experience, so I'll make up stories. In my work as a consultant, I've found that the truth is almost never as bad as the fantasies people have spun for themselves. By making up stories instead of just asking and getting clear, people perpetuate the fusion and add to the interpersonal mush in organizations.

Authority—Compounding the Problem

Authority amplifies the problems of fusion and anxiety because authority, just by itself, creates anxiety for many people. People who have authority over us can influence our lives for good or ill. We are also more fused with people in authority: we are more concerned about their approval, and our boundaries are not as strong around them. The reaction of authorities toward us has a bigger emotional impact on us simply because they have authority. That in itself is likely to make us cautious about being real. On top of this, most people have had a number of bad experiences with fused authorities at home, school, and work. We've had teachers and bosses who didn't react well when we told them the truth of our experience, and we learned that we had better be careful about what we say.

If you are a manager, some people working for you are going to feel more fused with you simply because you're their boss. Because of the anxiety, there will be even stronger filters between you and them, and their sense making about you will be determined less by the facts and more by their internal state. If you do anything that tells them it is not OK to be real around you, your authority will amplify the impact of your action. The slightest voice inflection, the most innocent remark, can land hard on those you have authority over, causing them to make up stories that support increased caution and distort further interactions.

On top of that, many people already come to interactions with a bias against authority—it is one of the central dilemmas of Western society at the beginning of the twenty-first century. Just think of the general contempt and distrust with which people view political, corporate, military, religious, educational, and judicial authorities these days. A lot of people expect to be treated poorly, unfairly, discriminatorily, and with callous disregard for their welfare by authority. Sense making makes it likely that they will perceive such disregard in their manager's behavior. Interpersonal mush makes it almost a certainty. Once you begin, as a manager, to learn what people who work for you are making up about your thoughts and feelings toward them, you will be astounded, I assure you. I still am.

Authority is really a two-edged sword. On the one hand, people who have it live in a fishbowl, where every action and utterance is scrutinized for meaning, and they are suspect until proved trustworthy. On the other hand, it gives managers greater visibility and greater prominence in the psyches of their subordinates. This influence can be very helpful in allowing managers to set the tone, the norms, and the climate of interaction. Because of their authority, leaders have much more influence over creating cultures of clarity. The higher up they are in a corporate hierarchy, the stronger the authority dynamics that swirl around them and the bigger the impact of their actions. The only people authorities can influence to be real with them are the ones with whom they've made an effort to personally interact and who have learned that the leaders are trustworthy. Those who do not get a chance to test an authority's trustworthiness will always be cautious around that leader. As discussed in chapter 1, managers who don't realize this are living in a fantasy world where they cannot see the consequences of their actions. The amount of distortion can be so great that a senior manager might believe everything in his organization is fine while the troops are looking for ways to bail out. It's not that uncommon.

Fusion Can Also Lead to No Leadership

Up to now, I've been concentrating on how fusion can cause one person to close down another person, creating interpersonal mush and making collaboration difficult to sustain. There is another consequence of fusion that interferes with a manager's ability to provide leadership. When a manager holds himself responsible for the experience of his subordinates, he will not be able to make hard decisions or stay focused on an objective. Anyone who tries to do anything significant when a lot of other people are involved is almost sure to encounter some resistance. This is especially true of change. The psychological dynamics of transition ensure that most people will experience some loss and grief with any change. Managers who are fused with their subordinates could be emotionally hijacked by other people's hurt or sadness. They may also be affected by anger and outrage, but I've found that people are more likely to get hooked by tears than aggression. If I am fused with you and believe that what I am doing is hurting you (taking responsibility for your feelings), then I am going to stop doing it or feel miserable myself.

Because of the nature of experience, everyone hears and reacts to things differently. Whenever someone tries to provide leadership by proposing a course of action, it is a virtual certainty that there will be a range of experiences about that proposal. Most of the time, some people will like the proposal and some people won't. If you are worried about how others are going to judge your proposals, and are only willing to suggest ideas when you are pretty certain that everyone is going to like what you say, you aren't going to be providing much leadership. That doesn't mean you shouldn't work at building agreement and framing proposals in a way that is most likely to get support. It does mean that people who worry too much about how others will react to their proposals don't propose much.

Managers who try to ensure that everyone likes them generally accomplish little other than stressing themselves out. In general, I've found that people initially love managers who create no anxiety for them, who make few demands, and who search for consensus on all issues. Over time, however, they get impatient with the lack of clarity and action from such managers. Collaboration is not about consensus. Outstanding teams and organizations require leaders who have a vision of the team or organization at its best and are willing to push hard to accomplish that. This sometimes means stepping on toes, maybe even a knock-down-drag-out fight. The clear leaders I've seen do not constantly try to ensure that everyone agrees with them. Not at all. They just want to know exactly where people stand and why, so that they understand the situation and don't cause unnecessary problems. A clear leader needs to be able to hear the misery she is causing people as she forces them to adopt a new and better technology and not lose her vision because of it. Clear leaders can't be fused with the people they lead or they will either cave in to other people's emotions or avoid hearing them altogether. In order to be hard-nosed leaders, some people therefore go to the opposite extreme: disconnection. Let's take a look at that.

Disconnection—A Different Kind of Reactivity

At the other end of the continuum is disconnection, which comes from choosing extreme individuality without any connection to others. When I am disconnected from you, I don't think at all about what might be going on in your head. Again, there is a continuum from the pathological disconnection of the sociopath to the everyday disconnection of not considering how others might react to something you say or do. Like fusion, a disconnected response comes from either intimacy anxiety or separation anxiety. It is easier to see disconnection as a response to fear of closeness, but it can also be motivated by not wanting to feel the pain of separation. Because I don't want to experience separation, I stay disconnected and therefore feel nothing.

When I'm disconnected, I have little sense of you. I don't notice that I'm not really thinking about what is going on in you. I'm aware of you as an object, a role, or a means to an end, but I have no curiosity about your experience, and I don't notice this. I don't much care what effect I am having on you, but that's not because I've decided to not care—a disconnected response is as unconscious as a fused one. When I'm disconnected, it doesn't even occur to me to pay attention to what effect I am having on you. I might even be embarrassed by my lack of curiosity if someone points it out to me. This is a crucial distinction. If I'm fully aware that I am closing myself off from you and can choose a different response, that is not the kind of disconnection I am discussing here. I am making a conscious choice, aware of what I am doing. Like a fused response, a disconnected response to another person is a reactive response. We don't think about it; we just do it. In a sense, we are out of control—the fusion or dis-connection controls us.

Because disconnection is a reactive state, it also creates interpersonal mush. A disconnected response, however, tends to be reactive to the whole person, while a fused response is more often reactive to the specific behav-ior. This means that if I am disconnected from you, I tend to do things to avoid being emotionally affected by you. The person who is disconnected from her colleagues doesn't make demands on others to get them to act in ways that make her feel OK. Instead, she enters and exits situations in order to control her anxiety. She avoids situations, interactions, and peo-ple that might cause her to not feel OK. She doesn't think about what oth-ers might be thinking or feeling about the things she says or the e-mails she writes or the decisions she makes. It just doesn't occur to her.

You could argue that disconnection is just a different manifestation of fusion. Underneath disconnection there is often the fear of becoming fused if we allow ourselves to get too close. It is also a case of weak bound-aries, but one that involves a sort of all-or-nothing state. We can keep our barriers up as long as we keep them up rigidly. If we relax them at all, the floodgates will open. But dealing with disconnection is quite different from dealing with fusion, and I have found that it makes more intuitive sense to people if I portray differentiation as a midpoint between the problematic form of belonging (fusion) and the problematic form of individuality (disconnection).

Disconnection appears to be quite prevalent among senior managers in organizations. It looks different from fusion in that the person is not likely to be emotionally hijacked and is not demanding that people express only certain kinds of experience. Rather, disconnected managers show little interest in their subordinates' experience. They give the appearance that other people's experiences are irrelevant to the business at hand. They tend to show no curiosity about the impact of their ideas or actions. They make it difficult to have the kinds of interactions that might surface uncomfortable feelings for them. For example, I once con-sulted for a large, well-established corporation that had been successful for many years. In order to meet with the CEO of this company, I had to take the elevator to the executive floor, where there was a woman sitting behind a desk flanked by two guards with machine guns (this was well before 9/11). She had to buzz me through a set of doors, and then I walked down a hall to where another woman at a desk had to buzz me through another set of doors to enter the C Suite (where the CEO, CFO, and so on had their offices). Then I had to get past the CEO's executive assistant before I could finally see him. In the CEO's office was an elevator that went directly to the executive parking lot, where his chauffeured limousine was always waiting for him. In other words, he could enter and exit his office without ever interacting with anyone but his chauffeur. Talk about disconnection! You will not be surprised to hear that this organization was smothered in toxic interpersonal mush.

There is another kind of disconnected interaction that managers can have, in which they solicit information about other people's experience but provide no information about their own experience. The new manager who talks to all his subordinates, solicits their opinions and views, says little about his own, and then suddenly announces a set of changes is operating in a very disconnected way. If he is managing his anxiety about what others might think and feel about his plans by closing off the possibility of being reasonably influenced, he's being disconnected. What he avoids is a discussion about his own experience—his thoughts, feelings, observations, and wants. It never occurs to him to ask others what they think about his experience.

The person who is disconnected is still sense making just like everyone else. She is making up stories about other people that she considers important, but she does it with even less primary information. If someone says something that creates a sense of closeness, the person using disconnection will find a way to distance herself from the remark—a glare, a joke, a change of subject. It's a knee-jerk reaction that is quite often outside the person's awareness. In a disconnected interaction, a person won't be affected by praise or by criticism; neither is really allowed to register.

A person who prefers to interact in disconnection from his partners makes explicit attempts to separate the business at hand from people's experiences. The problem is that his partners' experience determines how they make meaning out of the business at hand. The two factors are inseparable. People who say things like "Feelings are irrelevant to the decision" are just acting on the basis of their own fears or anxieties. Feelings are strong determinants of how people work together. The disconnecting person is afraid of connecting, so he talks as if it were not legitimate.

In Western organizations, disconnection tends to look more "professional" than fusion. In fact, I have found that some people equate disconnection with professionalism, contending that professional managers

keep a distance and don't allow themselves to care about employees. This
might work, even be effective, in command-and-control work systems,
but it is deadly to partnership-based organizations. In chapters 1 and 2, I
described how new, collaborative work systems create a very different interpersonal reality that requires managing interpersonal contact. I've also
described the problems of authority and hierarchy and how they create
interpersonal mush. Subordinates already tend to keep authorities in the
dark about the effect they are having and about the stories people are
making up about them. When authorities are operating out of a disconnected state, the combination ensures that they will have little chance to
provide the kind of leadership outstanding organizations require. Disconnection is a kind of professionalism that organizations cannot afford.

Rob is typical of a disconnected leader trying to create change in his
organization. He had been the CEO of this professional, knowledge-
based organization for about ten years and was strongly identified
with it by people inside and outside the company. It had been successful in pursuing a particular strategy, but Rob had decided that the
company needed to make a major adjustment to its strategy. This
meant that some parts of the organization that had been central under
the old strategy would now have a different role.

Rob made pronouncements about the changes and tried to explain
the logic behind them but experienced the anxiety his new vision created in others in ways that made him uncomfortable. I watched him
have a lot of difficulty listening openly to the fears and concerns of
people in the organization. As I got to know him, I learned that when
people described the problems they were having, he felt he was
responsible for taking away their fear. In addition, so many of these
fears and concerns seemed unreasonable to him that he created a
story that allowed him to dismiss them: "It's just resistance to
change," he said. "People will get over it once they see that the
changes are good for everyone." So he became more and more dis-
tant and difficult to communicate with. He had less and less time for
meetings. He was away more. It wasn't easy to get in touch with him.
He even stopped returning phone calls to his vice presidents.

In this vacuum of information, those involved with the changes
became increasingly anxious. Mario, the lead manager of the department most affected, reasoned that the lack of contact with Rob meant

that he was in imminent danger of losing his job, so he placed more pressure on himself to perform. He became less and less clear about what Rob really wanted, and the more anxious he became, the more he tried to please and the less competent he appeared. Mario's actions puzzled Rob, who believed that Mario had been a great asset to the company, but he began to resign himself to the possibility that Mario would have to go.

The people who worked for Mario felt even more unsure about the changes. They, of course, were aware of Mario's anxiety but had little information, so they made up stories about what was going on. Naturally, these were not pretty stories. They thought Mario and Rob were getting ready to downsize their department and lay people off. Actually, Rob thought that these workers were a highly skilled group and did not want to lose any of them. None of that was communicated, because Rob believed it was obvious and went without saying, especially with the problems they were having with other companies raiding their top personnel. Morale in Mario's department was sinking, and this was affecting the rest of the organization, which was increasingly unclear about the real nature of the now ambiguous changes. Rumors were rampant.

When people broached the topic of what the changes might mean for the department, Rob would act annoyed and reply in a brisk way. This was a manifestation of his unconscious anxiety, as he feared that if he listened to these people, they would try to talk him out of the change, and he would have a hard time standing firm. They, of course, only heard his annoyance and, already fearing for their jobs, stopped asking questions because they were afraid of his anger. By the time I was hired to do some executive development, the best people in the department, unbeknownst to Rob, were polishing their résumés and getting ready to leave. Rob knew there was some unease, but he assumed that Mario was communicating the actual nature of the changes and that people would quickly get comfortable with them. Everyone had a fantasy about what was going on, and everyone was, in some way, wrong.

Before this could change, Rob had to recognize his disconnection and understand that he was avoiding people because the interactions made him feel bad. That led him to see how his deep caring for the people who worked in the organization caused him anxiety when he had to face their discomfort. As we worked to uncover all the stories and experiences swirling through the senior levels of the organization, Rob realized that, ironically, his disconnection was causing the people he valued even more discomfort than the change in strategy he was pursuing. This was a major revelation for him. As Rob came to understand the logic of being separate and connected at the same time (self-differentiation), he began a process of learning how to stand firm on his principles, values, and vision and not take responsibility for the experiences other people created from that. At the same time, he needed to hear the experiences others were having so that he could influence those experiences, make them more realistic, stop wildly inaccurate speculations, and ensure that key people knew that they were, in his perception, key people.

Self-Differentiation—Resolving the Paradox

With self-differentiation, we find a place where belonging and individuality are not mutually exclusive, where I am separate from you and connected to you at the same time. Self-differentiation is about having clear boundaries, being clear on what my experience is and the difference between that and your experience. Self-differentiation requires knowing

Comparison of Fusion, Self-Differentiation, and Disconnection

FUSION	← SELF-DIFFERENTIATION →	DISCONNECTION
Too connected	Separate and connected	Too separate
No boundaries	Choiceful boundaries	Rigid boundaries
Reactive to the interaction	Choiceful during the interaction	Reactive to the person
Own experience based on other people's experience	Wants to know what others are experiencing but stays true to self	Doesn't think about what others are experiencing

the difference between the data I have and the stories I make up with it. Self-differentiation requires acknowledging that your experience will always be separate from mine and not needing you to have a certain experience for me to feel OK. Self-differentiation is about being true to myself and true to the relationship I have with you. It is about putting equal emphasis on my needs and our needs, whether "our" means two people, a group, or an organization. In order to do this, self-differentiation requires being aware of what my truth really is—knowing what my experience is and what is really motivating my thoughts, feelings, and actions. Obviously this is a lot easier said than done. As one of my friends says, self-differentiation is a razor-wire balancing act that you never get completely right. It is a commitment to living a certain way, with as much failure as success.

There are at least five elements to what I call "acts of differentiated leadership."

- When a person is acting in a differentiated way, she knows what her experience is, that is, being an Aware Self. She is aware of the choices she has and the choices she is making. Awareness is the basis of differentiation, and without it, differentiation may be impossible to achieve. I'll cover this in greater depth in the next chapter.

- A person acts in a differentiated way when she openly seeks to understand the experience others are having, that is, being a Curious Self. She notices when she is making up stories to fill in the gaps in her knowledge and asks questions to get more accurate information. She wants to know the impact she is having on others, not necessarily because that might change her mind but so that she will know what is really going on. She acts in a differentiated way when she communicates to others that she really wants to know the truth of their experience and can listen to them dispassionately, without judging their experience or needing to change it.

- A person is acting in a differentiated way when he is describing his experience to others, that is, being a Descriptive Self. This is not the same as being open, when you tell people whatever is on your mind. It is when you describe the truth of your experience, fully aware that it is only one experience and is no more valid or invalid than anyone else's experience.

- A leader is acting in a differentiated way when he is clear about his scope of authority, what he is responsible for, what he expects from others over whom he has authority, and the consequences of non-compliance. He is clear about what decisions he has made and expects to be implemented and what decisions he is making on which he is seeking others' input. He is clear in his own mind about issues on which he does and doesn't want other people's input and how much authority he is willing to delegate to others. He acts in a differentiated way when he makes his position on this clear to others.

- A person is acting in a differentiated way when she is clear about the basis of her actions and can describe these to others. Her actions are not motivated primarily by anxiety or other reactive emotions. She allows herself to be informed by emotion, to understand the message the feeling is sending her, but not to be overwhelmed or controlled by emotion or unconscious motivations. As I describe in the next chapter, she knows what her mental maps are, is willing to describe them to others, and is open to changing them as she and others learn from experience.

Learning to be self-differentiated is a lifelong journey. It is a life path, a way of being. Some people decide that they want it all: They want to be self-defined, true to their own needs and wants, yet also be in close partnership relationships that support their growth and self-definition as well as those of their partners. These people, whether they use the term or not, have chosen differentiation as the way they want to be.

Almost everyone is able to be differentiated in some interactions. The less emotional baggage we have in a relationship, the easier it is to be differentiated. And all of us have relationships that make it very hard to be differentiated. The most difficult are our intimate relationships, especially in our families. As we develop, we become differentiated in more and more of our relationships, but this requires conscious work and the strong intention to be differentiated in our relations with others.

Differentiation Is About Healthy Boundaries

The term *psychological boundaries* is increasingly used to describe and explain many of the psychological and relationship issues normal people face. Healthy boundaries are those that show I know the difference between what is me and what is not me and can choose what I let in and what I don't. They are a necessary part of being self-differentiated. For most people, it is not always clear what is really inside and what is outside. If I believe that a story I've made up about you is really about you, then I'm confusing me with you. If I think I am responsible for how you feel, then I am confusing me and you. Healthy boundaries also require that I not confuse my thoughts and ideas with the things they are meant to represent. As I describe in chapter 5, we all create internal representations, or maps, of external realities, and we are forever confusing the map for the territory. Self-differentiation also requires that I be able to separate my past from my present. Again, that is not as easy as it sounds. We are constantly reacting to things in the present with feelings, attitudes, and perceptions fueled by past experiences.

One of the ways that people often confuse the boundary between themselves and others is found in the phrase "you make me . . ." (angry, sad, happy, upset, mad, whatever). When I say this, I am saying that you are creating my experience. I am confusing you with the person who really creates my experience, me. The logical extension of the principle that I create my own experience is the principle that I am responsible for the impact you have on me. You are not making me feel or think or want anything. I make myself do those things. Let me give you an example.

Laurie, a new clerk, was transferred to my department. She seemed a little ditzy. Her manner of speaking was weird, like someone with a mental deficiency. She was pleasant and smiled a lot but sometimes seemed a little spaced out and appeared not to follow the conversations around her. I decided she wasn't too bright and left it at that. I avoided giving her work that was in any way complicated. For months she was fine doing simple work with a smile on her face.

One week she filled in for one of our senior clerks and gave me a first-class report write-up. Not only that, she hesitantly pointed out changes she had made to increase its clarity. They were excellent changes. I was a little shocked. This was not what I had expected. I started paying closer attention to her but still saw the same slightly spaced-out behavior and heard the same lispy speech. Then one day I noticed that she wore little hearing aids. I asked her about them, and she blushed and then confided that she had been virtually deaf from

birth but didn't like to tell anybody. From that point on, even though
none of her behavior changed, my experience of her changed completely. I have come to see her as extremely bright and courageous.

Notice that I created my own experience of Laurie. One minute she is
a somewhat spaced out, mentally deficient person. The next, she is brilliant and courageous. Her behavior didn't change at all, only my awareness. She didn't create the impact she had on me. I did.

A self-differentiated person takes the position "I am responsible for
the impact you have on me, and I am responsible for the impact I have on
you." You'll notice that whether it's me impacting you or you impacting
me, I take responsibility. This is a fundamentally empowering position,
and it is the position from which to lead learning in teams and organizations. It is not about blame. It is not about who did what to whom. As you
deepen your inner game of leadership, you'll come to realize that such
questions are of little value. Blame keeps you in a disempowered state,
feeling you are a victim of forces larger than yourself, and you learn nothing about how to get more of what you want.

At a certain point in personal development, most people become
interested in learning about the impact they have on others and modify-
ing their behavior so that they will have the impact they want. Fewer people, however, develop to the point that they understand they are responsible for the impact others are having on them. I am the one making
myself think, feel, and want what I do in reaction to you. This perspective
is the mark of a truly self-differentiated person and is a powerful stance
for learning in social interactions. For example, a young man joins our
office. He is bright, outgoing, self-confident, and playful—at least that's
my experience of him. Jeanette sees him as arrogant, self-absorbed, and
not serious enough. Who is having the right experience? Is he responsible
for Jeanette's and my very different experiences of him?

If he is a learner, he will be interested in understanding the impact he
is having on Jeanette and me and will learn from that. For example, he
might learn to notice when his playfulness gets in the way of others taking him seriously. If Jeanette is a learner, she will take responsibility for
the impact he is having on her and learn what predisposes her to label his
behavior as arrogance instead of the many other ways in which that same
behavior could be experienced.

More often, however, Jeanette will believe that the young man is responsible for the impact he is having on her—it's his fault and he needs to buck up. If she is a "good manager" she will give him some constructive feedback. If she is a "bad manager" she will just treat him poorly without telling him why. Either way, Jeanette learns nothing and won't be able to bring out the best in this young man, who will probably just feel confused by the feedback and get the message that he is not OK. He may then try to fit in, losing his creativity, confidence, and motivation, or become rebellious and lose his commitment to, desire to cooperate with, and concern for the system. Either way, both parties won't learn anything useful from their experience, and any chance for partnership will be lost early on.

Self-differentiation comes from realizing that what we see in others is mainly ourselves, reflected back to us. You can't lead learning in social systems if you don't understand this. If you are having an emotional reaction to other people who are not in an intimate relationship with you, it means that you are fused with them in some way, that you are not separating them from yourself. If you are the boss, you can probably get them to stop doing what you are reactive to, but you will lose some of their commitment and effort in the process. Most of us can find ways to avoid being around people we have a negative reaction to, and if we aren't interested in being in partnership with them, then there's not much point in doing anything different. If I need to be in partnership with this person, avoidance is clearly a difficult and ineffective strategy, but I can at least try, as Marv did with Holly, to minimize contact. I could demonize them in my mind, adding other negative traits that will allow me to feel morally superior to them. From there I can imagine punishing or banishing them, making them go away, or changing them.

Usually it's precisely the strength of my negative emotional reaction that makes it most difficult to take a learning stance toward my experience. Surely I'm not responsible for my experience in this case—any reasonable person would have the same negative reaction, wouldn't they? To make sure, I search out others whose opinions I value and describe the things that are bothering me. I'm usually able to get them to agree that a certain person really is bad or deficient in some way. Validated in my belief that the other person is the source of my negative experience, I can then safely hold on to my current point of view. And learn nothing. And be totally ineffective in dealing with that person, lose any chance of partnership, and even get in the way of my getting what I want.

If two people who are having a negative reaction to each other use the skills in this book to have a learning conversation, an almost magical transformation will occur and their patterns of interaction will be unalterably changed. (Even if only one of the two people does that, their relationship will change.) Both will discover ways in which they are confusing their stories with the other person's experience and will probably find out something new about themselves. It is almost always a profound learning experience because it is so rare and so tough to do.

The Boundary Between Past and Present

As I explained in the introduction and describe in more detail in the next chapter, our moment-to-moment experience is created both by things outside ourselves and by things inside ourselves. Because of these inner things, people who encounter the same situation have different experiences. A lot of the inner things that affect how we generate percepts come from our past. The way we experience the present is more or less conditioned by our past, and so we all have some problems with confusing the present and the past.

Of all the aspects of self-differentiation, untangling the past from the present is the most difficult to learn on your own. I have been immensely aided by others—coaches, therapists, and partners—who have helped me notice when my reactions to and perceptions of the present seem off. Maybe I am having strong feelings that are out of proportion to the situation. Maybe I'm having too little reaction to what is happening. Maybe the story I am making up has little relation to the actual facts. All of these responses are clues that the experience I am having is based as much—or more—on the past as on the present.

Most of the people I've met who are skilled at clear leadership have spent some time exploring how the past is affecting them in the present. Generally this means learning about the emotional baggage they are carrying with them from the past. They do this so that they can learn to separate the past from the present and not let it unconsciously affect their experience of the present or motivate their behavior. Increasingly, in my work with executives, I try to include sessions with a partner who is a psychotherapist so that leaders can develop greater awareness of the deep forces operating inside them. Let me give you an example of how important that can be.

Jeremy was the whiz-kid founder of a fast-growing start-up company. One of the seasoned members of his board insisted that he get some help with his leadership skills, and I was hired to work with him. In my contract with Jeremy, I stated that I wanted to work with him on both his outer game and his inner game. For his inner game, he would meet for one hour a week with me and a partner, and he would work on deepening his understanding of the forces inside himself, increasing his awareness and control over himself. He agreed. What I didn't tell Jeremy was that my partner was a very skilled psychotherapist, as the word "therapy" tends to scare people. But Jeremy figured that out after a few weeks.

We had been working this way for about three months when members of Jeremy's management team approached me with their concerns about Jeremy making promises he could not keep. For example, while on an overseas trip, Jeremy had agreed to send a joint-venture partner $5 million, but the company, which was caught in a cash-flow crunch, simply didn't have the funds available. They could not understand why Jeremy was making such foolish and unnecessary promises, and they were angry and scared about the long-term consequences for the company.

I confronted Jeremy with the issue during a psychotherapy session, and over the next three sessions, using techniques for accessing his deepest feelings and motivations, he came to realize that he had made these promises to older men because he was trying to please them. He realized that the person he was really trying to please was his father. In his interactions with older men he respected, he was confusing his need to find a way to thank his father for all he had done (the past) with the transactions he was having with these business associates (the present). Jeremy got clear about his desire to thank his father and how, exactly, he wanted to express his gratitude. He developed a realistic plan to do that, and we moved on to other issues.

This realization had a dramatic impact on his behavior and the organization. Over the next two weeks, Jeremy terminated three major joint-venture relationships that weren't really that good for the company. He had realized that he was in them simply because he wanted to please the older men he was confusing with his father. He stopped making promises he couldn't keep and became a much sharper negotiator.

You can see in this example not only the problem caused by lack of clear boundaries between the past and the present but the belonging–individuality paradox still at work. It is ever present. Jeremy was fused with the older men he was doing business with and could not say no to them because of the separation anxiety he would experience—but the source of that anxiety was separation from his father. His desire to please them was a manifestation of his desire for belonging. They were surrogates for being in relationship with his father. It was only when he got clear about his unconscious motivations that he could be more choiceful and self-defining in his encounters with such men. Developing a plan for dealing with the real issue, his relationship with his father, helped reduce any separation anxiety that might be created in future interactions with father figures, so he could operate more rationally and with more clarity.

Paying close attention to your here-and-now experience and noticing when the situation just doesn't seem to warrant your reaction is one way to figure out when the past is intruding on your present. But nothing substitutes for spending time working with someone who is skilled at helping people strengthen those kinds of boundaries.

Summary

In this chapter we've looked at one basic difference between those who can operate successfully in partnership-based organizations and those who can't. People who are too fused with, or too disconnected from, the people they work with are not able to create the interpersonal clarity needed to clear out the mush that inevitably creeps into important relationships. They can't create the culture of clarity people need to be able to collectively explore and learn from their experience. Instead, their actions are motivated by a desire to avoid the anxiety that comes out of the belonging–individuality paradox. Either they avoid finding out what others are experiencing, trying to sweep everything under the rug, or they send the message that only certain kinds of experiences are OK to have. Here are some examples:

When people on Wendy's team expressed fears about their ability to accomplish their objectives, Wendy gave them a pep talk, telling them not to dwell on their fears.

When people on Harin's team raised concerns about the strategy they were following, Harin told them not to second-guess themselves and to redouble their efforts.

When people on Sarah's team expressed unhappiness with the quality of their meetings, Sarah brought the meeting to an end and didn't call another one for months.

When people on Martin's team questioned their objectives, Martin said the goals had come down from on high and there was nothing more to talk about.

The same thing is happening in all of these cases: The leaders are showing no curiosity about the experiences others are having. They probably aren't even aware they are doing that. Probably they aren't aware that they are trying to avoid the anxious feeling these concerns and questions raise in them. By their actions, they make it much less likely that anyone will bring up those same issues again. Instead, people will take their fears, concerns, and questions to trusted others, and the mush will grow, and real partnership will diminish. There will be no learning about and from the collective experience of the team. Things will probably just get worse.

Self-differentiation is about noticing when you are not clear about what others are experiencing and being able to choose when you will be curious and when you won't. It is the foundation on which the skills of clear leadership are built. People can learn to talk the talk of clear leadership, but without some real self-differentiation, they often can't walk the walk. Self-differentiation requires not taking responsibility for other people's experience and not making them responsible for yours. It requires willingness to be a learner and curiosity about the experiences others are having so that you can understand your impact on them and how you create the impact they have on you. Unless you are able to build relationships in which people can learn from their collective experience, you can't sustain real partnership over the long run. Finally, self-differentiation comes from choosing both individuality and belonging and searching for ways to have both simultaneously. People who are using clear leadership are self-defined enough to be clear about their experience and what they intend to do. At the same time, they are connected enough to others to be able to see the consequences of their actions and be open to changing as they learn.

4

The Four Elements of Experience

The Experience Cube

In this chapter I provide a very detailed and more technical description of experience. This may seem far away from the hustle and bustle of organizational life, but I promise that if you learn to be fully aware of your in-the-moment experience, your ability to lead learning and create effective and sustainable partnerships, as well as your self-differentiation, will increase significantly. This model of the elements of experience is a key tool in three skills that follow: the Aware Self, the Descriptive Self, and the Curious Self. You need to be aware of your experience before you can describe it, and you need to know what experience is in order to use your curiosity well.

The Basics of Experience

The percepts (building blocks of perception) we generate are the basis of our experience. Percepts are images and urges that, for the most part, are below our level of awareness. They are the primary material we construct our experience out of. We are constantly generating a stream of percepts, with or without external sensory stimulation. These percepts then combine with things outside ourselves to create an experience. The same external stimulation can lead to very different experiences. Say that one morning I wake up and have grumpy percepts. I may or may not notice this—I sure don't say to myself "I think I'll be grumpy this morning." But as I head to the breakfast table, I see my seven-year-old dawdling over her food, which means we'll be rushed getting to school, and I get angry and yell at her to hurry up and eat her food. The next morning when I get up, I have happy percepts, and when I get to the breakfast table, my daughter is dawdling over her food once more, but instead of being angry, I feel playful, give her a hug and a kiss, and make a joke of her dawdling. What is going on outside me is the same. My experience is more a function of what is on the inside coming out than of what is on the outside coming in.

Where do percepts come from? That is the mystery of consciousness. They do seem to be affected by our history, our culture and language, our biochemistry, and our mental maps (the ideas, beliefs, and concepts we use for making sense out of the world). You can be clear without knowing where they come from or how they arise. You just need to recognize that experience is not what happens to you but what you do with what happens to you.

I have found it very helpful to think of experience as having four elements: observations, thoughts, feelings, and wants. In this chapter I describe each element of experience in some detail. In the model of experience I propose in this book, the key idea is that all four elements of experience are present in each of us all the time. At every moment, whether you are paying attention to it or not, you are having thoughts, feelings, and wants, and as long as you are awake and not in a sensory deprivation tank, you are having observations, too.

You may be thinking, "Wait a minute—I'm not feeling or wanting anything at this moment." The model of experience I am proposing contends that if you were a perfectly evolved Jedi master, you would know what you are feeling and wanting at every moment. Most of us have not put in the years of discipline and mindfulness required to be aware of all of our experience all the time. Instead, some of our experience is outside our awareness. That means that some of our experience is conscious and some of it is unconscious. Part of the work of developing clarity in yourself and in your relationships is becoming more aware of what your experience is.

You may find the idea of unconscious experience a bit difficult to grasp at first. Isn't experience, by definition, something you are aware of?

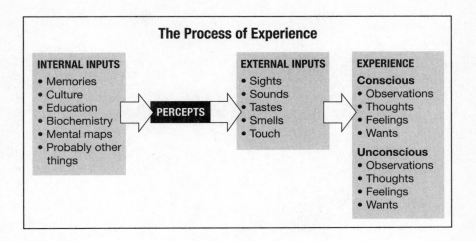

Let's examine that through the most objective form of experience, observations. I'm the kind of person who can walk through the same hallway a dozen times and not notice the color of the walls. Apparently I am not alone. My wife, on the other hand, can tell you the floor plan of every house she's ever been in. So she and I differ greatly in how aware we are of our observations. If I were to be hypnotized, I could tell you the color of the walls of any hallway I'd walked through—that information is in me even though I'm not aware of it. I have the experience; I'm just not conscious of it.

I've been trained to observe group process. I can be in a group for an hour and then play back pretty much who said what to whom over the whole hour. But to do that, I have to mentally turn on my observation switch. It's not my normal mode of existence. So anyone can be trained to develop greater awareness of any element of experience. All people have aspects of their experience that are close to the surface and easy to be aware of. And there are aspects of experience that are deeper down and more difficult to be aware of. This is summarized in the diagram I call the "experience cube," shown in the figure on the next page.

The experience cube is a road map to your experience. You can use it for deepening your awareness of your own experience and for focusing your curiosity into the experience of others. In the next chapters I describe how you use that awareness to lead organizational learning and create successful partnership-based teams and organizations. Here I want to focus only on what experience is.

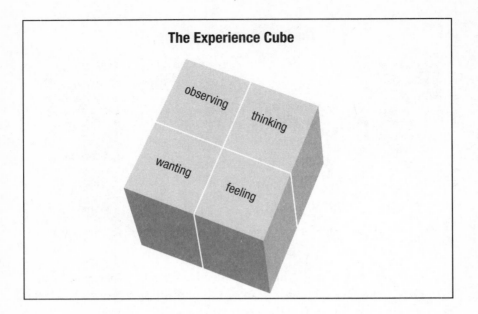

The Experience Cube

observing

thinking

wanting

feeling

The Elements of Thinking and Observing

Thinking involves all the cognitive processes. These include thoughts, judgments, perceptions, interpretations, calculations, beliefs, ideas, fantasies, visual images, internal dialogue, and daydreams. Of all the elements of experience, thinking is the one that is most developed in Western cultures. It is what we spend most of our time cultivating in school. We prize the capacity for good thinking.

Like every element of experience, people differ in their depth of awareness about what they think and the speed with which they access that awareness. Some people find out what they think as they talk, while others need time to think about what they think. We have thoughts that are outside our awareness; some of these we can bring to awareness if we want to, and some we can't. For example, when you drive your car, you don't think about everything you are doing (now lift my foot and press the brake pedal, now hit the turn signal, now take my foot off the brake pedal, and so on). Those thoughts are usually outside your awareness, though you probably could bring them into awareness pretty easily. Then there are thoughts that are much harder to bring into awareness, like the negative judgments of ourselves we picked up as kids and learned to repress but not quite get rid of. When I work with managers to increase their clear leadership abilities, however, thinking is the element of experience they usually need the least help with. Most people are aware enough of their thoughts to be able to create interpersonal clarity.

A more common problem is confusing observations with thinking. Consider each of the following statements and pick out the observations:

- I observe you are upset.
- I observe he is hungry.
- I observe her working hard.

None of them is an observation. They are all thoughts. They are interpretations of some behavior, a story made up about another person's experience, or a judgment about another person's behavior. One of the bases of self-differentiation is the ability to distinguish between the elements of experience. To get clear, you need to be able to tell the difference between what you think, feel, want, and observe. Of all those differentiations, the one most critical for leading learning is probably the ability to distinguish observations from thoughts. People who can't tell the difference between what they observe and what they think cannot learn from experience. Instead, they get lost in their own interpretations and judgments, seeing what they expect to see and missing what is actually happening.

What might you observe that would lead you to think someone was upset? Maybe he is pacing the room, or crying, or standing with his arms crossed and a frown on his face. Those are observations. Observations are what a video recorder would pick up, and for the most part, the key observations are what you see and hear. The other three senses (touch, taste, and smell) also contribute to observations, but for the purposes of organizational learning, what we mostly need to deal with are sights and sounds. A video recorder does not pick up that someone works hard, but it does pick up the length of time a person spends working. Whether or not that person is working hard is a judgment.

Observations are the only element of experience that have an objective quality. You did or did not do something. She did or did not say something. Unfortunately, no one sees and hears purely, like a video recorder. There are numerous barriers to accurate perception. Our observations are shaped by internal stimuli, which means they are influenced by percepts, and part of developing the skill of observation is removing the influence of your percepts (whether happy or grumpy) from what you are actually seeing and hearing. To be able to properly describe your observations, you have to give a description of what anyone in your position would have actually seen and heard, with as little of your personal biases mixed in as possible.

I think a part of interpersonal competence is being able to make accurate interpretations and judgments (while keeping in mind that they may be incorrect and need to be validated). I'm not advocating that you try to stop sense making and attend only to the facts. What I am advocating is that you be as clear as you can about what is observation and what is thought. This will enable you to do three things that will help you be more effective at leading people in collectively learning from their experience:

- You will be able to see how much or how little data you have for your thoughts and ideas and avoid getting too far out on a limb when you don't have that much to go on.

- You will be able to tell others about the actual observations that led to your interpretations. This is a key piece of your experience that will help others understand you. It is indispensable for having learning conversations.

- You will be more likely to make observations that are contrary to your beliefs and will therefore stay open to thinking about things more clearly and accurately even after you have developed a satisfactory story.

When it comes to other people, our judgments and interpretations are strongly shaped by our observations, though people differ greatly in their ability to be aware of what those observations are. None of us really knows how much more we depend on nonverbal cues than on verbal content when we interact with people, but everyone guesses that it is a lot. In our interactions, we make more meaning out of our observations of others than out of what they are actually saying. Whether we are aware of it or not, we are constantly attending to what people are doing with their hands, their facial expressions, how they move, where they look as they talk or listen, and so on to create our story about them and interpret what they are saying. Becoming aware that you are doing this is a huge first step toward separating what you actually know from the stories you are making up.

Good observation skills give you the ability to mentally record and play back what is said and done with as little bias as possible. It takes effort and practice for most people to develop these skills. Many find it difficult to both fully participate in interactions and observe them. The more you are able to watch yourself and others while you are fully engaged in an interaction, the more you will be able to learn from your experience and to lead learning in groups. This observer function is really just about awareness. The data are always there, the awareness less so.

Without good observation skills powering your thinking, you can't give people useful feedback, you can't explain the basis of your thoughts and judgments, and you can't confront others effectively. The reasons will become clearer as you read this book. The goal is to have the ability to observe what is going on inside you (I'm having this thought, I'm making up this story, I'm feeling this emotion) and outside you, moment to moment. When you can do that, you are well on your way to being able to lead learning in the midst of performing and build successful, sustainable partnerships.

The Element of Feeling

While Western culture has developed the element of thinking to a high degree, we are much less attuned to feeling. We have standards for good thinking, but what is good feeling? Does that question even make sense? In many work organizations, people hesitate to talk about feelings. Why does it matter? Isn't it better to just keep feelings to ourselves and operate on the basis of facts and logic?

I understand that position. Feelings are so subjective. They can be hard to handle. Many of us don't have a strong grasp on them. But here's the problem: They strongly influence our actions and our sense making. I would even go so far as to say that of all the elements of experience, feeling is the one we attend to most in others, and it has the greatest influence on the choices we make about how to interact with others. Say, for example, that you want to have a conversation with your boss about something sensitive. What's the first thing you check out before you bring it up? What mood is he in? What is he feeling at the moment? Unless we are very disconnected, we are constantly monitoring and making up stories about what others are feeling. How did what I just said land on him? Is he feeling OK about it? If we don't acknowledge and talk about feelings, they just go into the interpersonal mush.

Why do we pay so much attention to other people's feelings? I think it's because we know intuitively how powerful feelings are in determining what people decide and do. There is increasing scientific evidence to suggest that we feel first and then think. Studies of decision making support the position that people decide based on how they feel about things and then organize their thoughts to support that decision. People do it when they buy cars, and executives do it when they develop strategic plans. So if we don't acknowledge and talk about our feelings, we are leaving out a major source of information about what is going on. And if you don't tell people what you are feeling, they will just make up a story about it.

Feelings are composed of two things, sensations and emotions. These are both feelings because we actually feel them in the body. Emotions have sensations associated with them. If you can't feel it in the body, it is not an emotion. But emotions are different from sensations because a judgment about your state of being is associated with them. Emotions have an explicit message connected to them, whereas sensations don't. For example, if I feel love, the sensation is warmth around my heart. But knowing that I am feeling love tells me a great deal about my relationship with the object of that feeling, while warmth around the heart says nothing more, in itself, than that. If I feel anger, there is tension in my jaw and, if I'm really angry, a slight nausea in my stomach. Again, anger as an emotion has a lot more connotations than muscle tension and nausea.

I'll begin by describing sensations and their role in experience and then move on to emotions.

Body Sensations

Body sensations are the part of our experience that many people know the least about and pay the least attention to. Body sensations are things like hot and cold, pain and pleasure, tension and release. They are very basic to our experience and have a strong impact on our actions. For example, when we sense pain, we react quickly, often without any thought, like pulling a hand away from a hot stove.

Unless you have been trained to pay attention to your body though a discipline such as dance, yoga, vipassana, chi gong, or somatic psychotherapy, chances are that you've been trained to ignore your body and push it out of awareness. When I first started listening to my body, I was amazed to discover how much unconscious pain I had—sore muscles that I was numb to. If you want to find out whether or not you have unconscious body pain, get a therapeutic massage. If you are like most people, you will find that some muscles in your body are in a good deal of pain, but you are numb to it until someone touches them. I'm not talking about deep, hard massage—I'm talking about pain from a light, soothing touch!

We seem to start pushing body sensations out of awareness during infancy. It's as though the sensations are too big for our little bodies, and they overwhelm us. There is a lot of truth, at least in my generation, to the joke that the average twenty-year-old man has no sensation between his neck and his groin. In the rough-and-tumble of sports and school, boys (and, increasingly, girls) learn to control their reactions by pushing them out of awareness so that they will not show physical or emotional hurt and will always appear cool. We learn to sit quietly in our seats for six or more hours a day from the age of six onward. Doing this requires numbing ourselves to what would otherwise be incessant body sensations that would get us into trouble.

In our society, we don't have a language of the body, and there doesn't appear to be any point in listening to our body except to notice when we are ill. But it turns out that body sensations are the most primal form of experience, contain lots of important information, and have a big impact on how we think, what we want, and what we do. They are the only basis we have for validating subjective truth. It is difficult for many people to be certain what they feel or want. Some, if asked, can quickly tell you how they are feeling. Most people, however, never learn how to know or label their feelings beyond a narrow range.

In my teens, I learned that I was expected to have feelings, and I learned what feelings were appropriate to have in what situations. Later I went to classes and workshops where we talked about our feelings. But I didn't learn to pay attention to my sensations, to my body, so I didn't actually learn what I was feeling or wanting. Sometime in my late twenties, I realized that, in many situations, I knew what I didn't want but didn't know what I wanted. So I started listening to my body and found out I was having lots of sensations, feelings, and wants that were not registering in my awareness but were still affecting me.

Let me give you an example of someone whose unconscious sensations were causing him to destroy an important partnership.

Shauna worked for Milo and respected his abilities and his competence as a manager. They worked together for a number of years and developed a real sense of closeness and caring. After the first couple of years, Shauna found herself occasionally feeling bad after interactions with Milo. At first she wasn't sure why, but as she paid more attention to it, she came to believe that whenever she was feeling particularly close to Milo, he would put her down in some subtle way, as if he were trying to create less closeness between them.

One day, right after Milo had pointed out a problem with Shauna's work (even though the work had been hailed as a success by the client), she confronted him with her suspicions. Milo did not believe that he was doing anything more than offering constructive feedback when it was warranted. He did not believe he was trying to create distance, and there was no logical reason for it. From Shauna's perspective, however, the more she tried to get Milo to look at the behavior that concerned her, the more it happened. When I entered the picture as a consultant, it was getting to the point that Shauna was seriously considering leaving, even though she loved her job and felt that otherwise she and Milo were a good team. "It just batters my self-esteem too much, and I don't think it has anything to do with improving my performance," was how she put it. Milo was upset by Shauna's "touchiness" and had come to believe she wanted more out of the relationship than just work and that was what she was really complaining about. Their ability to be in partnership was spiraling downward.

I was most curious about the adamancy with which Milo dismissed, out of hand, Shauna's experience. When people have no curiosity at all about what others see, and dismiss it aggressively, that is usually a good indication that something unconscious is going on. In this case, I suspected that Milo was unaware of some part of himself, so I suggested we try an experiment, and both Milo and Shauna agreed to it. I asked Milo to stand in one part of the room and Shauna to stand at the other end. Then I asked Shauna to slowly walk toward Milo and asked Milo to notice if there was any change in his body sensations and, if something did happen, to ask Shauna to stop. As Shauna came within about ten feet of Milo, he cried out, "Stop!" I asked what had happened, and he said he felt like his guts were twisting. I asked Shauna to slowly back up, and Milo was amazed when the sensation went away after Shauna had walked backward a few feet. We tried having her move forward and back a few times, and each time the sensation would reappear when Shauna got within ten feet of Milo.

At this point, the implications were raining down on Milo's awareness, and he became angry with himself for having been so out of touch and for having this unconscious reaction to Shauna. Wanting to break through the twisting feeling, he asked Shauna to walk right up to him. This caused his throat to close down so much that he began to choke, and she backed off.

Milo learned that he had been reacting to the unconscious sensation of his guts twisting when he felt too close to Shauna and realized that his "constructive feedback" had been his unconscious way of reducing his discomfort by pushing her away. Now aware of the sensation, he was able to simply ask Shauna for space (literally) when he needed it instead of putting her down, and she was more than happy to give it to him. Interestingly, as he learned that he could ask for and get as much space as he needed, the gut-wrenching sensation slowly went away.

What I am trying to help you understand here is the power of body sensations and the extent to which they unconsciously compel our actions. These sensations do not exist randomly. In this case, you will recognize that Milo was unaware of the intimacy anxiety he was feeling toward Shauna or of what he actually wanted. But his sensations told the story. Sensations contain very useful information about what is going on inside us. Some people learn to listen to sensations that offer warnings, like a grumbling in the stomach, a pain in the neck, tension between the shoulders, and so on. Sometimes they are not even that aware of the actual sensation but have a nagging doubt that can't be put into words.

By learning to listen to the body, we can learn to become aware of the unconscious aspects of our thoughts, emotions, and wants. We can learn whether or not the stories we are making up about ourselves are true by developing an awareness of the internal BS detector built into our bodies. Subjective truths that we have been keeping at the unconscious level often first come into awareness through sensation.

Emotions

Emotions are sensations with a message. There are hundreds of emotional words in the English language, but the average person in my classes has a hard time listing twenty when given a few minutes to do so. If you want to see how rich your emotional map is, put down this book and list all the emotional words you can think of in one minute.

How many did you get? Now test them to make sure you actually listed emotions. Some people confuse judgments and feelings. They might say something like, "I feel OK." Where in the body does a person feel OK? This is actually a judgment (thought) about how they are feeling, not an emotion. Maybe they feel happy or excited or amused—three very different emotions that someone might judge as OK. Sensations like cold, hot, and hungry are different from emotions, though those words are sometimes used to describe emotions. The hot I feel from the sun is a sensation; the hot I feel when I dress up is an emotion. Check to see how many of the words on your list are also on the emotional word chart on pages 162–163 in Chapter 6. If they aren't on the chart, use this question to challenge each word: Where in your body do you feel this emotion? You may have to wait until the next time you are feeling it before you know.

After you've whittled down your words, how many valid emotions did you actually list? If you got more than fifteen, you have a significantly richer emotional vocabulary than the average college-educated North American. Sure, people will recognize hundreds of emotional words, but it's not the same as having them handy on your feeling map. Without the words, it is very difficult to describe our emotions to ourselves or to others.

Perhaps you know emotional words but don't think you actually feel them in your body. You have a sense of when you feel happy and angry, but mostly you're not aware of having much feeling. This is a common experience for men unless their capacity to feel has been activated. Robert Bly (who started the men's movement in the 1980s) contends that men generally learn how to feel their emotions only by having a close relationship with an older man who has learned to feel his emotions. That was true in my life. The birth of a child can also activate feeling in men, but the full spectrum only comes to those who are initiated into their feelings in some way. Bly also says that women don't seem to need that kind of initiation and that women cannot initiate men into their feelings.

The same circumstances that lead us to be numb to our body sensations lead us to be unconscious about a lot of the emotions that are too big for our small bodies and would overwhelm our experience. We try to not feel them, and many of us succeed. In some families, only certain emotions are allowed. It can be OK to express anger but not to express fear, OK to feel happy but not to feel sad (or vice versa). The permutations could be endless. We tend to be aware of those emotions that we learned were OK in our families of origin and unconscious about the rest.

Emotions have an enormous impact on our experiences and therefore on the decisions and actions that occur in organizations. In some organizations, the culture does not consider discussion of feelings to be legitimate. In my view, that is a sure way to reduce the ability to build successful partnership-based organizations. It's bad enough that so many people are operating on unconscious feelings. This in itself makes feelings a force outside awareness and choice. To then try to make them socially unacceptable and banish discussion of them is a double whammy. People have feelings, and those feelings powerfully affect what they say and do. Trying to ignore them simply pushes them underground and makes them much more difficult to manage.

Decisions often are not implemented because they violate people's feelings. How about the strategic plans of major corporations that call for radical changes and just get ignored? One company I've worked with developed a strategy that entailed widespread implementation of empowered (leaderless) work teams. It never happened. Executives who verbally agreed to this part of the strategy had very mixed emotions about it. They were uncomfortable with leaderless groups, but it wasn't OK to say so because, logically, the groups looked like a good idea. So they officially agreed on the strategy and then communicated plans that weren't followed. As a result, everyone felt just a little less sure about what to believe and what to do in the future. Who knows what the opportunity costs were for them? When an organization acknowledges feelings and integrates them into problem solving and decision making, it creates better plans that people will implement. That's about as no-nonsense as you can get.

I believe that the hallmark of emotional growth is the ability to fully feel one's sensations and emotions without being overwhelmed by them, to be able to contain them without diminishing them and so be aware of what they are while still acting rationally and purposefully. For me, this meant learning to feel my anxiety and take the risks anyway, learning to feel sorrow while taking aggressive necessary action, learning to feel my real caring for certain people while saying things that I knew would disturb them. That is part of what self-differentiation is all about.

The Element of Wanting

The fourth element of experience is wanting—the desires, intentions, motivations, aspirations, needs, and wishes you are having moment to moment as well as the objectives, targets, ideals, and goals you are pursuing. I believe that each of us is born with a clear sense of what we want at any moment. Just watch young children—they know exactly what they want. But the process of growing up in our society leads many of us to lose awareness of our wants. As children, we want many things that we are told we can't have, often for good reasons. To survive, we have to learn to repress our wants and do things like sit quietly in classrooms when we'd much rather be doing something else. Learning to delay gratification has many very good consequences, but it also has the negative consequence of making us less aware of our current wants. In addition, in our consumer society, we are inundated with messages about what we should want, which confuses us even more about our real wants. By the time we reach adulthood, most of us are so confused that we are often much clearer about what we don't want than what we do want. Sometimes we have to get what we think we want before we can find out if we really want it.

One of the things that gets in the way of our being aware of our wants is feeling cautious about expressing wants. Some people have been taught that it is selfish, or impolite, to express their wants. Others have learned that it causes problems in relationships when they talk about their wants, so it is better to just say nothing. In both cases, these are normal adaptations to being around people who react negatively when we say what we want. In chapter 3, I explained the problem of fusion. When I am fused with you, I am compelled to respond to what you say you want. It's not OK for you to just say what you want and leave it at that. When I am fused, I will think I must either try to give you what you want, help you figure out how to get it, or convince you that you don't want it or that it is not good for you. I feel burdened by your wants and may express my annoyance. Under these conditions, people learn that if they say what they want, then they have to contend with the reactive person's response. Better to just not say anything.

But, you see, the problem is not that you are expressing your want. There's only a problem if you expect me to satisfy it for you. A manager who thinks she has to satisfy or change every want that's expressed has a boundary problem, and the separation anxiety that fuels it gets passed back as a bad feeling and more interpersonal mush. How can a manager effectively motivate and lead people if she doesn't know what they want? She can't. It is impossible to build and sustain partnerships if people aren't clear about what they want, especially from one another. But the fused manager will feel so compelled to respond to the wants of others that she'll try to avoid hearing them in the first place by conveying the message that expressing wants, or wanting too much, is not a good thing.

In organizations, as in any other kind of relationship, people rarely get what they want unless they are clear with themselves and others about what they want. If people are not getting what they want, they won't want to be in partnership, so expression of wants is vital. You cannot negotiate good deals, develop win-win solutions to problems, or connect tasks to motivated people unless everyone is clear about what everyone else wants. It is as simple, and as difficult, as that. One rule of partnership is that people have to say what they want. The second rule is that they shouldn't expect to get it. People are not responsible for giving others what they want, but when they are in a partnership, committed to the mutual success of a process or project, they probably want to look for ways to make it more likely that those other people get what they want.

One terrible trap for managers is to let people say only what they don't want and still be responsible for satisfying them. I've seen this happen most often in union–management interactions, when the union says, "You are management—you propose, and we'll tell you if we like it." I have also found that managers ask subordinates what they think, and maybe even what they feel, but forget to ask what they want because the managers assume that the wants will be obvious once they know what their employees think and feel. Well, that's not always how it works. I am still often surprised by what people say they want after I think I already know. Trying to satisfy people's wants when you've made up their wants is as good a way to drive yourself crazy as letting them tell you only what they don't want.

Finally, there is the problem of thinking that our wants are not OK, that to want what we want is in some way wrong, illegitimate, immature, or whatever. Let's face it, there are lots things we want that we don't give ourselves. I may want to not get out of bed and go to work, but I do anyway. I may want to buy a totally impractical little red convertible, or you may want to buy a little black cocktail dress that you will wear only twice a year, but we don't. All of us are going to censor some of what we tell others about our real wants and motivations, if for no other reason than to avoid embarrassment. This can be dangerous in partnerships, however, if people are not saying what they really want just because they want to go along with the others. Jerry Harvey tells a now famous story of a family who drove one hundred miles to Abilene one dusty day to have lunch at a diner when no one really wanted to go there simply because family members didn't want to offend anybody and so did not say what they really wanted.[1] This kind of thing can happen because people are afraid to say what they want or because they really care about the others and are willing to go along with what the others appear to want. The family members in the story had good intentions but lousy skills. They were not telling the truth of their experience because they wanted to avoid looking selfish and to respect the stories they had made up about what the others wanted.

Sustaining partnership requires that you understand the wants and motivations of the people you want to be in partnership with. That might be your boss, colleagues, subordinates, suppliers, customers, whoever. As a clear leader, you have to lead in creating a culture of clarity by telling the truth about your own wants and being genuinely curious about the wants of others. People are only going to be as forthright as you are, so you need to think hard before censoring your wants, especially if you don't want others to censor theirs in return. And it could be good to let subordinates know that you, too, are human, have childish or impractical wants, and can express your wants without expecting that they will be satisfied!

Summary

Clear leadership assumes that all people create their own experience and that everyone involved in a similar event is having a unique experience. The experience cube is a model of experience and, as you'll see in the next three chapters, a very useful tool for clear leadership. Observations are what we see and hear, what a video camera would record. Thoughts are the interpretations, ideas, judgments, and beliefs we have. Feelings are the sensations and emotions we have in our bodies, and wants are the desires, motivations, goals, and aspirations that animate our actions.

The experience cube model proposes that each of us is having observations, thoughts, feelings, and wants in every moment. The sum of these four makes up our experience. You are aware of some of these and unaware of others. Learning from experience requires that people be able to access their full range of experience and describe it to others. That ability begins with awareness.

5

The Aware Self

Knowing Your Experience Moment to Moment

It has become almost a cliché for leadership books and courses to talk about the need for self-awareness—but what does that mean? My intention in this book is to make that as concrete as possible. The Clear Leadership model proposes that the key aspect of self-awareness is the ability to know what your moment-to-moment, here-and-now experience is. All other forms of real self-awareness flow from this.

Why is awareness a basic skill of clear leaders? Because in order to collectively learn from our experience, we first need to know what our experience is. You can't lead learning if you are not able to understand your own experience and uncover other people's experiences. You can't sustain partnerships if you can't learn, adapt, and adjust on the basis of your collective experience. A commitment to being self-aware is the first step.

The figure on page 110 shows my mental map of being an Aware Self. It says that the mastery of the Aware Self is knowing what my moment-to-moment experience is. Here are the best models and techniques I've found to do this:

- Fill in the cube

- Use clear language

- Talk about right here, right now

- Identify your mental maps

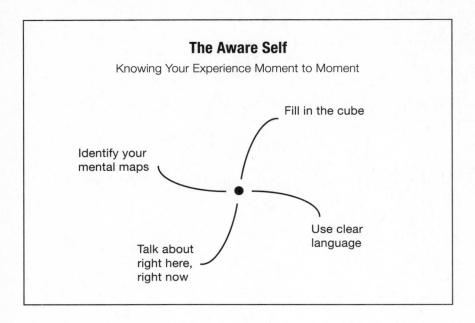

The sequence does not matter. All are important and should be used in parallel for the greatest possible awareness.

I'll begin by reviewing issues involved in becoming aware of different parts of the experience cube. Then I'll identify patterns in how we speak that mystify our experience to ourselves and others and look at how to correct that. Next, I'll explain the here and now and why an ability to be present is necessary for leading learning and sustaining partnership. Finally, I'll show how our experience is shaped by the architecture of our thinking and why awareness of that is crucial for leading organizational learning. At the end of the chapter, I'll offer some ways to practice increasing your awareness.

Fill In the Cube

Imagine that we all have four containers (the four elements of experience). At any moment, we can stop and dip into a container to see what is there. Different people are able to dip into different containers and to different depths. Some of us can dip into a couple of containers quite deeply and then barely know where to find the others. Others skim easily along the top of all four containers but can't reach down too far. There are endless variations in people's awareness of their experience, but I think we all have pretty much the same containers and can all learn how to dip deeper into each one of them.

Part of the problem of awareness is simply paying attention. The more people pay attention to all four parts of the cube, the more aware of their experience they become. Part of the problem is being able to be in the here and now. The more you pay attention to your moment-to-moment experience, the more you will learn just how much of your experience is outside your awareness but is affecting you nonetheless.

Each person has a different level of awareness in each element, and each person has a different speed at which he or she becomes aware. At one extreme are those who are fully aware of what they think in the moment. At the other are those who need time to be by themselves to figure out what they think. Some people know what they are feeling as they are feeling it. Others have no sense that they are feeling anything. And the same is true of observations and desires. There is a continuum of awareness in each element of experience, and we are all different in each area. The skill of being an Aware Self is to be fully aware, right in the moment, of what you are observing, thinking, feeling, and wanting.

Thinking

Thinking tends to be the most developed element of experience among professionals and businesspeople. People tend to be more aware of what they are thinking than of what they are feeling, observing, or wanting. Even so, there can be thoughts that are outside of awareness, particularly if these thoughts are in some way threatening to a person. The things I don't want to think about are still rattling around in my head, just outside my immediate awareness.

How do unconscious thoughts affect your decisions, choices, and actions? Let me give you an example.

Peter and Mosen were marketing managers in different parts of the same organization. They were responsible for marketing their organization's product in very different sales channels, and reported to different managers, but they both thought it was important to have an effective partnership. They'd been hired at this fast-growing firm within six months of each other, and they quickly developed a camaraderie and willingness to work together for their mutual success. They liked to joke together and often went out for drinks after work. Over time, however, Peter became less and less available. Mosen was troubled by what he called the "lack of communication" he experienced from Peter. Peter was making marketing decisions without consulting or informing Mosen. When they were together, things seemed fine, but Mosen started getting the distinct impression that Peter was avoiding him.

When the organization hired me to help explore possibilities for reorganizing, Mosen confided his concerns about the situation. He was convinced that Peter was competing with him for a promotion and wasn't sure he could trust him. When I talked to Peter, none of this came out. He described his admiration of Mosen's expertise and how much he appreciated the partnership he had with Mosen. I discreetly prodded Peter to try and understand what Mosen might be experiencing, but all I got from Peter was that the relationship was fine. I went back to Mosen and described what I'd heard from Peter. Then I suggested that something must be going on to create Mosen's experience of Peter and that it ought to be cleared up. With my urging, Mosen decided to ask Peter to have a learning conversation within the context of my coaching. Peter agreed to participate.

We started the conversation with Mosen describing his experience of Peter being less available and communicative. At first, Peter reacted defensively. He insisted that his behavior hadn't changed much at all and, if it had, that there were good reasons having to do with being busy. When Mosen described specific times when he'd been left out of the loop, Peter provided explanations and rationales that had nothing to do with Mosen. I then asked Mosen to describe how he felt and what he wanted, and Mosen described how much he missed the quality of their relationship and the fun he'd had with Peter. At this point, Peter became less defensive and more pensive. He said he was surprised by what Mosen was saying. As I explored Peter's experience of Mosen at work and away from work, he stopped, stared off into space, and finally said, "I've been trying to pretend that it's OK, but it's not OK. I didn't want to admit that I feel put down by you, so I've just been ignoring it. But I guess I started thinking you don't respect me." As it turned out, what to Mosen was just "joking around" had sometimes landed hard on Peter, but Peter didn't want to show that or admit to himself that it bothered him. He seemed to have a hard time just admitting that he was hurt.

They were both becoming pretty uncomfortable with the whole tone of
the conversation, and to lighten the mood, we joked about them being
like a married couple. Mosen was surprised and apologetic about the
impact he'd had on Peter. They reaffirmed their desire to be in partnership at work and decided to go out for a drink. Mosen later told me
that things got better after that.

An unconscious thought, feeling, or want can be a very powerful determinant of our experience, and, because it is unconscious, it is outside
our choicefulness. Peter wasn't aware that he thought Mosen didn't respect him. He didn't want to have that thought, so he kept it out of his
awareness. But that didn't stop it from influencing his behavior; he just
didn't notice that he was avoiding Mosen. That's what often happens with
unconscious thoughts—they influence our actions in ways we don't consciously choose. Other people notice the change in behavior, but we don't.
In this case, Peter's unconscious thought was causing him to behave in
ways that were at odds with his conscious desire to be in partnership with
Mosen. If they hadn't had this learning conversation, I'm sure their partnership would have continued to fall apart.

Peter's reason for keeping this thought unconscious is a subject for
psychotherapy and doesn't concern us here. I have found that people
don't need to learn why they make some part of their experience unconscious in order to become conscious of it. I offer some techniques for
increasing your awareness of your thoughts at the end of this chapter. For
now, what is important is that you understand that a portion of your
experience is composed of thoughts (beliefs, values, opinions, judgments,
cognition, and so on) and that some of your thoughts can be outside your
awareness but still part of your experience. Bringing these thoughts to
awareness almost always requires being in conversation with others. It's
much more difficult to do it by yourself.

Feelings

Some cultures value feelings more than others do. In those that don't,
people are subtly trained to keep their feelings out of awareness. A way to
repress feelings is to close down the diaphragm, that area in the center of
the body just below the rib cage. This stops feelings from traveling upward

into the chest and into awareness. When I was repressing my feelings in this way, my diaphragm was sore, but that sensation was usually outside my awareness until I poked my diaphragm. Another consequence was that the repressed strong feelings put force on the closed diaphragm, which caused the spine to torque subtly, which in turn led to lower back pain. For years I had lower back pain, which I don't get anymore. I wonder how much of the lower back pain in our society is caused by repressed feelings.

In organizations, the effect of repressing feelings is just as debilitating. Even when individuals are aware of their feelings, the organization may not encourage disclosure. "Decisions and plans should be based on sound analysis of facts and logic, not emotion and feelings" goes the mantra of organizational repression. But as I pointed out in the last chapter, feelings are a key part of our experience, and a lot of sense making revolves around them. People may talk about logic and analysis, but what they actually decide and do is based as much on their feelings as on anything else. By not talking about our feelings, all we do is keep them outside our awareness, where they can't be discussed and dealt with choicefully. The most powerful feeling, and one that rarely gets talked about in organizations, is anxiety.

The Role of Anxiety

After observing hundreds of groups make and avoid making decisions, I have come to the conclusion that the strongest force in organizational behavior is the avoidance of one feeling: anxiety. The profit motive pales in comparison. I have seen decisions taken that left millions of dollars on the table so that people would not have to deal with issues that made them feel anxious. These are common examples of anxiety avoidance: not confronting nonperforming managers or departments, not exploring new ideas that are outside people's competence or comfort zone, silencing views or perspectives that challenge the currently accepted view of things, ignoring signals that competitive threats are increasing, and avoiding making decisions when there are strongly held differences of opinion. Embarrassment is a common form of anxiety that we seem to want to avoid at all costs. The rule seems to be "Don't embarrass yourself and don't embarrass others." Those who consistently break this rule won't get very far in traditional organizations.

On the one hand, causing unnecessary embarrassment or anxiety is not an effective approach for working with people. In fact, leading learning requires you to be a nonanxious presence. That doesn't mean tolerating complacency or smoothing over concerns that need to be addressed for the system's good. Interpersonal clarity requires the willingness to look squarely at and confront anxiety-provoking issues. This, in turn, means that you must be able to tolerate your own anxiety—to be differentiated from it, not acting out of it but aware of it and acting rationally in spite of it.

Anxiety is a particularly difficult problem for successful people because many of them are not aware of being anxious. Learning to be unaware of anxiety has some very useful consequences for an ambitious person. Anxiety can be paralyzing. Anxiety can stop us from taking risks. Anxiety can make us tongue-tied, cause us to lose our wits when we most need them. We are able to appear courageous when we are really just unaware of our fears. The brashest, most confident, most seemingly self-assured people are the ones who typically get ahead in business. Anxiety doesn't look good, and visible anxiety makes others get in touch with their own anxiety, which is doubly unwelcome. As a consequence, there are a disproportionate number of senior managers in organizations who lack awareness of their own anxiety.

The downside of this lack of awareness is that anxiety affects behavior in unconscious ways. People don't even know that they are acting out of their anxiety, or, more precisely, their desire to avoid anxiety. Aside from the personal impact, such as addictive behaviors that exist primarily to keep anxiety and other difficult feelings out of awareness, the lack of awareness has two very negative consequences for creating partnership in teams and organizations. One is that such leaders are not acting rationally when they think they are. The other is that they tend to become increasingly disconnected from the people who work for them because unconsciously anxious people manage their anxiety by pushing away any source of anxiety. If a decision causes anxiety, it is put off. When someone is creating anxiety for them, they do something to make the person want to go away. All of this is done without awareness, so the unconsciously anxious people don't even realize what is going on. Even those who think of themselves as people-oriented and caring will act this way out of unconscious anxiety. They become, as described in chapter 3, disconnected. Here's a typical scenario.

A subordinate gives his unconsciously anxious boss an update on a project. There is bad news. The boss gets anxious as she hears the bad news and, without being aware of what she is doing or why, begins to tell the subordinate how to fix the situation even though she doesn't really understand it. Each time the subordinate tries to tell the boss that he has already tried her fix or starts to give her more information, she interrupts with more solutions. After a while, the subordinate just stops telling her what he really thinks, feels, and wants. He assures his boss that everything will work out and leaves feeling frustrated, unsupported, and demoralized. The boss, oblivious to what has gone on, thinks she has done a good job of getting her subordinate back on track. The interpersonal mush is thicker than ever, and the subordinate's sense of partnership is diminished.

Feelings affect what we think and want and motivate us to take action. Whether it is anxiety or any other unconscious emotion, we need to make sense of our actions to ourselves and will search for sufficient external justification for actions that are really motivated by feelings. For example, when I avoid dealing with someone because doing so would make me anxious, I could rationalize it any number of ways—I am too busy to deal with that person right now, other issues are more pressing, it's Friday afternoon so I'll leave it for Monday, I don't really have rapport with that person and so-and-so should probably deal with it, maybe dealing with it would just makes things worse so I'll just sit tight and watch it for a while to see what happens. And so on.

Like other aspects of experience, feelings that are outside our awareness exert a powerful influence that we cannot control. What happens when we acknowledge that our emotions are getting in the way of rational decisions and actions? We're able to act more rationally. By naming the feeling we reduce its power, and we can take it into account in making decisions, which are then more likely to be implemented.

Wants

Bringing wants into awareness is difficult for some people. I described some of the reasons for that in the previous chapter. We may be unaware because of simple lack of attention or because part of us doesn't want to know. And some people could be unaware because they lack the inner resources to know what they really need. At a critical stage in infancy, they rarely got what they needed and so never developed the ability to know what they truly need. These people don't know what they want until they get what they think they want and then see how they feel about it. If you are damaged in this way, learning to know what you want requires therapy with someone who is skilled in very early childhood developmental healing. But people can increase their awareness of their wants by assuming that they are having wants in every moment and then paying close attention to what is motivating them.

Some normal human motivations are socially acceptable, and some aren't. It's the unacceptable motivations that are most likely out of awareness. I'd rather not notice the part of me that wants to always win an argument—that's greedy, vengeful, and so on. I pretend that if I'm not aware of those parts of me, I won't act out of them either. So I won't notice when the greedy part takes more than I need just so I'll be sure to have enough, or when I'm arguing just for the sake of winning. As I become aware of these wants, I gain more control over my actions. I notice when I'm taking more than I need and then choose whether I want to leave some for others or be greedy. Knowing what I want doesn't stop me from wanting it, but it does make choosing my actions easier.

Uncovering all my less-than-perfect motivations and coming to accept them lead me to develop compassion for myself, and in turn I develop more compassion for others. It then becomes easier for others to own up to their less-than-perfect motivations in my presence. We can acknowledge the realities and limitations of our wants and needs and make choices that we'll probably follow through on.

A good technique for discovering your real motivations is to look at your results. Since you are creating your experience, and other people are having different experiences in the same situation, there must be a part of you that wants to have this particular experience. If you are constantly winning at something, there must be a part of you that wants to win. That seems obvious to most people. If you are constantly failing at something, there must be a part of you that wants to fail. That seems less obvious, yet in my experience it is nonetheless a subjective truth. Why would someone do something and want to fail? A very interesting question.

Early in my work life, I had a string of lousy bosses. At least, that was how I described it. More accurately, I had a string of experiences of bosses with whom I did not get along, who seemed incompetent to me, for whom I felt contempt, and who ended up firing me. After I'd had the same experience three or four times, it occurred to me that maybe it wasn't them—maybe I was doing something that caused me to have the experience of seemingly incompetent bosses. After I rooted around in the bottom of my wants bucket for a while, I discovered that I wanted to be the star in every authority's eyes. I wanted my bosses to immediately realize how outstanding I was, and I wanted to feel warm and close to them. When I got this from leaders, I became a great employee, but when I didn't, I quickly pulled away from them and started looking for reasons to lessen their authority and importance in my mind. Because they did not immediately see and embrace my competence, I wanted to believe that they were incompetent. I didn't want to work there anymore. And that was the result I created.

Some people have, I think, taken this perspective too far. They will say such things as "If you have cancer, you must want to die." I believe that people create their experiences out of what happens to them, but I also believe that things happen to people that they wouldn't choose. The flip side of "I create my own experience" is "shit happens." But it is a great aid to awareness to take the point of view that since I attract what I get into my life, it helps to look at what I'm getting if I want to know what my unconscious wants are.

A critical aspect of wants in any partnership are the things I want from you—things I want you to do, to say, to feel, and to want. I want people who work with me to have certain kinds of experiences. Most learning conversations get to a point that people talk about what they want from one another and from themselves. Just because I want something, however, doesn't mean I expect to get it. Knowing I want you to have a certain kind of experience, describing it to you, and being choiceful about how I act if I don't get it is a completely different thing from being fused with you. When I'm fused, I'm not really aware of what I am doing; I am simply reacting to my bad feelings and getting you to try to change what you say or do. There is no awareness in fusion. Being in partnership and leading learning require being clear about what I actually need—the absolute must-haves if I am to continue working with these people in this organization—and the difference between these needs and what I want. The more awareness I have of my needs and wants, and the distinction between them, the more I can ensure that my wants don't get in the way of working together. So I may still want to be the gleam in every authority's eye, but I know I don't need it. I can work just fine with someone who doesn't think I walk on water. And because I am clear about what I do need, I'm more likely to create experiences that allow me to get it.

Awareness is the first step, and our awareness is shaped in many ways by our language. A person's awareness increases when she stops using common errors of language that mystify her experience. Her thoughts become attuned to differences between subjective and objective reality, and her wants become clearer. This leads us to a second aspect of being an Aware Self.

Use Clear Language

There is something about the way we are taught to talk about our experience that leads us to confuse what is inside with what is outside. It leads us to mystify ourselves and others, and it reduces our awareness of creating our own experience. This seems to be a cross-cultural phenomenon. From what I can tell, people who speak different languages and have very different cultures do similar things. We all talk about the things inside us as if they were outside us.

For example, if someone enters a room and feels cold, he is most likely to say, "It's cold in here." Coldness is a sensation, an inner experience. I have canvassed rooms of people and found that some are cold, some are hot, and some are neither. The feeling of cold is inside the person. Notice how this common way of thinking and talking takes the origin of the experience out of the person and puts it in the room. What is inside is described as being outside. Since language shapes how we think, we are actually confusing ourselves into thinking that what is inside is outside. When I think, "It's hot in here," or "It's tense on that team," or "It's fun in this organization," I have confused inside and outside. It's not fun in this organization; I have fun in this organization. There are probably other people who are not having any fun. But when I talk in this normal way, I have lost the clear boundaries between what is in me and what isn't, and so I am less differentiated. If our language assumes that our experience (hot, tense, fun) is everyone else's experience, that will be how we think about it. We won't even see it as our experience, but rather as a quality of the place or group, and we'll assume that others are having the same experience. In effect, we are treating a subjective truth as if it were an intersubjective or objective truth.

One way we have of confusing inside and outside that really contributes to interpersonal mush is saying "you" when it's really about "I." Many people do this, and not only do they confuse the people they are talking to but they confuse themselves. Here's an example from my interview with an engineer who was talking about his disappointment that his new designs had not been enough to improve product quality.

When you go and see what they've done in that factory, you just want to cry about the mess they've made. We really worked hard to improve the machines and ensure a leap in quality improvement, but you look at their attitude and just have to shake your head. You think to yourself, "If I were running the plant, I could really make a difference," but it's not up to you, and there's nothing you can do about it. We tried our best, but it's out of our hands.

Obviously, the speaker is the one who just wants to cry about it. You-language is so prevalent that most of us have learned to translate it when we hear it. But who is this "we" who worked hard to improve the machines? It turns out it was the speaker, but that was not obvious until I asked. Notice how you-language and we-language mislead people into thinking that their experience is generalizable, that everyone else would have the same thoughts and feelings in the given situation. It's confusing trying to follow who is having what experience. Every time I say, "We think such and such," I confuse myself (not to mention the people listening to me) about who thinks what.

The rule of clear language is very simple—say "I" when you are talking about your own experience. It is so simple, yet the impact is so profound on both you and your relationships that if you don't currently use I-language, it may be the single most important thing you can do to increase your self-differentiation and ability to learn in partnership.

Inappropriate you-language makes it harder for people to engage with one another. If Jean is sitting at a meeting and Natalie says something like "You can't get Bob to listen without sitting on his head," and Jean doesn't have that experience, what happens? The only obvious way to engage in that conversation is to begin by disagreeing, when, really, it's simply that Jean and Natalie have different experiences. Natalie has presented her subjective truth as an objective truth. Most people would just let it pass, not wanting to start a disagreement. By using you-language, Natalie has made it more difficult for Jean to engage with and be curious about her experience.

You-language is so ubiquitous and seems so natural that even people watching themselves on videotape, trying to learn not to use it, will miss seeing it when they are doing it. Here are some common examples of hard-to-spot you-language, we-language, and it-language:

- It depends on how you look at it (when it really depends on how I look at it).

- We need to take a break (when really I need to take a break).

- We're glad you came (when really I'm glad you came).

- It's scary to tell the boss the truth (when really I'm scared to tell the boss the truth).

Why do we talk in ways that mystify ourselves, that make what is inside seem to be outside and mix up different kinds of truth? Some of us were taught that it is impolite or ineffective to talk about "I." As children, we were taught that it made us look selfish or self-absorbed. We're afraid people won't like us if we talk about "I." Or there are those who have been taught as adults that there's no "I" in "team." They believe they will engender more team spirit if they talk about "we" instead of "I." Does a manager who expresses his experience as "what we think" or "what we want" really create a greater sense of teamwork? I don't think so. I think it actually creates the opposite if the employees who are listening to the manager talk about what "we" think are actually thinking something else.

The thousands of managers who have taken the Clear Leadership course report that shifting from you-language to I-language improves their sense of connection and rapport with one another. Rather than creating the appearance of being self-absorbed, I-language makes them seem more disclosing and personal. Conversations are more interesting, people get to the point more quickly, and the whole point of what the other person is talking about seems much clearer. If the effects of I-language are so obviously positive, why do so many people use you-language?

One reason is that you-language makes it easier not to take responsibility for our experience. If it is outside ourselves, we don't have to hold ourselves accountable. When I say, "It's tense in here," I don't have to take responsibility for the tension I feel. I don't have to confront the possibility that there are other people who aren't feeling tense and ask myself why

I am if they aren't. Rather than making a statement about myself, which makes me feel a little vulnerable and exposed, I seem to be making a statement about the situation.

Another reason is that you-language and we-language helps us avoid responsibility for our opinions and judgments. The engineer in the example above did not have to look at whether he had really been effective in his attempts to improve product quality because, due to his way of confusing inside and outside, anyone in his situation would see that it was the plant's fault. By saying "we tried our best," he could even avoid a sense of personal failure by spreading it around to a "we" that didn't exist.

This way of confusing things helps people manage the belonging–individuality paradox because they avoid saying things that might separate them from others and yet do not give up their individuality. You-language allows me to state strong personal judgments in a way that is less threatening to my membership in the group. When I say, "It's scary to tell the boss the truth," I am saying something that could threaten my relationship with others, especially my boss. Saying it in this depersonalized, externalized way seems much less threatening than saying, "I'm scared to tell you the truth." But like all forms of fusion, it only appears to be helping because it reduces anxiety. Instead, it makes things worse because it creates interpersonal mush. The first statement ("It's scary to tell the boss the truth") mystifies my interaction with my boss by seeming to make a general statement about the way things are. It does not appear, on the face of it, to be a statement about my experience. We could debate its objective truth, but that would be irrelevant, because what I really mean is that I'm scared to tell you, my boss, the truth, but I am saying it in code. Maybe my boss will figure it out, and maybe he won't. Maybe I won't realize that not everyone is scared to tell my boss the truth, and probably we'll never even get close to discussing why I find my boss, the person, scary to speak honestly with. Only the direct statement "I'm scared to tell you the truth" brings real awareness and promotes a conversation in which we tell each other the truth of our experiences and can learn together.

When we use language that clarifies, we don't confuse objective, subjective, and intersubjective reality: we keep them distinct, and so make it easier to create both clarity and agreement with others. Occasionally, I hear someone disagree with another person's experience. I am always surprised when I hear it. One person is clearly talking about his own subjective truth and another will say, "I disagree." She doesn't mean "I don't believe that is your subjective truth," she means "That is not my subjective truth," but again she is confusing the nature of subjective truth. What is usually going on is that the person who is disagreeing has made a leap in her thinking—she is disagreeing with the story she has just made up about the other person's experience. In her mind, she has taken the other person's "I" and turned it into "you" or "we."

Correctly thinking and saying "you" when you mean "you," "I" when you mean "I," "it" when you mean "it," and "we" when you are referring to a group that includes you really helps avoid problems created by confusing different types of truth. It is one of the simple yet powerful clear leadership skills and will greatly increase your ability to create and sustain effective partnerships. Clear language increases your awareness and reduces the interpersonal mush you are building around you. It is easy to describe, but some people find that it is difficult to do and takes a lot of practice and coaching to master.

Talk About Right Here, Right Now

Some self-awareness comes from solitary reflection, but much of collectively learning from experience and building partnership comes from interaction. The back-and-forth of inquiring into our experience brings into awareness parts of our experience that were out of awareness. When I'm thinking about the past, I'm having a memory of my experience. It's almost impossible to uncover new aspects of my experience from my memories. Memories are shaped by my beliefs and mental maps, so I am only going to be able to notice the parts of my past experience that I'm already aware of. Only by paying attention to the experience I am having, while I am having it, do I get around my defenses against self-awareness. And perhaps even more important for organizational learning and partnership, it's often only in the here and now that I can understand the impact I am having on your experience. Let me tell you about one of my first experiences with an inquiry into a pattern of interaction that led to new knowledge and a change in that pattern.

When I was in my late teens, at university, some women labeled me arrogant. When they said this to me, I couldn't understand what they were talking about. My inner experience at that time, especially around women, was of being uncertain, vulnerable, scared, and confused, and I didn't see how that could come across as arrogant, which I thought of as being superior, know-it-all, and dismissive. When I would ask a woman why she had labeled me this way, she would talk about some interaction that had taken place with her or someone else and describe my behavior in a way that did not match my memory at all. I felt terribly misunderstood, and this, of course, increased my fear and confusion around women even more.

The student organization I belonged to organized a weekend leadership retreat that involved numerous experiential activities. In one activity, we were divided into two groups and asked to compete to build the best Tinkertoy tower. I was assigned to be a worker in one of the groups and was sitting in a circle with the other four workers when a facilitator came by and dumped some Tinkertoy pieces in the center of the circle. I started to pass the pieces out when the woman sitting across from me said, "There—you are doing it again!" I sat back, puzzled. "Doing what again?" "You're handing out the Tinkertoy pieces!" "Yeah, so?" "It's that arrogant part of you. Who said you were in charge and could hand out the pieces?!" At that moment, it was as if the clouds parted, a heavenly choir started singing hallelujahs, and I could finally connect my actions and intentions with the feedback I'd been getting. My experience of what happened when the Tinkertoy pieces were put in front of us was wondering how I could be helpful and thinking that the only thing I could do would be to hand out the pieces. Her experience was that I was taking control and putting myself in charge. While that was not my intention, I could see how my actions could have that impact—like, who said I could hand out the Tinkertoy pieces? I finally understood that it would help to get assent before acting on my ideas, even though I thought they were for the benefit of others.

That was breakthrough learning for me (and a breakthrough conversation in my relationship with that colleague), but I never would have gotten it if that conversation hadn't taken place in the here and now. Seeing myself as mainly interested in being helpful, how could I understand when others called me controlling or self-oriented? Without being able to put together the variety of experiences as they were happening in the moment, I don't think I would ever have understood it.

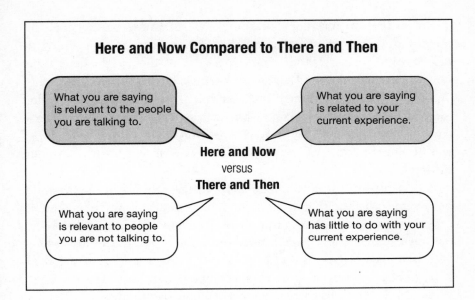

Here and Now Compared to There and Then

What you are saying is relevant to the people you are talking to.

What you are saying is related to your current experience.

Here and Now
versus
There and Then

What you are saying is relevant to people you are not talking to.

What you are saying has little to do with your current experience.

What is "right here, right now," and how is that different from what we normally talk about? The figure above identifies the difference between talking in the here and now and talking in the there and then. When I talk in the here, whatever I am talking about is relevant to the people I'm talking to. If I am talking about something that happened to me but is of little relevance to them, I'm not here. If I'm talking about people who are not in the conversation, I'm not here either. When I talk in the now, whatever I'm talking about is connected to my current experience. It's not simply the observations, thoughts, feelings, and wants I'm having at this moment; it's also anything that has happened in the past or that I'm thinking about in the future if it is influencing my current observations, thoughts, feelings, and wants. So if I am talking to you about something you did last week that is influencing how I am feeling today, that is very much a here-and-now conversation. If I'm talking to you about my thoughts about how a decision made six months ago affected the organization's success and is influencing my thinking about a decision we are making now, that is also in the here and now. But if I am talking to you about my concerns about another employee's actions, and the employee is not in the conversation, that is not in the here and now. If I talk about my ideas for how to improve service in my department, and you are not in my department, that is also not talking in the here and now.

In leading organizational learning and sustaining partnership, the most important part of talking in the here and now is your ability to talk to your partners about your experience of them right here, right now. Can you look them in the eye and tell them what you are really observing, thinking, feeling, and wanting in regard to them at this moment? Can you remain calm while your partner describes his experience of you right here, right now? Any limits to your ability to do so will be limits to your ability to become aware of and learn from your collective experience.

I've had people in my courses really struggle to talk in the here and now. Some have said that it's unnatural, but I disagree. Watch preschoolers—they are totally in the here and now. Being in the here and now is the natural state. We've just been trained out of it. I can attest from working with hundreds of groups that it takes only a few hours of talking right here, right now, describing and respecting one another's experiences, to create strong bonds of partnership between relative strangers.

Identify Your Mental Maps

Mental maps are the outcome of learning from experience. Soon after birth, we begin to develop internal representations of the external world. Some of these are about how to get what we want. How do I get fed? How do I get praise and attention? How do I avoid punishment? Some maps are about what things are. Who am I? What is good and bad? What am I good at? Answers to these questions form just a few of the hundreds, perhaps thousands, of mental maps we use. Developing a set of mental maps that allow us to successfully navigate through life is part of what we think of as growing up. Different theorists have called these "concepts," "theories," "formulas," "paradigms," "schemata," and "software." You may have read Peter Senge's book on organizational learning in which he refers to them as "mental models."[1] I like to use the term *mental maps* or just *maps* for short. Like any map, they are a symbolic representation of the territory, but, in the words of the great semanticist Alfred Korzybski, we often mistake the map for the territory. This is why understanding our maps is a significant aspect of the Aware Self.

Every time we enter a new situation, we begin building a map of it. When we are first developing a map, we are pretty conscious of what we are doing. Whether it's learning how to solve business problems, what's appropriate to wear, or how to deal with the front office staff, we learn as much or more from our failures as from our successes while slowly building maps that help us succeed at our endeavors. Once we get a map that works for us, and we use it over and over again, it tends to recede into the background, out of awareness. After a while, we don't even realize that we are operating from a map.

A well-ingrained map is the platform for our awareness and sense making. The stories we make up about people are not random. They come from the maps we have developed about people in general acting in the situation we are making sense of. These are often called "biases" or "perceptual filters." They have a profound effect on our experience. When we don't have a map, we feel confused, our sense making is more tentative, and we seek out other opinions. When we have a well-ingrained map, we apply it automatically, without even noticing that we are doing it. Good maps are valuable because they help us operate effectively. We don't have to relearn everything from scratch. But maps also cause problems because they focus our attention. We tend to see only what is on our maps and miss what isn't. When we mistake the map for reality and are not aware of doing it, that distorts our perceptions. This can cause us to see people doing things they didn't do and hear them saying things they didn't say as well as to not see things they did do and not hear things they did say.

Maps shape our awareness for good or ill. If something isn't on our maps, we don't know to look for it. It's hard to be aware of something we don't know exists. When we learn a new map, our awareness changes, too. This book has described a number of maps already and will describe more further on. If you've never thought of interpersonal mush before, or its impact on an organization, now you will. If you haven't paid much attention to the negative consequences of you-language, you may start to see them now. That's how maps work; they are both an aid and a block to awareness.

It's significant that many of the maps people create about others and their organizations result not from having checked out the validity of the ideas but from having avoided checking out the validity of the ideas. What does that mean? Let's say that I see my new boss get very upset at someone who is disagreeing with her, so I make up a story that she doesn't like it when people disagree with her, although there could be many other reasons why she is upset this one time I observe it. Am I likely to check this hypothesis out by disagreeing with her and seeing what happens? Not unless I'm self-destructive. Am I likely to ask her directly about it? Not in the normal atmosphere of interpersonal mush. More likely, I will avoid disagreeing with her and instead watch to see what others do. I'll notice that they don't disagree with her either (how often does someone disagree openly with a new boss?). I may talk to others about my story, and they may confirm that they, too, avoid disagreeing with her. Perhaps I will, at some point, feel a great need to disagree with her and think up some elaborate strategy for subtly getting her to see a different point of view. If I'm successful, this will only reinforce my map that people can't disagree with her outright but instead must be very subtle.

Karl Weick was the first to describe how organizational reality is created this way. He pointed out that a surprising number of maps exist not because people test ideas about reality but because people avoid the tests that would disprove their maps.[2] A lot of what people think of as the normal way of doing things is like that only because people are afraid to try doing things differently. This helps explain why innovations in social processes tend to come from newcomers—they don't know the way things are usually done. The clear leaders I've met tend to break these unwritten rules and almost always get away with it. One clear leader who was a first-line supervisor in a pretty stuffy and very large traditional organization was trying to get managers interested in a new technology. He called up and invited the general manager of another division, who was a champion of this new technology, to come to the plant and give a talk on it. Other managers were aghast. A first-line supervisor does not call a divisional general manager! Senior managers in the plant held meetings to discuss damage control. Should someone phone the general manager and apologize, or should they bluff it out? What retribution would the plant suffer because of this affront? Well, the general manager came, thanked people for inviting him, and gave a great talk. No one in the plant could remember ever having called a divisional general manager for anything before.

Not checking out the validity of our maps is just another form of interpersonal mush. Whether it's about people, tasks, or processes, people who work together may have maps that are inaccurate, invalid, out of sync, dissimilar, or at cross-purposes. So we need to put our maps on the table, look at them together, see what is causing problems, and change our maps when that is appropriate.

If it were only that simple, I wouldn't need to write this book. But the solution is difficult for several reasons: we are not aware of all of our maps, we have an emotional investment in our maps, and we have a tendency to forget that our maps are not the territory. People differ about what kinds of maps and what kinds of conversations cause them anxiety, but we all feel nervous about displaying and discussing our own maps when we are outside our comfort zones. You could say that leading organizational learning is mainly about containing the anxiety created by exposing and exploring our own maps and those of others, and you wouldn't be far off. It's also about helping people uncover and understand what their maps are in the first place. Cardwork is a technique you can use to do that, and I describe it in more detail in chapter 6.

If I think my map is the reality, I won't be interested in hearing about alternative maps. Others will see me as having strong opinions about the way things are. If I'm the boss, I'll probably make it uncomfortable for others to describe alternative maps, thus increasing interpersonal mush and eliminating partnership. Another problem is that people can identify with their maps and hold on to them pretty tenaciously. When they identify with their maps, they confuse who they are with their maps. One of the reasons people resist change is that change often requires a new map for success. When the environment changes so that the maps people are identified with no longer work, many will try to go back to the old situation so that their old maps will continue to work. Calls for more rules and regulations in groups, organizations, or nations are almost always motivated by this kind of resistance to change. I think the big reason for holding on to maps so strongly is that they reduce anxiety for us. Uncertainty makes us anxious. Maps get rid of uncertainty.

Three Kinds of Maps

I refer to three kinds of maps in this book. Stories about other people are a kind of map. Then there are maps that identify things, and maps of ideas about cause and effect.

Stories about Others

One map is the stories we make up about other people. We develop maps about each of the significant people we work with, and these include how they think, what they want, what they like and dislike, their biases and hot buttons, and so on. We've already explored this one in a lot of detail. Your stories of people are open to distortion, bias, and inaccuracy, so it's very important not to think your maps of them are the actual people and to stay open to being surprised by who they really are. When you are an Aware Self, you stay open to seeing new parts of people, things that aren't on your maps.

Identity Maps

A second kind of map is an identity map. It identifies what things are. At work, people have identity maps about goals, who has what role and what those roles are, the definitions of success, quality, and customer satisfaction, and so on. I have a map of clear leadership: it's composed of the four skills I'm describing in this book. For the most part, identity maps gain their validity because a large enough number of people hold the same map. Identity maps are an example of intersubjective truth. The accuracy of my map of a team's goals depends on how similar my map is to those of other people.

Here is another area where people can create problems for themselves if they try to treat these maps as objective truths. It is possible to create measurement systems for defining quality or success, but that only gives these goals the veneer of objective truth. The nature of either depends on the group of people defining it. For example, in one company, success means increasing return on investment; in another, it means increasing market share. When I wrote the first edition of this book in 1999, conventional maps of business wealth were being turned on their heads by Web-based companies that had hardly made a profit, had few hard assets, and were worth more than General Electric. There were a lot of hard lessons about the difference between the map and the territory in 2001! An Aware Self needs to be aware that his identity maps are not objective truths, and intersubjective truths can change when we're not looking.

Ideas about Cause and Effect

A third important kind of map consists of our ideas about cause and effect: how to make things happen, how to accomplish tasks and goals. Chris Argyris and Donald Schön coined the term *theory of action* to describe these kinds of maps.[3] I have a theory-of-action map about how to sustain partnership through clear leadership—that's part of what this book is about. If I am trying to help leaders create partnership in their organizations, this map guides my actions. Every goal-oriented action you take is based on some theory you have of how that action will lead to that goal. You may be fully aware of your theory, or you may not, but it is there. If we are trying to accomplish a goal together, it's helpful to be operating from a common theory of action.

Muriel was the founder of an unusual and successful retail store that had grown so large—to twenty-five employees—that she found the business was now taking up more of her time than she wanted it to. She had been trying to have a life for a few years and had come to the conclusion that she needed to change her management style, so she hired me to help her out. I soon learned that every time she brought someone in to run some part of the store, before long she was back, deeply involved again. Sometimes she had reversed decisions the new manager had made, making people confused and upset. She had tried promoting people from inside the store and hiring people from outside the store, but she had not been able to find anyone who seemed competent enough to take over any facet of the business.

It would have been easy to make up a story about Muriel not being able to give up some control, and many of her employees had. I began by working with her on redesigning the structure of her organization and reengineering some of the store's work processes. Of course, all these work processes had just evolved, willy-nilly, over the years, and there hadn't been a lot of thought about how they might be designed to work most effectively. We thought that by doing that, she might be able to identify areas that could run themselves without her involvement. Trying to understand the work processes forced Muriel to become explicitly aware, for the first time, of what she was actually trying to accomplish. Obviously the store was there to make a profit, but that wasn't Muriel's main goal, nor had it ever been. Muriel had never been interested in being a successful retailer. She had always wanted to see herself, and her store, as a resource for the community. As this got clearer, the logic behind her actions and her problems with what had seemed to her to be incompetent managers became clearer.

The key was Muriel's identity maps and her theories of action. Managers hadn't worked out because they weren't operating from the same theory of action as Muriel. For example, if a manager's theory of action was that increasing profit was the way to succeed, he was operating from a different map than Muriel. Muriel wanted to make a modest amount of money and reinvest a certain amount back into the store. Beyond that, a part of her felt guilty making a profit, as if she were ripping off her clients. Providing a valuable service at the lowest possible cost was an important part of her theory of action, and unless a manager understood that, his actions would not seem right to her.

Muriel wasn't aware of her theories of action, so she couldn't explain them to others. All she knew was that people didn't seem to do it the way she wanted it done. Once she could describe her theories of action and identity maps, she was able to train people who could take charge of some parts of the store so that she could focus her energies on what interested her most.

___

When we work together to achieve some outcome, our effectiveness depends on our ability to describe, compare, and learn together about our identity and theory-of-action maps. If we are unaware that we have maps that guide our actions, we are likely to confuse our maps with reality. In Muriel's case, she confused her maps with her managers' competence. Since she couldn't describe her map, she and the others couldn't learn together. There was just a succession of failed managers.

Muriel owned the store and had the right to decide what the goals were. She had a success map that she needed to share with her subordinates. And she had developed a set of ideas, theories of action, for how to accomplish those goals. Her theory of action for managing employees was somewhat unique, and her theory of action for selecting products was entirely idiosyncratic. Once she became aware of what she was trying to accomplish (identity map), the people who worked for her could start to devise new and better ways of accomplishing it (theories of action). After seeing and believing that her new managers were operating from her success map, she became a lot more flexible with their way of doing things, and it became clear that Muriel did not have a problem giving up some control.

We do not have to have the same experience in order to be in partnership or be an effective team. But partnership and teamwork require some common maps. Authorities in partnership-based organizations must have clear maps about what they want the team, department, or organization to do. We call this kind of map "vision." This vision is an identity map, and leaders will probably need to hold on to it against the inevitable attempts of others to change their minds. Collaborative organization is not a free-for-all, with everyone getting an equal say. But when it comes to theories of action, leaders need to be flexible if they are going to sustain partnership. Managers with strongly held theories of action could stifle creativity and innovation if they think their way is the only way to accomplish an outcome.

Using Espoused Maps and Theories

Every moment at work, I am having an experience. My maps are an input, part of what creates that experience. They are also an outcome, as I create and modify my maps based on my experience. Most of this cycle of map–experience–map is taking place outside my awareness.

I don't usually pay much attention to how my maps are creating my experience or are being modified by it. What happens is as natural as breathing. Because my maps are, for the most part, outside my awareness, I have imperfect knowledge of them. At any moment, if you asked me, "Why did you do such and such?" I could probably give you a rational answer. But it wouldn't necessarily be a valid answer, and therein lies one of the biggest impediments to organizational learning. It's also another reason why learning to pay close attention to your in-the-moment experience is so useful.

More than thirty years ago, Chris Argyris and Donald Schön identified one of the key blocks to organizational learning: the difference between what people describe as their theories of action (their "espoused theories") and what their theories of action really are (their "theories in use").[4] Our espoused theories are the stories we make up to explain our actions to ourselves and others. Our theories in use are the real reasons, our real mental maps, the actual basis for our experience and actions. Sometimes the maps we say we are using and the maps we are really using are the same, sometimes they overlap, and sometimes they have little resemblance to each other. There are many reasons why we might be unaware of our theory-of-action maps, ranging from psychological defense to simple inattention. For our purposes, the reasons aren't that important. We just need to understand and acknowledge that we can't always be sure that the maps we think we are using really are the maps we are using.

It turns out that most people already have an intuitive sense of this. It is not all that unusual to question, in our own minds, whether other people know why they do what they do. As you listen to someone give what sounds like a rationalization for his behavior, you might occasionally find yourself making up a story about the real reason. Maybe you think he is not telling the whole truth, or perhaps you think he doesn't really know himself. If the latter, then you are making a distinction between his espoused theory (his story) and his theory in use (what you think the real reason is).

This is one key reason that normal attempts, by people committed to partnership, to discuss and change problem patterns fail. Even if a person is willing to describe her maps, others may not believe that those are the maps she is using. In an intellectual discussion, there is no way to know for sure. More likely than not, people keep their doubts, and the stories they make up about their doubts, to themselves. Rather than clearing out the interpersonal mush, abstract discussions about why things happen may just create more.

In a situation like this, the ability to track your experience moment to moment is invaluable. By working at being an Aware Self in the here and now, you sidestep the problem of espoused maps and increase your awareness of your real subjective truth. Through paying close attention to your experience, you find out what your maps in use really are. Let me give you an example.

Rose was the CEO of a small rural hospital, and Chuck was her second in command. The hospital had been in the community for more than fifty years, and there was a feeling of family among the staff. It was part of a chain that was going through the same cost crisis all U.S. health care providers were experiencing at the time. Rose was fifteen years younger than Chuck, but he respected her visionary abilities in a time of great turbulence in the industry. For Rose's part, she respected Chuck's experience and operational acumen. They considered themselves a great team, but things had started to go sour over the past few months. Chuck began to notice a disturbing pattern. Even though he and Rose agreed that the hospital had to run more efficiently if it was going to survive in the long run, Rose was forgiving departments that ran over budget. Each time she did this, he pointed it out to her and explained his concerns about the implications of her actions. His theory of action was that people were going to have to feel some pain before they started getting serious about operating more efficiently. Rose didn't disagree. She shared the same map. But every time she found some contingency money to rescue a blown budget, she gave him a good reason for what she had done. Chuck thought each explanation was reasonable but found the overall pattern troubling. When he tried to discuss it with her, she agreed with his maps and his theory of action but then went ahead and did something different.

At the time, I was consulting with the headquarters staff and interviewing senior managers throughout the larger organization. When Chuck described his concerns about Rose to me, I suggested that I might be able to help them have a different kind of conversation about this issue. I talked with Rose about it, and she didn't see what good it would do, but she was concerned about her deteriorating relationship with Chuck and agreed to get together with him on the off chance that it might improve things.

We met in Rose's office, and I started by having Chuck describe his experience. He talked about the four incidents that had occurred in the previous six months. I asked Rose just to listen while I asked him to describe what he felt in the moment as he talked about this. He described his fear for the organization and his confusion about Rose's behavior. As I probed further, he got in touch with his resentment that she came off looking like the good guy and he got stuck being the bad guy, holding the line on budgets. He felt saddened and hurt by her behavior, almost as if she were betraying him. He quickly added that this was "nonsense," but it was part of the baggage he was carrying around. I asked him what he wanted, and he said that he had thought he wanted Rose to hold the budget line, but he now realized that he wanted even more to feel, once again, that he and Rose were on the same team.

I then turned to Rose, who was visibly affected by what she had heard. She quickly launched into an apology, assuring Chuck that she had no intention of betraying him and hadn't realized the impact of her actions on him. Before she got too far into this, I asked her to stop for a second and just pay attention to what she was sensing in her body. She paused for a few seconds and said, "I have a sinking feeling in my stomach." I asked her to look at Chuck, who was sitting across from her, sad and glum, and to notice what was going on inside of her at that moment. "What do you want right now?" I asked. "I want to take

his hurt away. I want to make it all better," she replied. I then asked
her if the sensations she was having were at all familiar, if she could
remember having them before. She paused for a few seconds, looking
down at the floor, and then snapped her head up and said, "Yes. I feel
the same way when a department head who's gone over budget is sitting in that same chair [pointing at Chuck] with the same sad look on
his face."

Rose was bright, and the implications of the insight she'd gained from
paying attention to her here-and-now experience were immediately
apparent. "Oh my God," she said, "is that what I'm doing?" It was
clear that Rose's espoused theory of action, which matched Chuck's
theory in use, was not her theory in use. At that point, she became
embarrassed and wanted to disown the compassionate (fused?) part
of her and promise never to do it again. However, I insisted that we
look more closely at the positive intent behind her actions and try to
understand what her real theory of action was. We found out that one
of her maps said that part of her job as CEO was to get resources for
people and departments. Another map said that maintaining the family
atmosphere in the hospital was important for patient care and overall
effectiveness. She didn't want people to feel unnecessary and arbi-
trary pain. The need for cost-cutting was so apparent and overwhelm-
ing that she hadn't been aware she was holding contradictory maps.

Chuck agreed that maintaining the sense of "everybody being in this
together" was important to the hospital's overall effectiveness and
agreed that their previous theory of action (induce enough pain to get
people to change) might have a negative effect on that. He also
agreed that Rose's past rationalizations for supporting cost overruns
had each had some merit. But the pattern would have to change if
they were going to control costs. Chuck and Rose found themselves
caught between the contradictory assumptions of managing organizational effectiveness through teamwork, cohesion, and a sense of
belonging, on the one hand, and through impersonal controls and
hard discipline, on the other. Because they couldn't come up with one
theory of action that fit all situations, they agreed that in the future
Rose would not forgive a budget overrun without first fully consulting
Chuck, and together they would find a decision they both agreed to
on a case-by-case basis.

Rose and Chuck could have kept on having logical, rational discussions about the best way to run the hospital for a long time, but nothing would have changed. Rose was not aware that her map in use was different from her espoused map. Each time she acted in a way that didn't match her espoused map, she had a good reason for it. That's how sense making works. We can always come up with sensible, logical explanations for our behavior, but that doesn't mean our explanations are valid.

When you learn to track your here-and-now experience, moment to moment, you get around the problem of espoused maps. You put aside rationalizations and explanations and just focus on what is actually going on inside of you, here and now. If you do this sincerely and pay attention to your sensations as well as your thoughts, the real feelings and motivations that underlie your actions become apparent. Your real maps are put on the table, and real learning and change occur. That is the promise of the Aware Self.

Exercises to Develop Your Aware Self

Each skills chapter ends with a section for people who would like to increase one or more of their clear leadership skills. Most of these exercises require a practice partner. Since these are skills of partnership and learning collectively from experience, that's probably not surprising. People who read the first edition of this book tell me they have been able to apply the insights and skills they learned from it in their working lives. I find that very gratifying. However, all the people who have taken the Clear Leadership course say they understand the skills and concepts at a much deeper level than they did after just reading about them. Experiential learning will help you get it, so I encourage you to find a teacher who can coach your skill development. If you are going to try and develop these skills without a teacher, I strongly encourage you to do it with one or more people who have read this book and want to develop their skills as well.

Exercise 1: **Knowing Your Experience, Here and Now**

Sit across from your partner and, for an agreed-upon period of time, notice your moment-to-moment awareness. Say whatever you become aware of as you become aware of it. Start with a one- or two-minute time frame in which you just talk out your stream of consciousness while your partner listens. Then switch roles. As it becomes easier, increase the amount of time until you can go on indefinitely.

- It may help if you preface each statement with "Now I'm aware . . ."

- When people first try this exercise, they often begin with their observations (e.g., "Now I'm aware of the green color of the walls. Now I'm aware of the chair you're sitting in. Now I'm aware of the hum coming from the lights"), but after they've exhausted that, they have to turn inside for awareness.

- The partner's job is to listen and notice which of the four elements of experience the person is mostly aware of. The listener points this out to the speaker when the speaker is finished. Practice bringing all four elements into awareness.

Exercise 2: **Being Aware of Each Element of Experience**

In this exercise, which is similar to the one above, you focus on a specific element of experience for an agreed-upon period of time. Your partner asks you for your awareness of that element, and then you answer. Your partner thanks you and then asks again. Start with a one- or two-minute time limit and increase this as you get better at it. Here's an example:

Partner: *What are you feeling* [observing, thinking, or wanting] *now?*

You: *Irritated.*

Partner: *Thank you. What are you feeling now?*

You: *I'm not sure.*

Partner: *Thank you. What are you feeling now?*

Try to avoid getting stuck in long periods of silence. Say something and move on. Then switch roles.

Exercise 3: **Timed Awareness**

This may be the most useful skill practice you will do. After every three to five hours of interaction with your learning partner, describe your here-and-now experience of each other. At first, these conversations are likely to be filled with appreciation and "good" experiences. The real rub will come when you are having a not-so-good experience of your partner. Watch how your sense making stops you from talking in the here and now—the story you make up about the consequences of saying what is really going on inside you is what initially stops you. Say it anyway, but make sure to describe only your experience, not your judgments of them (more on this in the next chapter). If you or your partner have trouble with not getting defensive, make an agreement with your partner that when you do this exercise, the listener is not allowed to comment on what the speaker has said for at least an hour.

Exercise 4: **Developing Your Observer**

The ability to record and play back exactly what you and others said and did pays off tremendously in all sorts of ways. You will be much more capable of learning from your experience. The key skill you need is to be able to record while you are fully involved. To develop this skill, you simply need to practice it. Two or three times a day, after you have been in a meeting or interacted with another person and have a few minutes to yourself, go back over the meeting or interaction and try to recall exactly who said what and in what sequence. If you are like most people, you will be surprised at first by how little you can actually remember. But the intention to learn and constant practice will make the difference. Over a short time, you will find that you are remembering more and more. When you can leave a one-hour meeting and then play back what happened and in what sequence, you will have mastered this skill.

Exercise 5: **Knowing Your Real Wants**

For this exercise, you should be alone in a place where you can talk out loud without anyone hearing you. Think of some outcome or result that you don't really like. This could be a problem pattern you are in with someone at work or in your life, or some specific interaction that left you upset. Ask yourself, "Why did I create... [fill in the blank]?" and then say out loud the first thing that pops into your head. It is critical that you not censor or prejudge the first thought you have—just say it. You're doing this alone so that you won't have to worry about what people might think of your reason. It will probably be something you are not proud of or are embarrassed by. That's why it's unconscious in the first place. If you don't say it out loud, it will quickly recede back into the unconscious. Like dreams, unconscious content rapidly fades from memory, but if you say it out loud, it will stay conscious. Here is an example.

Richard found that he constantly felt angry after interacting with a co-worker. Over time, he came up with a number of explanations for his anger, all having to do with the co-worker's inadequacies. He had to work with this person, who was effective and influential in the organization, so he resolved to mellow out and not get so worked up. But that didn't help. Having just taken a course in clear leadership, he decided to see if he could figure out his part in this situation, so he closed the door to his office and asked himself out loud, "Why do I always get so angry around Emma?" What immediately came out of his mouth was "Because she's a stupid fucking girl."

Whoa! thought Richard. Where did that come from? Richard prided himself on his sense of equality and on treating people the same regardless of gender or racial differences. He couldn't be putting Emma down just because she was a woman, could he? But because he'd said it, he decided to try it on a little longer and see what it felt like. That's when he noticed that he had the same ambivalent feelings around Emma that he'd had toward some girls in high school to whom he was attracted and who used to scorn him. Richard realized that he was a lot more attracted to Emma than he'd allowed himself to realize and that his anger was his way of defending himself from his fear of being scorned by her. His unconscious want had been to protect himself from feeling put down. Once he realized that, his anger went away and he could be choiceful about what he wanted: a good working relationship with Emma.

If you accept the fact that you create your own experience and sincerely ask yourself in this way why you are creating a certain experience, you will almost always get an answer.

Exercise 6: Increasing Your Awareness

Undoubtedly, journalizing is the most effective way to learn about yourself without the aid of a skilled therapist. Ira Progoff is a remarkable teacher who has written books on how to use journals to increase self-awareness, and if you are interested in trying this, you should get one of his books. In journalizing, you keep a written record of your experiences, observations, thoughts, feelings, and wants on a regular basis. Then every now and then, you go back over what you have written and analyze the underlying themes and patterns of your experience. This can be a great aid in uncovering what you really think, feel, and want in life.

Exercise 7: Using Language That Clarifies Rather Than Mystifies

The only way to practice this is to try to use appropriate pronouns (I-language) and then get feedback on how well you are doing. Watching yourself on videotape is very helpful. Probably your best option is to ask your partner to point out each time you use pronouns inappropriately. It's much easier to notice other people using mystifying language than to notice it in ourselves.

If there is someone at home or at work who thinks quickly and is willing to be a spotter for you, make an agreement with that person to let you know when you are using mystifying language.

For example, whenever you say "you," "we," or "it" instead of "I," your partner asks, "Who?" It will take a few weeks, but your language will really start to change, and you'll notice an impact on your sense of differentiation, too.

Summary

In this chapter, we explored the skill of being an Aware Self. We saw how being able to describe your moment-to-moment experience is the key to self-awareness. We've looked at how to become aware of your experience by breaking it down into four elements. Knowing your experience means knowing what you observe, think, feel, and want from moment to moment. For most of us, a great deal of our experience is unconscious, outside our awareness. That doesn't mean it doesn't influence us. Instead, our unconscious experience influences us in ways we do not choose and have no control over. Increasing the skill of self-awareness is about becoming more aware of what is going on in each element of experience and how your maps are influencing that.

The Aware Self uses language in a way that clarifies, for herself and others, the origin of her experience. She avoids mystifying her experience. Through clear language, she increases her awareness. And she is aware that her maps are, at best, intersubjective truths whose validity depends as much or more on what other people think as on any "objective" truth. She knows that her maps are influencing her awareness and tries to avoid being blinded by them by keeping them in sight and not mistaking them for the territory. She realizes that it can be difficult to know what her maps really are and that she can make up satisfactory stories that may not be valid—another person could believe one thing is motivating her while something else really is. Moment-to-moment awareness of experience is the only reliable guide to seeing your real theory in use and to understanding what is really going on.

Why develop an Aware Self? There are many reasons. Perhaps the most important is that awareness equals choice. Without awareness, we are pushed around by forces that are outside our choicefulness. Becoming aware of your experience is a route to being more differentiated if you, like many people, tend to be fused with your feelings or wants. Most adults realize that we are not our observations or our thoughts, but some people forget that we are not our feelings or our wants either. When I blur the boundary between myself and my feelings, then I am controlled by them, and other people will be afraid of my irrational actions. When I am my wants, I am self-centered and driven by the need for gratification.

Differentiating myself from my experience (being separate from it but still connected to it) helps me to be less reactive and more choiceful in my responses to others. It becomes easier for me to differentiate myself from other people.

The Descriptive Self

Reducing the Mush by Making Me Understandable to You

Clearing out the interpersonal mush and creating interpersonal clarity requires that people get clear about their own experience, the experiences of others, the maps they are all using, and the differences in their maps. This demands the skills of awareness, which I discussed in the previous chapter. Another necessary set of skills belongs to the Descriptive Self. The ultimate skill of being a Descriptive Self is noticing when others might need to make up a story about you and stopping the mush by giving them the information they need to have an accurate picture of what is going on in your head. The most difficult part of that is telling others your experience of them when you have a problem pattern with them, and doing it in a way that builds the relationship rather than makes them defensive, hurt, or angry. I've found the following models and techniques helpful in developing the skills of the Descriptive Self:

- Be transparent, not intimate
- Make statements before asking questions
- Describe the impact before responding
- Describe experience, not judgments

Let's explore these aspects of the Descriptive Self in detail before moving on to the exercises at the end of the chapter.

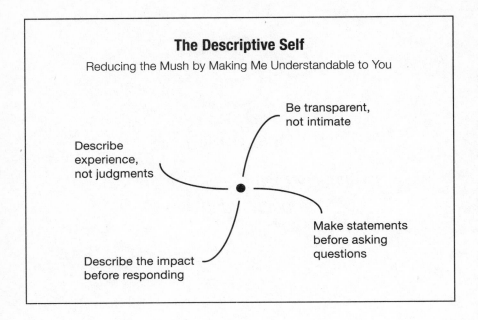

Be Transparent, Not Intimate

Partnership with people at work does not require intimacy. Being a Descriptive Self is not about telling your life story, exposing your secrets, or "letting it all hang out." It's not about being close and personal. It's not about being open in the conventional sense of the word, meaning you talk about everything that is on your mind. Being descriptive means just that, describing to others what is going on in your head so that they have more accurate information for their sense making. You can choose to be friends with people you partner with, or not, but that has nothing to do with the skills of clear leadership. Friendship is not the issue. Being pleasant or charming is not the point. Clear leaders don't needlessly upset people, but they are not charm school graduates either. If I had to use one word to describe their commonality, it would be "integrity," or maybe "sincerity." You can trust clear leaders to level with you.

When people are first learning these skills, many find the distinction between transparency and intimacy difficult to grasp. Being transparent, telling other people your subjective truth, sounds like a very intimate thing, but the way I am using the word here, it is not. One distinction some people find helpful is the difference between the here and now and the there and then. When you are being descriptive, you are talking about your here-and-now experience. "Here" means that what you are talking about is related to the people who are listening. "Now" means that you are describing what is going on in your head at this moment. "There and then" is when you talk about people or events that are not related to the people who are listening to you. Let me give you an example:

I was working with a group, and one member, Mark, was taking a big risk by telling the truth about his desire to influence and give leadership to the group. It was a touchy subject but very important to the members, who were paying rapt attention. At that point, Mark was being transparent as he described his excitement, his ideas, and his wants. Then he started to talk about why he felt driven to be influential, about leaving the country of his birth and finding it difficult to provide for his family in this new one. Mark was visibly distraught as he disclosed his concerns. When he did that, he had shifted from being transparent to being intimate, and the effect on the group was dramatic. People stopped listening to him, and some physically pulled back. They began making up myriad stories about why he was saying what he was saying. I was able to stop Mark and ask people to describe the stories they were making up about him at that moment. These ranged from thinking Mark was trying to get support for his leadership through emotional blackmail to thinking he was trying to get others to display their own softer emotions. Actually, Mark wasn't sure why he had gotten so personal and thought it really wasn't relevant to the points he was trying to make. Hearing Mark say that helped people get back on track and start listening to him again.

Being warm and friendly and intimate, telling people about what you did over the weekend or about your kids or your past, is generally irrelevant to a learning conversation. What is relevant are the thoughts, feelings, observations, and wants going on inside you that help the other person understand your experience as it pertains to the issues you are dealing with. So the proper attitude is transparency, not intimacy.

Some partnerships include intimacy. Marriage would be the clearest example, but any partnership can include friendship. We want to tell our

weekend stories to some of the people at work and listen to theirs. There
is nothing wrong with that; it just doesn't have much to do with interpersonal clarity. In nonintimate relationships, it can even get in the way. It's
as though every relationship has an intimacy comfort zone—the amount
of personal detail that the other person expects to hear. If you go outside
the boundaries of this comfort zone, the other person becomes uncomfortable. In an intimate relationship, that discomfort may come from not
getting enough personal details. In a nonintimate relationship it may
come from getting too much information. I've noticed that when someone goes outside the intimacy comfort zone and gives others too much
information, any interest in getting clarity and clearing up the mush goes
out the window. Instead, as in the story about Mark above, the mush
machine gears up as people start making up stories about why the intimate information is being shared. When I am being transparent, I am giving you information about my here-and-now experience to fill in the gaps
so you don't have to make up a story. When I am being intimate, I'm
going beyond the here and now to tell you about my life, other people in
it, and so on.

Another important difference between intimate relationships and
work partnerships is in the way feelings are expressed. In intimate relationships, it is usually appropriate, and perhaps even necessary, to express
feelings. When you express an emotion, you act out the intensity of the
emotion itself in nonverbal as well as verbal behavior. If I'm overcome
with joy, I might jump up and down and do a little dance. When I'm hurt,
I might cry. When I'm angry, I might yell or at least speak in an angry
tone. But that is not useful for gaining clarity, especially in nonintimate
relationships. Instead, you must describe the emotion without expressing
it. So if you are angry, you say, as calmly and dispassionately as you can,
that you are angry. The distinction between describing and expressing
emotions is very important to being a Descriptive Self. You are not being
an effective Descriptive Self if your description shuts others down, damp-
ens their curiosity, and/or causes them to make up even more stories
about you. Yet that is often the result when people express their emotions
in a work context. When that happens, the emotion is controlling them,
and that causes other people to get cautious. Any interest in clarity van-
ishes, to be replaced by an interest in containing the emotion. For these
reasons, it's always a good rule of thumb to avoid expressing emotions
when you are trying to be a Descriptive Self. By calmly describing your

feelings instead, you provide important information that others need in order to understand the rest of what you are saying and doing. That is transparency.

Make Statements Before Asking Questions

When you are describing yourself, you use statements. When beginning a conversation with a subordinate who is part of a problem pattern, many well-intentioned managers are likely to ask questions instead of making statements. Sometimes they even appear more skillful by doing so. Certainly, a person asking questions seems to be listening more than a person who just makes statements. Leaders need to listen, but there is a time for listening and a time for talking. Questions are fine when you are listening. Being a Descriptive Self, however, requires declarative statements.

What happens when someone, especially someone with authority, asks you a question? If you are like most people, you start to make up a story about where the question is coming from, why the question is being asked, what kind of answer the person is looking for, and so on. When you ask a question without first making a statement about the context and reason for the question, you create interpersonal mush.

For example, "Do you support our plans or don't you?" seems to be a straightforward question, but what kind of sense making will it generate in the person who hears it? One might infer undertones of distrust. Another might begin trying to imagine why the question is being asked. A third might think that her reservations about the plans are clearly not welcome. Questions lead to more clarity all around only when they are preceded by descriptive statements. For example, "Yesterday you seemed really committed to our plan when you were describing it to Sally, but today you keep hedging on your commitment. I'm feeling confused. Do you support our plans or don't you?" Make a statement before you ask the question.

Some people hide behind questions. As long as they are asking questions, they don't have to reveal themselves. Some use questions rhetorically. They really are making a statement but mask it as a question. The most notorious of these are the "Don't you think . . ." type of questions. The person who asks "Don't you think . . ." often means "I think you should . . ." but feels less vulnerable and, perhaps, not as pushy phrasing it as a question. But it has a different impact on the person who hears it. The person who gets the "Don't you think . . ." question hears the implicit judgment in it and is well aware of what the "right" answer is. I think this actually creates a certain amount of distrust in the person being asked such questions. At the very least, they create mush as the person who's expected to answer makes up a story about what the questioner thinks, feels, and wants. You support clarity by simply stating your belief before asking other people for their opinion.

Some managers have concluded that when they talk first, they don't find out what others really think. They've learned that their authority causes people to pretend to agree with them. Their mental map is "I get more honest answers if I ask people questions before making my own views known." I think that map gets in their way. It may be true that some people will tell the boss only what they think she wants to hear, but that only happens if the boss has made it uncomfortable for people with different views. If you really want to know what people think, and tell them that, and thank them for their different views, you don't have to worry about telling them your views first. In fact, it makes it easier for them because they have some context for answering your questions and can describe what they agree and disagree with and what parts of your views they don't understand.

When it comes to organizational learning, when we need to talk about our problem patterns, this is even more of an issue. Most people find it risky to describe their experience of others, especially if this has not been a common practice in their organization. In a risky situation, the leader has to go first, or she is not leading. A manager cannot expect subordinates to answer questions about their maps or experience if she herself has not fully described her maps and experience and answered their questions first. If you are going to lead learning, you need to be the first to make statements about what is going on inside you before asking others about what is going on inside them. And to keep clearing out the mush, you need to preface questions with declarative statements about why you are asking the questions. Letting people in on what is going on in your head before asking questions reduces the amount of inaccurate sense making they might do and helps contain the anxiety they may be creating for themselves. Before asking a question, tell them the purpose of the question. This also models the kind of descriptive, "telling the truth of my experience" information you want from them.

Describe the Impact Before Responding

In any conversation, two things exist simultaneously—the content of the discussion and the experience of the conversation. When you say something to me, you have an impact on me beyond the content of your statement. When I am being a Descriptive Self, I describe the experience I am having as we talk, before I respond to what you just said.

What do I mean by the difference between the content and the experience? Below is a quasifictional dialogue between Sue and Bob, two people at work having a normal phone conversation. I say "quasi" because one of the people involved related it to me, and I made up what the other person said. Sue is leading a cross-functional team, and Frank, who reports to Bob, is a member. Here is their conversation.

Sue: *I'd like to talk with you about how we're managing the ABC project.*

Bob: *Sure, what's on your mind?*

Sue: *I think we agree that this is a really important project for the long-term success of the company.*

Bob: *Yeah, probably true.*

Sue: *So it deserves our best attention and resources.*

Bob: *And your point is . . .?*

Sue: *Well, I've had more complaints about Frank not doing his part properly, and I really think we need to do something about it.*

Bob: *What's the problem this time?*

Sue proceeds to describe two instances in the past two weeks when people in other parts of the organization noticed discrepancies in Frank's figures. Frank is also late with some of his reports.

Bob: *OK, I'll have a talk with him. I'm sure there's a good explanation for these problems.*

Sue: *Well, I appreciate that, but, you know, this isn't the first time you and I have had this conversation, and I was wondering if you'd consider some alternatives.*

Bob: *Like what?*

Sue: *Well, I know your department has other priorities right now. Perhaps you'd consider just taking Frank off the project and transferring the work to me.*

Bob: *That's an interesting proposition. Let me think on it and get back to you. I should probably at least talk to Frank first, don't you think?*

It seems like a normal conversation that could happen in any organization, right? But what was the impact they were having on each other as this discussion took place?

In the right column of the table below, I list some of the impacts each person is having during the conversation.[1] Those impacts come from the story each is making up about the other. In this example, Bob doesn't express many of his impacts. If he did, he would be more honest but would probably risk making Sue angry and alienated. Most of Bob's impacts are judgments, and, as discussed in the next ground rule, judgments don't aid learning conversations. The impacts are the experience Bob is having, the story he is making up, which is leading him to a series of feelings and judgments and wants. That is the impact he needs to be able to describe if he is going to learn from this experience with Sue. The same holds true for Sue.

The Unseen Impact	
How they responded to each other...	**And the impact each was having . . .**
Sue: *I'd like to talk with you about how we're managing the ABC project.*	Bob: *Oh yeah, what's bugging you now? I can just feel myself tensing up because every time you are on the other end of the phone I have more problems to deal with. I'd sure like to just once have a different conversation with you.*

Bob: *Sure, what's on your mind?*	Sue: *You seem to be in a good mood today. Maybe I can finally break through to you about Frank. I feel like a runner poised for a race. I really want to come up with a long-term solution to this problem, and I know I'm starting to bug you, and I don't want that.*
Sue: *I think we agree that this is a really important project for the long-term success of the company.*	Bob: *Yep, she definitely wants something from me. I can feel my guard going up. I just hope it isn't about Frank again. The guy is two years from retirement, and I'm stuck with him, and, damn it, people who put in thirty-five good years deserve to be treated decently.*
Bob: *Yeah, probably true.*	Sue: *Uh-oh, he's getting defensive. How can I get him to be open about this? Sometimes I feel so helpless about making a dent in his attitude.*
Sue: *So it deserves our best attention and resources.*	Bob: *Oh shit, it is about Frank. What's he done this time? I just feel sick at the thought of having to give him grief one more time. I've got more important things to do than deal with this crap.*
Bob: *And your point is . . . ?*	Sue: *Yep, definitely not with me now. I guess I just better plunge in and try to make this work.*
Sue: *Well, I've had more complaints about Frank not doing his part properly, and I really think we need to do something about it.*	Bob: *I wonder if you've really had complaints or if they are just your complaints. What have you got against Frank anyway? Sure, he's a little slow, but he's a decent guy and tries his best.*
Bob: *What's the problem this time?*	Sue: *Well, at least you asked. Maybe you're becoming more open to looking at this issue. I feel a little ray of hope.*
Sue proceeds to describe two incidents in the past two weeks when people in other parts of the organization noticed discrepancies in Frank's figures. Frank is also late with some of his reports.	Bob: *So there are a couple of numbers off, big deal. Those should be double-checked anyway, no matter who does them. I'm actually relieved that it's such a little thing. I wish you would just chill out. Not everyone is as much of a perfectionist as you.*

The Unseen Impact cont'd

How they responded to each other...	And the impact each was having . . .
Bob: *OK, I'll have a talk with him. I'm sure there's a good explanation for these problems.*	Sue: *Oh no. That's what you said the last two times, and things didn't get any better. I don't think you really understand the project's potential to make a huge impact on our profitability. OK, try plan B. I hope you go for it.*
Sue: *Well, I appreciate that, but, you know, this isn't the first time you and I have had this conversation, and I was wondering if you'd consider some alternatives.*	Bob: *I know you'd like me to put someone else on this project, but I can't. We are totally under-staffed as it is, and it would take another person at least two weeks to get up to speed. But I don't expect you to take no for an answer. Why don't you just learn to work with Frank? He's got strengths as well as weaknesses. Use them.*
Bob: *Like what?*	Sue: *I know you don't have the manpower to replace Frank, and because you supervise him, he doesn't really feel any of the heat I'd put on him to get results. My first choice is that you transfer him to me, but I know you'd never consider that, so I'm willing to come in on Saturdays and make sure the work gets done correctly. Don't you understand that every time we issue an incorrect report, our credibility goes down, and ultimately the project will have no impact if that happens?!*
Sue: *Well, I know your department has other priorities right now. Perhaps you'd consider just taking Frank off the project and transferring the work to me.*	Bob: *Whoa, hold on there. I'm not sure I want to be completely out of the ABC project, and any-way, my department is responsible for those num-bers. Just what is your game here? Can I trust you, or are you trying to climb over my back? You don't seem that type to me, but now I feel I have to watch myself around you.*
Bob: *That's an interesting proposition. Let me think on it and get back to you. I should probably at least talk to Frank first, don't you think?*	Sue: *You're not buying it. Shit. I've got to find some way to contain the damage Frank is doing. I know you're stuck with him, but I wish you wouldn't fob him off on me. If you insist on doing that, at least give me some authority to make sure he does the work right. This is so depressing.*

If Bob and Sue are going to have a learning conversation, some of the stuff in that right column needs to be said. Not all of it—that would be openness—but some of it. Bob and Sue have a problem pattern. They keep having conversations about Frank, but nothing happens. In Sue's mind, Frank and Bob are the problem. In Bob's mind, Sue is the problem. Actually, the problem is that they are not leveling with each other about their experience or their beliefs about the situation, so the pattern doesn't change.

When people describe impacts, they disclose their here-and-now observations, thoughts, feelings, and wants in a calm, dispassionate way. They do this in a way that does not attack, criticize, or blame the other person. Instead of simply responding to the content of the conversation, they put their experience on the table for both parties to look at. Then they respond to the content. When both sides do this, the sense making that is causing the problem pattern becomes visible.

In day-to-day conversations, we don't need to describe to each other what is going on in the right-hand column. That would take too much time and probably drive us crazy. And we probably don't need to do that with people we don't want to be in partnership with. But when we want to be in a relationship in which everyone is committed to the success of the project or process, we need to talk about impacts when a pattern of interaction becomes a problem. During a learning conversation, we have to describe the impact others are having on us in the here and now—as it is happening. That is the only way for them to get an accurate picture of what is going on inside us. Otherwise, they just make it up based on their inaccurate stories, which are probably causing the problem pattern in the first place.

To illustrate, here is a snippet of a learning conversation Bob and Sue might have if they describe the impact each is having on the other before responding to the content of the conversation:

Sue: *I want to have a learning conversation with you about our pattern of talking about Frank and nothing much changing.*

Bob: *I agree that we have a problem pattern, but the impact of your bringing it up is that I feel myself getting tense and guarded. I guess part of that has to do with how many times we've been around this and how I feel about Frank. I think ABC is a good project, and I want to help you out, but not at the expense of Frank's dignity or the other work my department has to do.*

Sue: *I find myself getting tense and guarded, too, but I also feel a little relief and some hope now that you're leveling with me. I can understand that you don't want to jeopardize the other work you must do, and I want to find a solution that doesn't do that, but I want to feel assured that you do support the ABC project and see that there really is a problem here. I'm a little surprised by what you just said about Frank, and I guess I don't really understand how you feel about him. I'd like to understand that more.*

Bob: *When I hear that you respect my need to get my department's work done, I feel myself relax a bit and realize I've been thinking that you only care about your project and don't really care about my problems. Maybe that's not true. As for Frank, he's worked here for thirty-five years and made a real contribution to this company. He's only got a few years left until retirement, and I don't think those should be a living hell for him. Sure, he's a little slow, but he's also got a lot of experience and wisdom. I don't think you've really tried to get to know him or his strengths. I'd like you to put more effort into making the project work with Frank, and I wish you'd deal with him directly and stop putting me in the middle.*

Sue: *I respect your attitude toward Frank. I agree we shouldn't treat people who've put a lot of good years into the company poorly, but I don't think we can allow our success to be jeopardized by them either. I'd like to make the project work, with Frank or whoever. I believe he's competent to do the job, but I don't seem to be able to get his attention. The reason I call you is that he reports to you and seems to only care about what you tell him. Really, I'd rather not have to go through you, but I thought you wanted to keep control over Frank. I've thought the real problem is that I don't have any authority over Frank's time and so he doesn't pay as much attention to the project's needs as I want him to.*

Bob: *Oh, I'm getting a different picture of the situation now. I thought you just thought Frank was incompetent and wanted me to replace him. It's true that I have Frank working on some other things now, and he may not be clear about the importance of ABC. It sounds to me like we're going to need Frank to participate in a three-way conversation to really work out a solution. But before we do that, I wonder if you and I need to get clear about anything else that's gone on over this . . .*

Does this seem like a normal conversation at work? If it does, you work in an organization with a culture of clarity. For the most part, people don't have learning conversations at work. That's why the interpersonal mush is so thick. But you can see how such a conversation is essential if Bob and Sue are going to get their partnership back on track. To lead learning and sustain partnership, you have to be able to create these kinds of conversations, even with people who don't know anything about the ground rules of being Descriptive Selves.

I'd like you to notice two things about the conversation. Before Bob or Sue responds to the other's content, they describe the impact on themselves of what the other person just said. For example, before Bob responds to Sue's question about his feelings toward Frank, he tells her the impact her statement about not jeopardizing his department's work had on him. This is what I mean by "describe the impact before responding." In a learning conversation, I describe the here-and-now impact you just had on me—the experience I created from what you said—before going on to respond. In this way, both people are able to track, moment to moment, the experience they are having and ensure interpersonal clarity. As I explained in the previous chapter, it is often through looking at the here-and-now experience people are having with each other, moment to moment, that new insights into the really thorny problem patterns emerge. It's the best path to finding out what our unconscious experience is.

The second thing I want you to notice is that Bob and Sue are using the four elements of experience to describe their experience to each other. In almost every statement, they describe what they are thinking, feeling, wanting, and, if appropriate, observing. They share their maps of the situation. That is what being a Descriptive Self is all about.

Describe Your Experience, Not Judgments

This ground rule is a key to improving people's relationships and patterns of interaction. It is what makes this approach to organizational learning different from the human relations approach of being open and honest. For many years, as I was training to be an organization development consultant, I attended courses that told me it was better to be open and honest. Usually, after a couple of days, I would decide, "OK, I'll be open and honest. Let's see what happens." Invariably, I would upset people and quickly retreat back to being cautious and careful about what I said. I've come to realize that when I said what was on the top of my mind, I was usually expressing my judgments about people and their behavior. If you go back to the original conversation between Bob and Sue, you'll see what I mean. Bob and Sue have made a series of judgments about each other. If they were open and honest about these judgments, it might sound something like this.

Bob: *Oh no, you again. You only call when you have problems.*

Sue: *You're already getting defensive, and you don't even know what I'm calling about. There've been more complaints about Frank's work.*

Bob: *I'm not being defensive. It's just that you always call me to complain about Frank. Have there really been complaints, or are these just your complaints? What have you got against him anyway?*

Sue: *Me? What is it with you and Frank? I know you're stuck with him, but why do you keep running away from these problems?*

When I describe my judgments, I talk about "you": You only call when you have problems, you're getting defensive, you've got something against him, you keep running away. In effect, I am talking as if my story about you is "the truth" instead of my truth. This is a crucial difference. Implicit in your judgments is that I am right or wrong, good or bad. When I hear your judgments of me, I want to argue and defend myself. Instead of getting more clarity, we just end up hurling our judgments at each other without ever inspecting the stories we are making up that lead to those judgments. More than likely we walk away hurt and angry, and our relationship is in worse shape than if we had said nothing at all.

I think this is one of the main reasons for the prevalence of interpersonal mush. We learn time and time again that if we tell "the truth" (i.e., what we really think), we make other people upset, and things get worse instead of better. But what is really going on here is that we don't understand just what truth is and we lack some simple skills for saying it. My experience and the judgments I create from it are my subjective truth, not yours. When I hurl my judgments at you, I am acting as if my subjective truth is some kind of objective or intersubjective truth, which of course it is not. My judgments are just the outcome of my sense making. So I need to show you the stories and information I am using for sense making. And I need to do it with the attitude that this is simply my truth, which is probably not the same as your truth. When I do that, I make myself understandable instead of making you upset.

When I describe my experience, I talk about "I." I acknowledge that my thoughts are based on a story I have made up and that my story may or may not be accurate; it's just my story. Sure, my story is going to contain judgments about you, but when I am describing my experience, I express these judgments as things going on in my head that I am letting you see so you can correct me if I'm wrong. I use the experience cube to guide me: Only when I've described my observations, thoughts, feelings, and wants have I fully described my experience. Here are some examples.

Describing Judgments Versus Describing Experience

Judgment	Experience
At this rate, you aren't going to have the report done properly and on time.	I haven't heard from you once this week [observation (O)], and it confuses me [feeling (F)] since I don't understand how you can make progress on the report without discussing it with me [thought (T)]. I want to be assured that you will have the report done properly and on time [want (W)].
You're ignoring me and trying to control this meeting.	I have some ideas about what we should do and how we should do it [T], but the last two times I tried to raise them, you interrupted me [O], and it's starting to annoy me [F]. I think we all have equal say in how this meeting goes [T], and I would like to know that you will listen to and consider what I have to say [W].
I don't think you are giving your best effort.	The story I'm making up in my head about you right now is that you aren't putting your best effort into this. Am I right? [T] No? Well, let me describe to you what I'm seeing that is making me think that way . . . [W]

As you can see, when I describe my experience, I don't make assumptions about your thoughts, feelings, and wants. I check them out. I show you that I am aware that my maps about you are just my current story and demonstrate that I am willing to change those maps if you are willing to tell me your truth.

Describing Maps

One of the skills of being a Descriptive Self is the ability to describe your maps to other people in simple and understandable ways. A number of approaches to map making available today range from the disciplined and rigorous (such as fish-bone diagrams or systems thinking) to the intuitive and creative (for example, mind mapping). Some excellent software has been developed for individuals and groups, and it keeps getting better. Each has its uses, and I encourage you to develop as many mapping tools as possible. Some years ago, Tom Pitman and I developed an approach to describing mental maps that I find quite useful. It fits the clear leader's need to be able to clarify and articulate his maps and those of other people in simple, direct ways. Research has often compared the schemata—the academics' term for mental maps—of experts with those of novices (for example, how different people think about how to teach, manage people, fix a car, and so forth). The one consistent finding from this stream of research is that novices tend to have long lists of issues and activities that are not well integrated. Experts, in contrast, tend to have much shorter lists, with items that are more abstract and integrated. While the novices' theories of action are literal and linear, the experts' theories are holistic, relativistic, and metaphorical. Cardwork is a technique that helps uncover and describe the genius in each of us. In a sense, it forces you to think like an expert. At the end of this chapter, I'll give you a detailed explanation of how to create cards.

There are two kinds of cards—identity cards and theory-of-action cards. Every card is a complete map in itself. For example, this book is based on an identity card. It's my map of the skills necessary for partnership in collaborative work systems. My card is shown in the figure on the next page.

For this card, I reduced the complexity of my map on leading organizational learning down to four spokes on a propeller so that I can

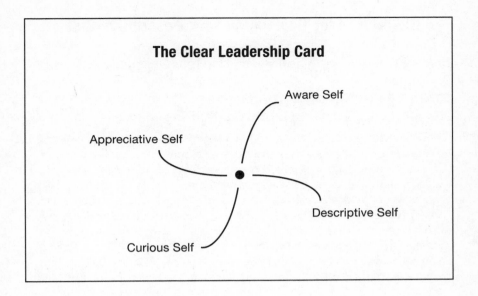

explain it in fairly simple terms. Each spoke of the propeller can be turned into additional cards. I have done that in this book as well. Each skills chapter is based on my theory of action about how those skills create and sustain partnership, and the card that describes the theory is shown at the beginning of each chapter.

Clear leaders know what their theories of action are and can explain them in simple, direct ways to the people they work with. This is another very important part of being a Descriptive Self. If you manage others or are expected to give leadership to a team or work group, I urge you to determine your key theories of action and talk about them to the people who work with you. A good basic set of clear maps on topics like success, teamwork, quality (or customer service), dealing with conflict, managing your boss, and getting ahead should be at any manager's fingertips. Experiment with different variations on titles (e.g., success, we succeed, succeeding together), as these can bring up important differences in maps. Put them on the wall where others can see them. Keep updating them as you learn. Encourage others to come up with better maps. Learn together from your successes and failures. Keep working on becoming more aware of your maps and your real theories in use.

Exercises for Developing Your Descriptive Self

Here are five exercises to help you develop your Descriptive Self.

• Exercise 8: **Describing Your Experience**

Walking the cube is a great way to practice this skill. Use masking tape and make a cross on the floor that represents the experience cube. Tell your partner about something that recently happened to you, and as you tell your story, stand in the part of the cube you are talking from. As you continue talking, move to the element you are speaking out of each time your story shifts. When you are describing your thoughts, opinions, judgments, and interpretations, you should be standing in the thoughts square. When you are describing feelings and emotions, you should be in the feelings square. When you are describing what you saw and heard, you should be in the observing square. And when you are describing your motives, intentions, desires, and needs, you should be standing in the wants square. Notice which square you spend most of your time in and which squares you spend less time in. Try to fully explore and describe your experience in each element. Your partner should point out when you are standing in the wrong part of the cube and help you figure out which square is the right one. Your partner can also ask questions intended to help you fully explore those parts of the cube where you've spent the least time.

The physical act of walking around helps get the notion of the experience cube into the body. Many managers who have taken the Clear Leadership course tell me that they put cubes on the floor in their offices or meeting rooms. When things get heated up or confusing, people take turns walking the cube.

Exercise 9: **Describing Your Feelings**

Feeling is the element many people have the most difficulty describing. It's easier to know we are feeling something than to know what to name it. There are hundreds of feelings, and learning to be able to name each could take a lifetime of introspection. For this reason, it is useful to start with a handful of basic primary feelings.

If you are among those who can barely discern their feelings, here's the starter pack: mad, sad, glad, hurt, and scared. A lot of emotions can be distilled down to those five at some level of intensity. I have found that even people who say they have no idea what they are feeling can find words in the starter pack to describe their sensations.

The next level up, for those who are more able to identify sensations in their body but have some trouble labeling them, is the Emotional Words Chart, shown below. In it, I have categorized what I think are fourteen primary emotions and other feeling words that correspond to each primary emotion at varying levels of intensity. If it's difficult for you to label feelings, just begin with these fourteen. Whenever you are wondering what to call your feeling, you can almost always find a word on the list that fits. After it becomes easier to identify each of the fourteen, go on to subtler shades and intensities. If you really want to work at this, I advise you to type or write the fourteen words on a piece of paper or photocopy the diagram and carry it around with you so you can look at it when you're trying to figure out what you're feeling.

Emotional Words Chart

Emotional Word	Related Feelings
Friendly	Appreciative, caring, concerned, warm, loyal, loving, lustful, attracted, curious, interested, respectful, brotherly
Glad	Content, elated, happy, ecstatic, up, cheerful, inspired, joyful, complete, bemused, marvelous, fabulous, peaceful, satisfied, moved, giggly
Scared	Afraid, anxious, terrified, frightened, worried, bothered, troubled, concerned, threatened, nervous, doubtful, suspicious, horrified
Surprised	Confused, puzzled, doubtful, amazed, fooled, tricked, betrayed, shocked, dumbfounded, perplexed, lost
Mad	Irritated, angry, enraged, disturbed, furious, frustrated, disappointed, annoyed, pissed off, petulant, defensive, unsatisfied, resentful, righteous, indignant
Desirable	Beautiful, feminine, pretty, flirtatious, sexy, handsome, hot, wanted
Shy	Timid, bashful, introverted, hesitant, tentative, unsure, unclear, tremulous, small, weak, insignificant
Lonely	Alone, isolated, abandoned, cut adrift, anchorless, displaced, stranded, solitary, detached, disconnected, separate
Embarrassed	Ashamed, aghast, abashed, remorseful, guilty, regretful, shamed, put down
Hurt	Wounded, wronged, broken, pained, sore, harmed, crushed, beaten, defeated, destroyed, used, abused

Exercise 9: **Describing Your Feelings** cont'd

Tired	Rushed, busy, worn-out, harried, used up, sleepy, passive, languid, apathetic, sedentary, lazy, bored, indifferent, lethargic, flat, wooden, stilted
Confident	Competent, strong, assured, composed, proud, skilled, able, fit, ready, poised, sure, certain, convinced, courageous, brave
Excited	Charged, alive, feisty, energized, motivated, enlivened, playful, raring to go, extroverted, bursting, bubbly, coltish, giddy, swept up, vital
Sad	Depressed, down, melancholy, sorrowful, disturbed, blue, tearful, nauseated, awful, grief-stricken, mournful, unhappy

And a couple of important feelings not covered by these primary words: thankful, grateful, awestruck

---

Work with your learning partner to describe the feeling you are having about different situations in your life. As you do this, your partner needs to be alert to when you are using the feeling word but not actually describing a feeling. Sentences that begin "I feel that . . ." or "I feel like . . ." or " I feel as if . . ." are dead giveaways, as what follows next is almost never a feeling. It's either a thought or a want.

Exercise 10: **Describing the Impact Before Responding**

This exercise will help you learn the difference between responding and telling your experience. Have your partner tell you something very controversial about you. If you think you can stand it, have your partner say something that really pushes your buttons. When he does, say the first thing that comes to mind. Notice what kind of statement that is. Now have your partner say the same thing to you again, but this time look inside, notice your experience, and describe what you are observing, thinking, feeling, and wanting in the moment. Here are some statements your partner could use.

- You're not very bright, are you?
- If I were you, I'd just give up.
- The best thing we could do is just nuke those stupid (insert a group).

Exercise 11: **Describing Experience, Not Judgments**

A fun way to practice this skill is to talk to your partner about someone you have a lot of judgments about. Pretend your partner is that person and for five minutes just fire away with all the judgments you have of that other person. Really let yourself go. Get it all out. When you are finished, take a few minutes to describe what that was like and how you are feeling now. Ask your partner what it was like to be on the other side of your judgments. Now talk to your partner as if she were that other person again, but this time describe your experience instead of your judgments. Instead of saying "you" say "I." Again, stop after five minutes and debrief what that was like for you and your partner.

Perhaps the most difficult part of this skill is the ability to give other people in-the-moment descriptions of the experience you are having in relation to them. There is a lot of room for anxiety, vulnerability, and embarrassment in doing that, so you really do need to practice doing it before you launch into a learning conversation with someone who is in a problem pattern with you.

A good way to begin practicing is to work up to it with your practice partner. Spend a few minutes discussing what you both think about the idea of having skill practice partners. Then move on to describing your experience of each other as skill practice partners. Then—and this is what you are working toward—describe your experience of each other right at this moment, in the here and now. Notice what thoughts, feelings, wants, or sensations you didn't mention. Notice why you didn't bring them up. Tell that to your learning partner, too.

Once you have done this a few times and feel comfortable with it, use Exercise 1 ("Knowing Your Experience, Here and Now") but do it in relation to each other. Describe your stream of consciousness beginning with the phrase "Right now as I experience you, I . . ." for an agreed-upon length of time (up to five minutes per person). Say it over and over. Work your way around the experience cube systematically, saying what you are experiencing in relation to what you observe, think, feel, and want. As you get more comfortable doing this, just let your experience come out of you naturally.

Exercise 12: **Using Cardwork to Describe Maps**

Cardwork is about making your identity maps and theories of action explicit so that they can be described, discussed, and tested. It's also a way of getting clear about other people's maps. You can also use it to practice getting clarity about theories of action even if you don't explicitly use it at work.

Flow diagrams and critical-path charts are one way of capturing a theory of action. They depict a series of activities toward some end. Cardwork is quite different. I use 3-by-5-inch blank cards. Well-constructed cards have the following characteristics:

Five or six parts. A theory-of-action card has a title, a subtitle, and three or four phrases (never more than four) connected by a spinning-propeller-like image.

Complete in itself. The title describes what this theory of action is about. The subtitle captures the outcome of successful action. The phrases compose a complete theory of how to reach that outcome.

Spinning in all directions. The phrases each capture a crucial facet of how to accomplish the goal, task, or action, but they do not have to be in a step-by-step sequence. Each phrase can "spin" and have more than one relevant meaning.

Poetry rules. The title, subtitle, and phrases are constructed to evoke as many useful associations as possible. Use wet, sticky, metaphorical language as opposed to dry, precise, intellectual language. You can use this rule for knowing when a card is completed: reading from the top right, it should sound like a poem. For example:

> Five or six parts,
> Complete in itself.
> Spinning in all directions,
> Poetry rules.

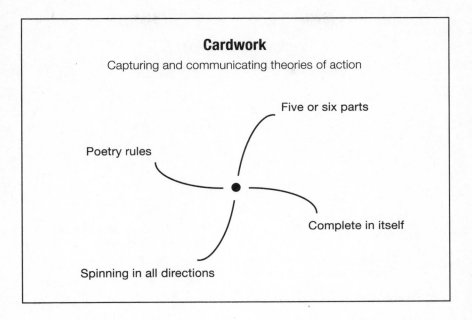

Cardwork

Capturing and communicating theories of action

Five or six parts

Poetry rules

Complete in itself

Spinning in all directions

I have found cardwork very useful in trying to understand my own theories of action or identity maps as well as those of other people. An identity card is constructed the same way as a theory-of-action card but doesn't have a subtitle. Helping another person make a card usually leads both parties to develop a much deeper insight into their maps and contributes to good working relationships.

Practice by using cardwork to identify some of your own theories of action. A few good cards to start with are "leading teams," "influencing others," and "satisfying customers." Pick a title. Then decide what the outcome of effective action is. If you are doing a card on "leading teams," what do you think excellent team leadership produces? The answer would be the subtitle. Next, brainstorm all the things you think a leader must do to produce that outcome. Once you are finished brainstorming, go back over the list and whittle it down. Combine ideas that are similar and eliminate redundant ones. Do this until you have reduced the list to no more than four key points. Arrange these so that the card reads more or less like a poem and then draw your card. If you find this practice useful, you may want to make a list of all the areas at work in which you must be operating from a theory of action and make yourself a deck of these cards.

Here's my theory-of-action card for sustaining partnership:

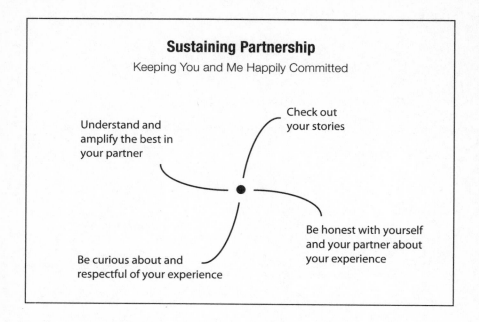

Sustaining Partnership
Keeping You and Me Happily Committed

Understand and amplify the best in your partner

Check out your stories

Be curious about and respectful of your experience

Be honest with yourself and your partner about your experience

The card says that the outcome of successfully sustaining partnership is keeping you and me happily committed (to whatever project or process we are engaged in) and describes the things that I think have to happen in order to do so. As you can probably tell, this mental map is woven throughout this book.

Summary

Being a Descriptive Self is describing your thoughts, feelings, wants, observations, and maps in a way that helps others see what is going on in your head so that they can give you the information you need for developing a more accurate story. One of my colleagues, Joan Mara, illustrates the proper attitude toward being a Descriptive Self with a demonstration. First, she has people play-act a snowball fight. Snowball fights are like hurling judgments. People try to nail one another while trying to avoid having anything land on them. By the end, all the snowballs are lying on the ground, melting. Then she has them play-act a game of catch. When people play catch, they throw the ball so that the other person can catch it. That's what you have to do as your Descriptive Self—toss what you "really think" to others in a way that lets them catch it!

Part of the skill of clear leadership is knowing when others need you to be a Descriptive Self and when they are most likely to be making up inaccurate stories. People are most apt to make up negative stories during times of stress, uncertainty, and confusion, so those are the times when we need to get really descriptive with the people we want to be in partnership with. It's a useful habit to ask "What do you think I just said?"—especially when the relationship is new and the other person is operating from a different map—and then repeat what you meant until the person hears it accurately. By speaking as Descriptive Selves, we replace interpersonal mush with interpersonal clarity, but only if we are listening to each other. Being a Descriptive Self is only half of a learning conversation. Being a Curious Self is the other. So let's turn to that next.

7

The Curious Self

Uncovering Other People's Experience

One of the things I have noticed about effective leaders is that they are naturally curious. They are always open to learning and will take every opportunity to gather different people's observations and opinions. Everyone has some curiosity, but disconnection, fusion, and reactions to unconscious anxiety can push a person's curiosity away. Clearing out the mush requires a balanced ability to be descriptive about you and curious about others. Being curious is both openness to hearing what goes on in other people's heads and the ability to find out. The mastery of the Curious Self is the ability to help others become aware of and tell you about their maps and experience. There are two parts to this. One is just getting people to be willing to tell you the truth of their experience. But people are not always aware of what their experience is, and some parts of their experience are outside their awareness. The Curious Self uses skills and techniques to help other people become more aware of their experience even as they are talking about it.

All people can increase their curiosity skills. The following techniques and models are helpful in understanding and developing your Curious Self:

- Make it appealing
- Park all reactions

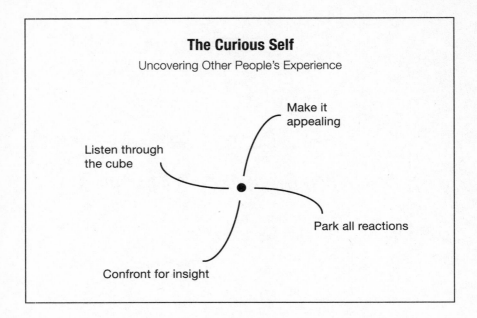

- Confront for insight
- Listen through the cube

After learning more about these aspects of the Curious Self, you'll have the chance to practice developing some skills by completing the exercises at the end of the chapter.

Make It Appealing

When you are being curious, you are inviting others to be Descriptive Selves. Being a Descriptive Self is not all that common. In addition to lacking the skills they need to do it, people have had painful experiences that have made them wary of being descriptive. Most have to be convinced that you are sincere about wanting to hear their experience and can be trusted with it. It's difficult to demand that people tell you the truth of their experience. It's easy for them to conceal what they really think, feel, or want, and you don't have any way of knowing what they aren't telling you. Telling the truth of your experience is a voluntary activity, and people are more likely to do that if they believe that what they say is going to be treated respectfully and with some dignity. Dignity—now there's a word you don't run into much in management textbooks. Dignity is about being treated as if you deserve to be here (in this group, this organization, this world) and that your experience is valid for you. We strip people of their dignity when we threaten, at least in their minds, their social identity and, by extension, their memberships. (I discuss this in more detail in the section on shame.) The hallmark of being a Curious Self is that others sense a real openness to hearing their inner experience in a way that won't diminish it or them.

Letting people have whatever experience they are having is the most fundamental and, for many people, the most difficult part of making it appealing for others to tell you the truth of their experience. Listen to their thoughts without trying to change their minds. Listen to their feelings without trying to make them feel better. Listen to their wants without feeling responsible for satisfying these wants for them. It sounds simple, and it's a simple concept, but I have found that it is one of the most difficult things for managers to do. It's as though we believe that when others tell us about their difficulties, fears, concerns, and confusions, our job is to give them advice—to fix it for them.

In my courses, I joke about how this seems to be a particularly male problem. In my early relationships with women, I always seemed to get in trouble when I listened to two or three minutes of some issue they were having at work, or with a friend, and then told them how to fix it. They would get annoyed! Women nod their heads knowingly when I tell this story. It took me a while to realize that they didn't want me to fix it (or them); they just wanted me to listen, to understand their experience. Women seem to be able to hold back longer before trying to fix things, although of course they do it, too. I think this is the main reason why a lot of men prefer to talk to women rather than to other men about their problems. They figure that if they tell their men friends, they'll start getting advice after a minute or two. What's it like to provide a few minutes of information about your experience and they have others start giving you advice? "Oh geez, thanks. It took me twenty years to get into this mess, and you're going to tell me how to fix it in ninety seconds. Wow, I must be a real idiot." As soon as I start giving you advice on how to fix it, I create a one up–one down situation in which I am the wise all-knowing one and you are the one who needs fixing. This is not appealing. At best, it's annoying and makes you want to stop talking. At worst, it strips people of their dignity. Either way, this kind of response makes it unlikely that people will want to tell you the truth of their experience in the future since they'll end up having to fend off your advice. It's different when a person comes to you expressly for advice, but most of the times when it is appropriate to be a Curious Self, that isn't what is going on. Usually, the Curious Self initiates the conversation.

The urge to give advice, to take away the bad feelings, to fix other people's experience for them so they will have a better one comes from a caring place. It also comes from a fused place. Many people report that they become physically agitated when they listen to someone else's experience without being allowed to express their opinions about it. So I have to wonder if their desire to fix the other person's experience is based on concern for that person or is really an attempt to take away their own anxious feelings. The Curious Self needs to park that kind of reactivity. And it is even more difficult to let other people have their experience when they are describing their less-than-perfect experience of you—which is most likely exactly what you are going to hear about in a learning conversation.

A learning conversation involves people talking about problems they are having in their patterns of interaction. You are going to be telling me your story about me, which most likely will include something I did, said, felt, or intended and that I believe is not accurate. It would be natural for me to want to stop you at that point and say, "Oh no, that's not what I meant," but that will destroy the learning conversation. Possibly the most important technique for creating effective organizational learning conversations is to simply listen to and explore the other person's experience of you, and demonstrate that you fully get it, before you say anything about your experience.

Pouncing on someone else's inaccurate observations or faulty logic will just shut that person up in the future. So will turning learning conversations into a win-lose contest by trying to figure out who's right and who's wrong. Being a Curious Self is not about being curious just long enough to figure out other people's misperceptions or inaccurate assumptions. It's about being willing to fully understand and explore what their experience is—to stand in their shoes and look at the world as they see it so that you can make sense of their sense making. Inviting another person's Descriptive Self into the room means you have to be willing to acknowledge that his subjective truth, whatever it is, is valid for him.

For many people, being a Descriptive Self is an act of vulnerability, so you need to make it safe. When you have authority over others, that does not happen quickly and easily. Setting up a time and a place where others don't feel pressured or threatened, especially with people who are not used to being descriptive with you, will be important in getting to their truth. Many people want to wait until they can interact one to one before they have a learning conversation. That makes sense in terms of reducing the threat factor, but people also need to consider whether it might be better to include all those who are affected in the learning conversations. The strongest teams are those in which people can talk out their issues with everyone present. The ground rule is that the only people who can fix relationship problems are the people in the relationship. You and I can't fix your problem pattern with Bob. Only you and Bob can. And if the issues involve three or more people, they all have to participate in a conversation if they want to turn mush into clarity.

It's also useful to tell people why you are curious—lead with being descriptive yourself. When people are reluctant to open up, help them see the benefits of being descriptive. Tell them what you get from it, why you want more of it, and what you would like from them. If you want them to be descriptive more than once, however, it would be better if they enjoyed the interaction, or at least did not suffer from it. They will need to test your trustworthiness before they really let it all hang out. They will test to see how well you actually listen, how much you accept what you hear without reacting to it or getting fused with it, and what you do with the information once you have it. Beyond that, one of the things that makes it appealing for people to tell you the truth of their experience is to see that you really value hearing it and don't judge the quality of their thinking, how neurotic they are, or whether their wants are acceptable—in other words, that you really believe their experience is valid for them.

Before going any further, I want to make one point very clear. While I don't think it's effective to demand that others be descriptive, I do think it is appropriate for managers to say that using clear leadership skills is a job expectation. Managers are responsible for outcomes. If they believe that those outcomes are best accomplished using the skills of clear leadership, they are as entitled to demand that as they are to expect fulfillment of any other performance parameter. But if authorities abuse their power and/or abuse the information others give them, people will close up and interpersonal mush will reign.

Park All Reactions

Somebody says or does something that pushes my buttons. I react—usually by saying something with an edge to it. The other person reacts back. Maybe we have a discussion. Maybe we have an argument. Maybe we just disconnect and go away, nursing our reactions to each other by ourselves. The key thing that happens when I act on my reaction is that I stop understanding the other person. Parking my reactions is about stopping myself from acting on my reactivity and staying curious instead.

There are probably a lot of reasons why people react before they fully understand another person. Some of the more common are an unconscious separation or intimacy anxiety that just got triggered, a feeling of embarrassment, and a desire to correct the other person's misperceptions. The knee-jerk reaction in each case is to find some way of stopping other people in their tracks and getting them to change their experience—change their perception or judgment, their feeling or want. When people first start trying to have learning conversations, a common mistake is to listen to the other person's experience for a minute or so and then, without hearing the whole experience, start to describe what they see differently. The Curious Self hears the other person out fully before doing this.

I think reactivity is one of the key reasons we have learned not to be descriptive about our experience. In the past, when we've told people "the truth," some have gotten reactive—angry, defensive, upset, and so on. So we learn to be very cautious and parcel out our truth in small bites, to see what happens. If you get reactive while other people are describing their experience to you, the game is over. So it's imperative that you learn to park your reactions and not act on them. I have found that people have an easier time doing this if they understand where their reactions come from. This is so important that I have developed a separate card for it (shown on facing page).

While it is easy to see reactivity in others, it is often difficult to see it in ourselves. I don't label myself as reactive. Normally, when I am being reactive, I think I am justified in whatever I am doing or saying. I'm trying to change your experience because it is inaccurate. I'm angry because you just insulted me. I'm being quiet because I'm embarrassed by what you are saying. The key behavior that lets us know we are being reactive is that we are no longer curious about the other person's experience. Curiosity goes out the window, and I'm either trying to get you to change

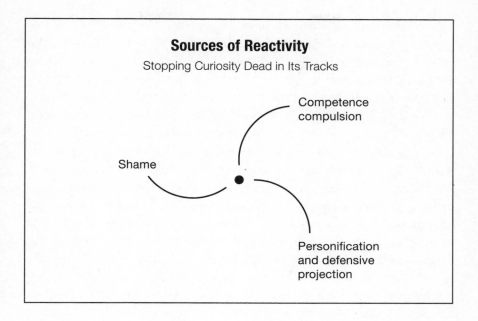

Sources of Reactivity

Stopping Curiosity Dead in Its Tracks

Competence compulsion

Shame

Personification and defensive projection

what you said or withdrawing from the interaction. If I can notice that I've stopped being curious even though I really don't understand your experience, I can park my reaction and reengage my curiosity. That is a tremendously powerful skill to develop.

As I've tried to understand my own and other people's reactivity, particularly the kind of reactivity that drives out learning in organizations, I've come to see that much of it comes from one of three places: competence compulsion, personification and defensive projection, and shame. I'll describe each of these in some detail.

Competence Compulsion

While sense making can be very individualistic, there are some patterns to sense making in organizations, and one of these is the competence compulsion. Simply put, this is the compulsion most people have to make sense of anything that happens to them at work in a way that ensures that they see themselves as competent and that others see them as competent.[1] Since learning and performing are inversely related, the compulsion to see themselves, and to be seen by others, as competent can make people reactive to information they need for learning. Rather than get curious about it, they get defensive.

When people are learning, they do not perform very well. When people are performing very well, they probably aren't learning much. This inverse relationship between learning and performing creates numerous problems for managers who are trying to increase organizational learning, and it is one of the reasons why really efficient, high-performance organizations have such a hard time learning, adapting, and innovating. People who can't tolerate poor performance are allowing no room for learning. In such a situation, what happens when someone brings up something I've done that's not so great? Rather than get curious about it, I'll feel an urge to explain my actions so the other person will see that I am actually competent or, failing that, to interpret the situation in a way that makes their observations inaccurate or not worth my attention. In either case, I'm not getting curious about the observations and trying to learn more about the other person's experience.

This may be one of the reasons why it is particularly difficult to bring up issues with one person in front of other people. In a work environment, my need to maintain an image of competence in front of those other people will affect my sense making of the interaction. If you bring up issues that threaten that image, I could get quite reactive, even if your intention is to support and enhance my competence.

In order to be effective as a Descriptive Self, it is useful to understand all the sources of reactivity listed here. If I want to tell you about my experience of you, and you might appear to be less than competent when I do so, then I need to think about how to do that in a way that won't trigger your competence compulsion. But my main point in this chapter is that it's important for you to recognize your own competence compulsion and know how to park it so that you won't get reactive. It is mostly a matter of intending to be curious and nondefensive when someone brings up something that is invalidating and questions your mental maps. It's easiest to do this, I think, in a formal process of inquiry, like a learning conversation, and when you have prepared yourself to remain nonreactive in the face of disconfirming information. It's harder when it comes at you all of a sudden and you are not expecting it. Try to notice when you are disregarding someone's experience because it threatens your image of competence and park your reactivity—engage your curiosity instead.

An organization's culture can have a dramatic effect on the amount of reactivity or learning that takes place at work. The competence compulsion will be operating in most people, but if leaders punish people for incompetence or mistakes, then that will likely amplify the problem. In contrast, leaders can reduce the effects of the competence compulsion if they create a culture in which being seen learning is viewed as a mark of competence. Leaders do this when they actively seek learning—that is, they seek disconfirming information, they get curious when people express contrary views or opinions, they surface and discuss the less-than-perfect results of their decisions or actions in order to produce better outcomes next time. And they amplify the effect of their actions by making it known that they consider these sorts of behaviors in others a mark of competence. Leaders can reduce a lot of the defensiveness to organizational learning in these ways. The other two sources of reactivity are a lot more difficult to deal with, and a lot more personal.

Personification and Defensive Projection

In my early days as a university professor, I found myself getting quite reactive toward an older professor I'll call Derek. In meetings, I often became upset by what he was saying. Our values and priorities seemed so different that I was pretty sure he had a lot of negative judgments about me, so I tried to avoid him. I took routes to get around campus that were longer but didn't cross his path. I had daydreams in which I imagined having debates with him that he would lose. This went on for quite a few months until it occurred to me that I really didn't know what Derek thought of me. Why did I think he had such negative thoughts and feelings toward me?

One theory of how the imagination works is that we choose others to personify attributes of ourselves, and they show up in our dreams and daydreams. It's quite informative to think that everything we're imagining is really made up of parts of us, clamoring for attention. According to this theory, we pick others—real, fictional, mythical—to personify different parts of ourselves to ourselves. It turned out that I had personified my negative judgments about myself in Derek. For whatever reason, I had chosen him as the figure who saw the worst of me. So whenever I was in his presence, what I saw reflected back in his eyes were the parts of me that I didn't like! No wonder I was reactive to him.

If you find yourself spending a lot of time talking to certain people in your head, you may be using them to personify some aspect of yourself to yourself. And if these are aspects you don't like, and are trying to avoid or deny, then you are likely to be reactive in their presence. Why would you get curious about the experience of someone who personifies the worst in you? In such cases, it is very important to separate your sense making from the facts. How do you know these people have these judgments about you? If they haven't actually expressed these things to you, then the judgments must be stories you have made up and projected back onto them.

I briefly discussed projection in chapter 1—it is one of the sources of the stories we make up. Defensive projection is a process that helps people keep the parts of themselves that they don't want to acknowledge out of their awareness. If I don't want to see my own pettiness, for example, it takes some energy and effort. A part of me wants to be aware of my pettiness, and another part doesn't. Defensive projection is a kind of mental sleight of hand that lets me take my pettiness and put it onto you. You carry it for me so I can be aware of the pettiness, but instead of seeing it in me, I see it in you. I dislike you for being petty, but at the same time, I find ways to encourage your pettiness so I can continue to project it onto you. The study of this process has taken up thousands of pages in psychology books, but because the whole purpose of defensive projection is to keep things out of awareness, it is extremely hard to notice in ourselves.

Let me describe one of the ways I've noticed it in my own life. I tend to be unaware of my anger until I blow up, and I've had a number of interactions with my wife that go like this:

Gervase: *Are you angry?*

Carmen: *No, I'm not angry.*

Gervase (after a moment): *Are you sure you're not angry, because you seem angry to me.*

Carmen: *No, I'm not feeling any anger.*

Gervase (after a longer moment): *I don't know, but I'm really sensing some anger in you. Are you sure you're not repressing your anger?*

Carmen (speaking angrily): *Will you stop with the angry thing?*

Gervase (to myself, or, if I'm really looking for a fight, out loud): *See, I knew you were angry.*

In this situation, I'm actually the one who is angry, but I'm keeping it out of my awareness by goading my wife into getting angry so that I can see my anger in her. I've since learned to assume, after the first or second time she says no, that I'm really the one who is angry, and when I do, I've found that I can notice the anger in myself and get clear on what it is about.

There has got to be something about the other person that hooks the projection in the first place. We don't project a quality randomly. The other person usually has some characteristic that makes the projection seem to fit. Before I project my jealousy onto you, I have to see you doing something that looks jealous. But I am not really seeing your jealousy any-more, just my projection. And here is the kicker: Because you are doing a good job of helping me avoid seeing it in myself, I want to keep that pro-jection in place. I will look for evidence that supports me in seeing you act jealously because that relieves me of having to confront my own jealousy. So on top of the normal sense making process of seeing what I believe, projection gives me a motivation to not see anything that might change my story.

Projection is different from personification, but as sources of reactiv-ity they are like two sides of the same coin, and both were going on in my relationship with Derek. I was projecting some negative aspects of myself onto him as well as personifying parts of me I didn't like by using him in my imagination. So after a few months of being very reactive toward him, I sat down and made a list of all the things I didn't like about Derek. Then I asked myself if I had any of those attributes myself. I had to admit I did, and I realized that I was probably projecting them onto Derek. When I did that, a miraculous thing occurred—I was no longer reactive toward him. In fact, I started to discover things I liked about him. When we served on the same committee, I discovered that we agreed on numerous things. Over time, I actually became fond of him!

People are going to have negative judgments about others, but that doesn't mean they are engaged in defensive projection. Reactivity and the unwillingness to be curious about their experience are the signs of defen-sive projection. If you find you need or want to be in partnership with someone but your reactivity makes it difficult to be a Curious Self with her, try this test: Think of the negative judgments you believe she has about you and then see if that isn't a list of your negative judgments about yourself. If it is, then you know you are using her to personify those parts of yourself to yourself. You can say to yourself, "I don't know what her judgments of me are. I'm just making this up. Maybe it's time to actually find out." It's more difficult to list your negative judgments of other people and then see if you can own that those things are also true of you to some extent. I call this "eating the projection." If you can see those things in yourself, then you will stop needing to use other people to defend yourself from awareness. When that happens, you will no longer be so reactive to them, and you can be a Curious Self about their experience.

Shame

From my clinical studies of people who are learning and using clear leadership skills, I have concluded that shame is the number one impediment to well-intentioned, normal people having learning conversations. If you are going to lead organizational learning, you must able to circumvent the shame that fuels so much of the negative fantasies and reactivity in organizational life. Part of what you need to learn, in being a Descriptive Self, is how to describe your experience of others without shaming them. The other part, in being a Curious Self, is learning what your shame buttons are, how you normally defend yourself against your shame, and how to park it.

Shame is that part in each of us that feels unworthy, small, and inadequate. Guilt is the feeling that we have done something wrong, but shame is when we are what is wrong. In most of us, there is a deep-down core of rot—a place where we are convinced that we really don't belong here, that there is something terribly wrong with us, and that if others knew who we really were, they would not accept us. That is our shame. For some people, that shame is ever close to the surface and they are always aware of it—we might call them "shame-based personalities." Others might have their shame buried deep, far away from their awareness. Most of us fall somewhere in between. I imagine that there are people who don't have that core of rot, but I have never met any. No matter how successful or powerful or beautiful people are, they probably carry shame. In fact, shame can be what compels a person to work so hard at being successful or powerful or attractive.

Each of us has some shame buttons. These are images we carry of ourselves as being less than, deficient, or inadequate in some way. Common ones are not being smart enough, not being caring enough, not being likable enough, and not being attractive enough, but the range is as wide as human experience. People vary, of course, in how much shame they carry and how close to the surface these buttons are, but we all have them. When you push my shame button, an image of myself that is painful to me is brought to my awareness. At that moment, what I feel is the pain of it—like a stab in the gut—and then I react to the pain and want it to go away, which usually means I want you to go away. Probably the last thing that would occur to me is to get curious and inquire into your experience of whatever it is that shames me. Yet if I can separate my experience (the pain) from you, realize that I'm the one, not you, who has this terrible judgment of me, then I can park it and be more open to understanding just where you are coming from.

If I try to insult you about something that you don't buy into, it will just roll off your back. The only insults that hurt are the ones you buy into. And since you carry around these images of yourself, I can bring them to your awareness without even naming them. Say you have a painful image of yourself as being disorganized, and I walk into your office and look around at the haphazard piles of documents with what appears to you to be an air of disgust—wham, you feel your shame. Who is making the judgment here? Maybe I am, but at this point you don't really know that. All you know is that you are feeling hurt. If you let your shame govern you, the last thing you'll probably want to do is find out what my judgments are.

When you think about it, infancy is a setup for shame. We arrived on the planet full of energy, vitality, and curiosity, but our parents wanted a "good" boy or girl. They were not as thrilled as we were by all the neat stuff our bodies create. They didn't think it was so great when we wanted to share the wonder of our loud screaming voices. In fact, we were severely reprimanded when we followed our exuberance onto a busy road. As we grow from infancy to childhood, we are told in myriad ways that our experience is not right—think different thoughts, feel different feelings, want different wants. Much of that is necessary survival training, but it has other consequences. Gershen Kaufman has argued that the number one way a child learns shame is when she asks a question and doesn't get a response.[2] Now how common is that—a child tugging at a parent's leg while the parent is trying to have a conversation with someone else and being shushed and ignored? Who can blame the harried parent? But what happens is that the child thinks to herself, "If I were worthy, I would have gotten a response." That sense of shame is dumped into a "shame tank" that she carries with her at home and at school, storing all the times when she gets the message that she just isn't right or good enough. Over the years, her shame tank becomes just something in the background, so much a part of her that she doesn't even notice it anymore. The question is not whether you have a shame tank, but how full it is and what you currently do with your shame.

When someone touches our shame buttons, it causes us to react in a defensive way that will usually stop curiosity dead in its tracks. More often, however, shame is what stops a person from even starting a learning conversation. When I'm not sure that I'm worthy or good enough, the last thing I want to do is be a Descriptive Self. Instead, I will want to fade into the background and figure out what would be the "right" thing to say or do before I say or do anything.

It's not just the shame, but the ways we learned to defend ourselves against shame when we were children, that make learning conversations difficult. Shaming someone can close down a learning conversation, but the defenses most of us have learned make it likely that we won't even begin a learning conversation. Shame-based behaviors create disconnection. Here are just a few of the common shame-based responses that make learning conversations difficult:

- Wanting not to appear foolish, stupid, or inept
- Wanting to get it just right before I say or do something
- Wanting others to agree with me so I'll feel accepted
- Always looking for what is "wrong" in others
- Wanting to know what others think before saying anything
- Wanting to be fully in control of the impression I give others
- Berating myself whenever I am less than perfect
- Feeling intimidated by people
- Creating really high standards for myself

Each of these responses is based on one of the seven basic ways in which I have seen people defend themselves against feeling their shame. Kaufman has described them as withdrawal, perfection, contempt, anger, power, humor, and shaming others.[3] These responses become lifelong habits unless we work at getting rid of the underlying shame. Each drives out learning, sometimes by reducing our willingness to be descriptive but most often by reducing our willingness to be curious. I'll briefly describe each and detail how they make learning conversations difficult. See if any are familiar to you.

Withdrawal. If I am not visible, I won't be shamed. So I fade into the background. Being a Descriptive Self is the last thing I would consider doing. It's way too scary—people will make fun of me! If someone asks me my subjective truth, I'm most likely to say something innocuous until I can figure out the safe thing to say.

Perfection. If I am perfect, you can't shame me. So I work to get the perfect job and have the perfect partner and wear just the right clothes and live in a perfect house and produce perfect reports and so on. It's a very precarious thing, being perfect, so I only engage in activities that I know I can be perfect at (or close enough to it). I have to control myself and the situation, and a learning conversation is too uncertain an activity. There's too much chance for my lack of perfection to be noticed. If you start to bring up things about me that I know aren't perfect, I will quickly say "I know" and try to close down the conversation before any real learning happens.

Contempt. If I don't have any respect for you, then you can't shame me because your opinion isn't worth considering. This defense can be a lot more subtle than the word *contempt* implies. In my head, I just notice that you don't really have much knowledge or experience or that your values aren't ones I admire. Why would I be curious about the experience of someone I don't think much of? Why would I care what your subjective truth is or bother trying to get you to understand mine?

Anger. If I become enraged when you try to shame me, I'll scare you into stopping. Perhaps you know people like this—you feel like you have to walk around them very cautiously for fear their anger will erupt. A person who has developed this strategy will become angry whenever someone gets close to his shame buttons. Then he either scares others off with his anger or puts his effort into keeping his cool, making it difficult to be curious at all.

Power. If I have power, then you won't dare to shame me. I will work at getting the resources others want or the authority that will ensure they are very careful about what they say around me. I use my power to make it very clear that you had better not shame me, or else— which makes bringing up issues and wanting to have a learning conversation with me very risky. If you touch my shame buttons, I will not get curious; rather, I will use my power to shut you down.

Humor. If I keep everything light and a joke, then you can't shame me. If I make you laugh, I can deflect any concerns you might have with me. If you try to bring up a problem pattern in our interactions, I make a joke instead of getting curious. Self-deprecating jokes work really well at ensuring that no serious conversation takes place.

Shaming others. If I do some mental maneuvering, I can avoid shame. Whenever some shame comes at me, I just pass it along before it can land. You push my shame buttons, and, wham, I shame you back. If you are too scary a target, wham, I shame the person next to me. If we are having a learning conversation and I start to feel shamed all of a sudden, you'll find yourself being attacked by me, and that brings the learning conversation to a bad end.

I hope you have noticed that while each of these responses may be effective at stopping us from becoming aware of painful images we have of ourselves, they also make sure that no learning takes place. Most of us have developed more than one defense against shame. It's useful to know what yours are so that you can catch yourself when you are using them and park them. There is, of course, something beyond skill alone, some quality of character or ego strength, that makes it possible for people to engage their curiosity despite the pain. Like many of the skills in this book, it seems that people learn to do this by "faking it until they can make it"—that is, noticing their shame, gritting their teeth and holding in the pain, and trying to pretend that they are still curious about the other person's experience. By recognizing your own shame-based defenses, you can catch yourself when you are starting to react and realize that you are reacting to your own stuff, not what the other person said or did. When you do this, you strengthen your own container, your ability to feel your anxiety or hurt and still do what needs to be done. If you do this often enough, it won't be so difficult after a while, and a little later it will feel natural.

I'd also like to point out that the more we understand and accept our own shame, the easier it is to understand and work around other people's shame. Recognizing the shame that underlies another person's arrogance (contempt), fear (perfection), tantrum (anger), accommodation (withdrawal), or intimidation (power) helps me be less reactive to his behavior. When I focus on the wound instead of the annoying behavior, I can feel my compassion increase and my reactivity decrease. I can be more of a nonanxious presence. I pay more attention to where his shame buttons are and avoid them when I want to have a learning conversation with him. And this is important, because sometimes I want to discuss something that is most likely to push the other person's buttons.

I have spent some time trying to figure out why people shame others. It is rarely a desire to attack or hurt the other person, although that does happen. We may shame someone as a defense against being shamed or to counterattack when we feel shamed. We may respond this way when we feel scared, want to push someone away, or are trying to get power over someone. Shaming may also be used to get attention or affection, to protect a third party, or to obliquely express anger. But the number one reason people use shame is to try to motivate change.

It goes like this. I notice that Sam is frequently late, and that starts to bother me. One day, when Sam's tardiness is really causing me problems, I say something sarcastic about it. My hope is that he will stop being late. Instead, one of three things almost always happens: Sam goes away feeling wounded and makes up nasty stories about me, we get into an argument in which I try to show Sam how late he always is while Sam defends himself, or Sam zings me back and we escalate our attacks until we pull back and go off separately to lick our wounds. It is ironic that even though shaming is such a common strategy for trying to change others, it almost never works. Sure, you can get people to change their behavior with enough negative reinforcement, as long as you are watching. But shame generally reinforces the part of the person that contributes to the behavior you are trying to change. For example, Sam wouldn't have felt his shame if there weren't a part of him that believed he was late too often. When I shame him by noticing and validating its existence, I am reinforcing the part of him that has trouble being on time.

Could I talk to Sam about my experience of his tardiness without shaming him? Yes, I could, and that is essential if I want to have a learning conversation about it. But I must do it in a spirit of curiosity, not

descriptiveness. If I confront Sam about his lateness in a spirit of "constructive feedback," I have taken the position that my truth is the truth. This
will almost always result in a reactive response. Instead, I need to bring up
the experience I am having in a spirit of curiosity, taking the positon that I
want to find out if Sam sees things the same way I do.

Confront for Insight

Confronting for insight is one way of getting around another person's
shame response. How do I bring up difficult issues if I think doing so
might push your shame buttons? Remember that we shame a person
when we bring to his awareness an image he has of himself that is deficient, unworthy, bad, or inadequate in some way. This is a very important
definition. It points out that shaming always reinforces a belief or map
that the other person already has of himself. If he doesn't buy into what I
am saying about him, no matter how negative, it doesn't push his shame
buttons. So there must usually be a kernel of truth, subjective or objective,
for shaming to occur, and that is why it is so difficult to deal with it.

When I am confronting for insight, I bring to awareness (in myself
and/or in the other person) an incongruence or discrepancy I've noticed
and ask him if he's noticed the same thing.[4] That could be a discrepancy
between actions and words, the ideal and the actual, goals and results,
what I think we both want and what we are getting, and so on. A confrontation results in a sense of clarity, not psychic pain. Confronting for
insight does not diminish the other person. Rather, it is an invitation to
help me understand his experience. A successful confrontation results in
increased awareness while maintaining or enhancing the quality of the
relationship.

When I confront someone, I put my observations on the table so that
both of us can look at them. When I shame, I am operating from the judgments and inferences I have made about those observations. I have already decided that he is the problem. In contrast, when I confront, the
discrepancy is the problem, not necessarily the other person. This is crucial, because I will feel certain that this discrepancy is real, but if he
doesn't see the same discrepancy, then any attempt to discuss it is going to
go sideways fast. So first I need to find out whether he and I both see the
same discrepancy. In the example above with Sam, I might say something

like this: "Two weeks ago, I thought you had agreed to produce a report on staffing by yesterday, but I haven't gotten it yet. The same thing happened a month ago, with a meeting you said you were going to plan. Do you see it that way?" In this case, I would be confronting for insight, wanting to find out about his experience before going further down the blame path.

If Sam agrees that this discrepancy exists without getting reactive, then I've sidestepped the shame reaction and opened a space where we can have a productive conversation about it. If Sam doesn't see the discrepancy, then there might be something else going on. I might discover, for example, that my unrealistic deadlines or unwillingness to listen when he says he can't meet them contributes to my experience of him being late. By focusing on the discrepancy I want to deal with, coming from a place of curiosity, being open to seeing my part in it and extra-sensitive to the other person's shame buttons, I can often discuss difficult things without provoking reactive responses.

Sense-making processes being what they are, however, there is one more difficulty. Someone may take a perfectly innocent remark and use it to shame herself. When shame buttons are close to the surface, people may interpret statements as put-downs even if there is no intention to shame. It's also true that people could shame another person unconsciously—human beings can block that kind of intention from their awareness pretty well. So if someone feels shamed by me, and I don't think I purposely shamed her, how can I know if it's her or me? If there are witnesses, ask them. When a person shames another person, everyone present feels it. That's one of the really interesting things about shame. The witnesses can tell you if your remark was innocent or loaded.

Like many other problems involved in developing interpersonal clarity, this one is amplified by authority. People are most sensitive to their shame around authority and can feel put down by a casual observation from a person who has authority over them. This puts an extra burden on leaders who want to confront subordinates and engage in learning conversations with them without pushing their shame buttons.

Those who are excellent at confronting for insight seem to be guided by a belief that every individual is his own harshest critic. People who become defensive when they encounter criticism are attempting to disarm their own internal critic by getting angry at you. If this happens, the confrontation has been less than effective. In the most effective confrontations, people do not experience themselves being confronted by you; rather, they experience you as an ally in exploring the patterns of interaction in which you both are involved.

Listen Through the Cube

Using the experience cube to guide your curiosity helps you fully understand the other person's experience. That is what "listen through the cube" means. Lots of companies and management programs offer a module or two on listening skills. Usually, these focus on something called "active listening," and the main skill is learning to paraphrase back what people are saying to you. Taking these courses for the first time usually provides a good lesson in how difficult it is to really listen to others. Listening is not a simple or passive thing. It takes concentration and effort. Paraphrasing back forces you to pay attention and ensures that you understand the meaning of what people are saying, not just the words. Listening through the cube takes it one step further, from actively listening to uncovering the experience of others.

Active listening is a technique, and like any listening technique, it rests on an understanding of why listening is so difficult and an intention to work at listening to others. Some of the difficulties of listening are caused by our mental maps. When it comes to listening, maps create three problems. First, we listen for what is on our maps and tend to not hear what isn't. If you are trying to tell me about something that isn't on my map, I will have to listen extra hard to hear it. Second, many of us have listening maps, things we expect to hear when interacting with others. As a professor, I am aware that I sometimes use a listening map when students come into my office. I'm listening for "the question"—something about the course material they need me to answer for them. If they come in just after I have handed back an assignment, I have a different map—I'm listening for the change in grade they're going to request. When I use this listening map, I'm not really paying attention to what they are saying as much as wondering which question from one of my listening maps I'm going to have to answer. As soon as I hear it, or anything that sounds remotely close to it, I stop listening and work on my reply. I care about my students and try not to do this, but I know that I sometimes fall into this trap of listening for instead of listening openly.

If you think about it, you will likely discover that you have all kinds of listening maps. You probably have listening maps for subordinates and another one for your boss. When they enter your workspace, what do you listen for? You may have listening maps for certain people at work and for other people in your life as well. These maps are not necessarily bad. We have them because they've been proved accurate enough in the past to be useful. But when we decide to enter into a learning conversation, they get in the way. A conversation creates learning when it adds something to a map that wasn't there before.

Third, when we enter a conversation with a map of where we want the conversation to go and how we want others to respond, we spend a lot of time talking to ourselves (thinking) instead of listening to the other person. This is particularly true when my purpose is to persuade you. Instead of listening to you, I am preparing my next persuasive argument while you talk.

In a learning conversation, we need to put our maps aside and just listen openly. We are not there to persuade each other of anything. We are there to clear out the interpersonal mush and get to interpersonal clarity. The willingness to put aside your maps and inner dialogues and just listen openly is more important than any technique anyone can show you.

Three Levels of Listening

Assuming that you are willing to listen openly, there are a couple of techniques that can really boost your ability to have productive learning conversations. These involve listening at all three levels. At level 1, you listen to the other person talk about something, usually her story about some event or issue. At level 2, you listen to the person's experience of it, using the experience cube to guide you in making sure you really understand her experience. At level 3, you listen to her experience of herself. At this level, you are exploring her personal maps with her so that you can really understand her and her experience.

The ability to listen at levels 1 and 2 is essential to learning conversations. This means that you should be able to summarize back other people's experience in all four quadrants of the experience cube and understand the maps they are using. Level 3 listening is not always necessary or appropriate, but it can be a very powerful aid in helping other people deepen their awareness of their experience.

Level 1: Active Listening

Active listening is the ability to understand the meaning of what a person is saying and to communicate that understanding to the person. When you listen actively, you hear not only the person's words but also his feelings and attitudes and the unexpressed meanings behind the words. By expressing this level of understanding, you help the person better express his thoughts, feelings, wants, and observations, and he also feels that someone has listened to him. It gives you an opportunity to put yourself in that other person's shoes and understand his world. Active listening is critical to a learning relationship. How do you do it?

- Face the person and maintain comfortable eye contact.
- Be aware of the other person's body language.
- Listen for the meaning behind the words.
- Don't confuse content and delivery. Assume the person has something to say even if he is having trouble saying it.
- Try to put yourself in the other person's shoes.
- Don't key in on one thing the person says and miss the whole message.
- When you find that your short-term memory is full, stop the person and summarize what you have heard. This will empty your short-term memory, and you can then resume listening.
- When you summarize, tell the person as completely as you can what you heard him telling you but don't just parrot back his words.
- Try not to add to or subtract from the other person's message.
- Check that the person feels understood, and then check out any hunches about things he has left unsaid.

The ability to summarize or paraphrase back what a person has said is critical to learning conversations. It is not the same thing as parroting what he said, which is usually just annoying. When you are actively listening to someone's experience, you need to stop him now and then and summarize back what you have heard. This does four very important things. First, you get to check out that you have understood the other person's experience. If you have missed or misunderstood something, he can tell you. Second, it gives the other person an opportunity to reflect on what he has said, and that sometimes jogs his awareness of other aspects of his experience that he hasn't yet described. Third, you demonstrate to him that you understand his experience. This makes it much more likely that he will be willing to listen to your different experience. Finally, most people find that they can listen for only so long before they start to lose the thread of what they have already heard. When you stop and summarize, an amazing thing happens—everything you have heard goes into your long-term memory, freeing space in your short-term memory for more information.

Level 2: Listening to the Other Person's Experience

When we listen at level 2, we inquire into the other person's thoughts, feelings, wants, and observations using the experience cube as a guide. At level 2, listening is more than just active—it is an inquiry. As you listen to the other person, are you able to describe all four elements of her experience? If not, then you need to ask questions about the missing elements. Initial questions are simple ones: "What did you observe?" "What did you think about that?" "What did you feel when that happened?" "What did you want?" This is the beginning of listening to the other person's experience of a situation.

In addition, you need to listen to the important maps that are a part of the other person's experience. It is especially useful to listen for her purpose and theories of action. Questions about purpose and theories of action are a little tricky. Purpose comprises the overarching wants the person attaches to the situation and situations like it. Your questions should be sensitive to the person and the nature of the experience she is discussing. Something like "In the big picture, what do you want out of a situation like that?" may be used in many listening interactions. Theories of action are the maps people have of how to get what they want. Here you are listening to the person's ideas of how to act in the world in general and, in particular, in the situation she is describing. These questions have to be carefully worded so that the other person doesn't feel defensive or think she is being judged. A question like "Why did you think doing A would cause B?" could be perceived as a negative judgment (e.g., only an idiot would think A would cause B). The phrasing of such questions should communicate belief in the other person's competence and sincere curiosity about what she thinks of her actions. A question like "When you did A, what did you expect to happen?" helps you understand her theory of action.

When you are listening at level 2, you go beyond actively listening to the other person to helping yourself and the other person get clear about her experience and the maps that are helping to create that experience. By the time you have finished listening, you should be able to fully describe her experience. The ability to do that is essential to having effective learning conversations.

Level 3: Listening to the Self

At level 3, you are asking the person to describe what he observed, thought, felt, and wanted about himself in relation to his experience. Use the experience cube to guide questions, but instead of asking about his experience of it, ask about his experience of himself. The basic questions here are "What did you observe about yourself?" "What did you think about yourself in this experience?" "What did you feel about yourself in this experience?" "What did you want from yourself in this experience?" Often, this quality of listening will lead the person to new insights about himself. This is one of the ways partners help each other get clarity and work on their own issues. They don't take on their partners' problems, but they also don't turn their partners away and insist that they solve their own problems. Instead, by listening to those you want to be in partnership with in a way that leads them to new insights about themselves and the problems they're facing, you strengthen and sustain your partnership.

Here's an example of the power of level 3 listening.

I was teaching a course on change techniques to organization development consultants, and one participant began to talk about her best experience of being a consultant. My focus was on helping her to learn more about being an effective consultant. We started at level 1, with her describing a client system she had worked with and the work she had done. As we moved to level 2, she described how different this experience had been compared to other consulting work because she had really felt a partnership with the client system, a sense of belonging that she had not often experienced before.

At this point, she had not told me anything that she hadn't thought about before. When we moved to level 3, however, she got in touch with her belief that OD consultants should not be looking after their own needs when working with a client system and that in this case she had allowed herself to have needs, too. This turned out to be a very emotional revelation for her, and she decided that it was really OK for her to have needs and get her needs met while working in a client system. In fact, she realized that doing so had led her to be a more effective consultant. My listening had helped her generate new awareness about her experience and new insights into her role as a consultant, insights that reframed her experience and led her to a different map of how to be effective. And I had never given her a word of advice.

Level 3 questions are more intrusive and more personal, so it is up to you to decide whether that level of information is useful or needed in the learning conversation. When I teach this material to managers, a number always voice their concern that these questions are too personal, too touchy-feely, and will generate a negative reaction in others. But when they try it out and listen, practicing level 3 skills, they almost never get that reaction. Instead, they're told that it was wonderful to be listened to so well and to be asked such interesting and thought-provoking questions.

Exercises to Develop Your Curious Self

These exercise will help you develop the skills discussed in this chapter. Each one requires a learning partner.

Exercise 13: **Make It Appealing**

Practice listening to someone else's concern or problem without giving advice or trying to change that person's experience in any way. You can do this with your learning partner or anyone who is willing to talk to you about something that is going on in his life right now that is of concern to him. Explain that you want to practice listening without giving any advice. As you listen, use the experience cube to guide you in asking questions so that you can fully explore that person's experience. Make sure you aren't asking questions that guide him to think about something the way you want him to think about it. Avoid having any agenda whatsoever—simply explore his experience as fully as you can. Make a commitment that even if you have some great advice to offer him, you won't give it for at least one hour after the exercise is over. That is critical, and if you can't keep to it, you need to really question what is making it so difficult for you to just let the other person have his experience. Also, before offering any advice, ask the other person if he wants it.

Exercise 14: **Park Your Reaction**

Talk with your learning partner about the people who consistently push your buttons at work. After identifying one or more, list the negative judgments you think they have of you and test the data you have that support your belief. If you have none, go over the list and see if these are actually negative judgments you have about yourself. If they are, and you have identified people you want to be in partnership with, make a commitment to your partner that you will have a conversation with these people and ask them what their judgments of you actually are.

Then make a list of the things you dislike about them. See if you can't "eat your projections"—that is, acknowledge that you have those attributes as well. If you are using defensive projection with these people, it will be difficult to see at first that you have any of these attributes since the whole point of projection is to protect you from that awareness. Your learning partner can help you by asking questions about where some of these negative attributes might show up in your life. For example, if you say that a certain person always yells and you never yell, your partner could ask, "Even with your children?" Or if you say that another person is so angry and you never get angry, your partner could ask, "Even when you are driving?" If you can acknowledge those aspects in yourself, you will be able to stop projecting them onto other people. It doesn't mean that other people don't have those attributes, too, but when you are projecting, you aren't really seeing them, just yourself projected onto them. And that is causing the reactivity. Once you take back the projection, you might still notice the behavior you don't like, but it won't push your buttons anymore.

Exercise 15: **Confront for Insight**

Think about someone you are having problems with. If you are like most people, when you talk about the issue, what comes out are your judgments about the other person. Spend some time thinking about the discrepancy that underlies the problem you have with this person. With your learning partner, work at coming up with a question that identifies the discrepancy but does so in a way that doesn't assume why it exists. Rather, the questions should be phrased in a way that makes it easy for the other person to describe a different experience if she is having one. Try it out by asking that person your reframed question and work at staying curious, especially if her experience is different from yours. Remember, when you practice being a Curious Self, your job is not to convince other people that your experience is right; your job is to understand how they could be having an experience that is so different from yours.

Exercise 16: **Listen Through the Cube**

Listen to your partner describe some recent experience. Use the experience cube as a guide in asking questions to ensure that you fully understand what his experience was (level 2). Try to understand any important identity maps and theory-of-action maps that are relevant to his experience. As you are listening, notice when you start to lose track of what your partner has already said. This is when you should stop him and paraphrase back what you have heard up to that point. This will help you retain all the information you have heard and renew your ability to absorb more.

Notice when you stop listening or when you want to offer your opinion or help him fix a problem. Do not offer any of your thoughts and feelings. If you are having reactions, park them. Just listen.

Once he is finished telling you about his experience, describe it fully back to him. If you have listened well, you should be able to summarize all four quadrants of the experience cube. Your partner will then give you feedback on how well you did at fully paraphrasing back the meaning of whatever he was telling you. He should also give you feedback on how welcoming your listening was. Did you make him want to open up, or did you make him want to be less open? How did you do that?

Exercise 17: **Listening at Level 3**

Once you have mastered listening at levels 1 and 2, practice listening at level 3. Your partner should talk about something she needs more clarity on, such as troubling issues, opportunities she's not sure of, and confusing experiences. She should focus on getting clearer about what her experience really is.

Begin by listening at levels 1 and 2 but look for opportunities to ask level 3 questions such as "How did you think about yourself...," "What did you observe about yourself...," "How did you feel about yourself...," and "What did you want for or from yourself...."

Again, you should be able to paraphrase back, at all times, what your partner has said. Completely avoid giving any advice or opinions for the duration of the listening exercise.

Your partner will give you the same feedback as in the previous exercise, evaluating your ability to fully paraphrase back the meaning of what she told you and describing for you how welcoming your listening was. In addition, for this exercise, she should tell you which questions really helped her increase her clarity or deepen her understanding of her experience and whether she ever thought you were giving her advice or making implicit judgments.

Exercise 18: **Using Cardwork to Understand Other People's Maps**

Once you've gotten the hang of making your own cards (described in chapter 6), make a card for your partner that depicts one of his theories of action. It takes some good listening to make a card for someone else, as you try hard to understand how the other person sees the world and avoid letting your own beliefs and ideas intrude.

First, decide with your partner what the card is about. For example, the card may be about something like cutting costs. So "Cutting Costs" becomes the title. Then help your partner get clear about the outcome of effective cost cutting from his point of view, maybe something like "spending less money without sacrificing service." This becomes the subtitle. When you make someone else's card, you have to take an appreciative stance, assuming that the other person has a genius for accomplishing the goal or action. Interview your partner about his theory of action, keeping a running list of all the fragments and images he uses to discuss his map. Use your intuition to ask questions about the beliefs and ideas your partner may not be conscious of and bring these together into words and phrases that capture and communicate batches of these fragments.

Once your partner feels that he has said all he can, craft a card, using the rules of cardwork, that best captures his theory of action. Go back over the list of ideas, eliminating the nonessential and consolidating common ideas until you have no more than four points. Draw a card, give it to your partner, and ask whether the card accurately captures his theory of action. If he doesn't accept the card, work with him to craft a card that is acceptable. The "poetry rules" part of cardwork is perhaps the least important, but every time I have used cardwork with managers, the person whose card has rich images and evocative phrasing is the one who has the biggest impact on others. It is important that the subtitle describe the outcome of successful action and that there are no more than four phrases describing how that will be accomplished. Most important, the card really must reflect your partner's map and not have your map mixed in.

At work, you do not have to formally make cards for other people, but you do have to know how to ask them questions to find out what their maps are. Making other people's cards is a great way to develop that skill. Leadership is a lot about influencing people, and you cannot do that if you don't understand their maps.[5] Cardwork is a simple and effective way of thinking about and checking out other people's maps.

Summary

The Curious Self is interested in getting the objective facts, understanding other people's subjective truth, and becoming aware of the impact of her own actions on others. All of these truths are necessary to get to clarity. The mastery of the Curious Self is not only the ability to make it easy for others to be Descriptive Selves, to be willing to tell you what their subjective truth really is even when they aren't too proud of it; it's also about helping them to become even more aware of what their experience is. The Curious Self listens fully until she can describe other people's experience to their satisfaction. She must also make it appealing, so that the opportunity to be descriptive is painless as well as enlivening, even fun.

The biggest obstacle to being a Curious Self is our reactivity, the tendency to want to respond and fix things before other people have finished telling their truth. If you learn to notice when you have stopped being curious, even though you still don't understand their experience, and can park that reaction until they have finished, you increase the likelihood that they will tell you their complete truth. It's important to recognize that inquiries into the less-than-perfect aspects of your interactions with others are just as likely to create reactivity in them as in you. Confronting for insight, rather than insisting that your truth is the truth, is indispensable in dealing with the tricky issues that could make others defensive. Maintaining curiosity is most difficult when others are telling you their experience of you and it does not fit your experience of your intent or your image of yourself. But the ability to stay curious may be the most critical skill required to create organizational learning conversations.

The Appreciative Self

Creating Spirals of Positive Partnership

Using the skills of the Aware, Descriptive, and Curious Selves to engage in organizational learning conversations will go a long way toward creating and sustaining the partnerships you want in your work life. Spreading that out beyond individual relationships to include whole teams and organizations requires creating a culture of clarity. A culture of clarity can exist only where people assume that everyone is having a different experience, that all people are entitled to their own experience, and that talking about and listening to the here-and-now experience of other people is useful and fulfilling. The two most important determinants are (1) the leader's ability to model being a learner and (2) the leader's ability to see beyond differences and difficult people to the positive intents and potentials in people and situations. This chapter is about that second point.

Simply put, people are much more willing to "get real" with each other when their partners see and amplify the best in them. A culture of clarity requires leaders who take an appreciative approach to managing. Using an appreciative approach, managers focus on what they want more of—and not so much on what they don't want—from people, processes, and outcomes. For example, the Appreciative Self doesn't focus on a person's annoying way of stating his wants but instead focuses on the intent that person has to be clear and create a partnership in which all those involved get what they want. The Appreciative Self doesn't focus as much on a

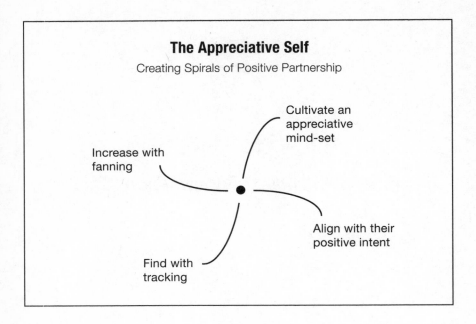

person's limitations in knowledge and skill as on her capabilities and motivation to become more skilled and knowledgeable. The Appreciative Self looks at the positive potentials that can unfold from people and situations and acts to increase the likelihood that they will unfold while creating ever stronger partnerships. My map of how the Appreciative Self does that is shown in the figure above. These are the best models and techniques I've found for mastering the appreciative self:

- Cultivate an appreciative mind-set
- Align with their positive intent
- Find with tracking
- Increase with fanning

The Appreciative Self cultivates an appreciative mind-set, an orientation toward paying attention to what she wants more of and seeing how it can unfold from the situation. The Appreciative Self assumes that people are the heroes of their own stories, and that they are operating out of positive intent no matter how negative their impact might be. Through tracking and fanning, the Appreciative Self creates more of what she wants, helping to build effective working relationships and cultures of interpersonal clarity. I'll describe each of these in more detail.

Cultivate an Appreciative Mind-Set

The first, and perhaps most difficult, step in being an Appreciative Self is developing an appreciative mind-set. As it turns out, this is not that easy for many people. We are all heirs to a deficit mind-set, which may have increased in Western culture in the past century.[1] Our society trains us to see the glass as half empty, to notice what is broken, lacking, needs fixing, and isn't good enough. In organizations, a lot of the drama of management is taken up with the identification and quantification of the gap between what is and what should be, the actual and the ideal, the goal and current performance. We are fixated on problem-solving. As soon as current performance gets close to the goal, we more than likely move the goal line. As a result, much of the time people in organizations live in "gap land," that place of "not good enough." Some try to put a positive spin on it with words like "challenge" and "opportunities," but most people see that the ground their managers stand on when they use those inspirational words is gap land. So they feel the gap, not inspiration.

Most people understand the critical role of self-esteem in the lives of people who accomplish and succeed. Without self-esteem, even the most talented fail. We know that if we constantly criticize a child, telling her she isn't good enough, setting standards she cannot meet, and never lavishing our praise upon her, she will develop an inferiority complex. What happens to a team or organization that gets the same message? What happens to people when most or all of their organizational lives take place in gap land?

I've come to believe that organizations also develop inferiority complexes, and when that happens, there is no chance of outstanding performance. One large company I consulted with had been very successful in the past but had spent the last ten years continuously failing to meet the standards and goals its executives set. This company was going through a major transformation in its industry. It had lost market share and wealth but had made numerous positive changes that no one was focusing on. Instead, there was a pervasive sense of inferiority. People were even embarrassed to tell their neighbors what company they worked for. In meeting after meeting, I encountered a phenomenon I came to call "pulling the rug out from underneath ourselves." For the most part, meetings were full of cynicism and doubt that the company could do anything right. Every now and then, a group would start to get excited by an idea for something positive it could do, and then someone would voice the collective doubt that these people really could pull it off, and the energy would instantly deflate.

In such an atmosphere, there is not a lot of value in having people describe their experience to one another—they just reinforce their own defeatist attitudes. Desire to be in partnership wanes when the partnership fails to perform. This company requires a leader who can see the positive potentials in the situation and get people focused on what can be done, on the future they prefer instead of the undesirable past.

Preston took over the management of the SBD division at a time when no one else wanted to. SBD was a small, almost insignificant part of a large furniture manufacturing company. The division's products were aimed at the lower end of the office furniture market, and the dot-com bubble had just popped, creating a huge hole in the entire office furniture market at the same time that the failure of so many Internet start-ups was flooding the market with cheap office furniture. All their competitors were feeling the same revenue pressures and were slashing prices, cutting into what little margins they had. People in the SBD division were feeling the pain of lost revenue, a collapsing market, and not much support from the rest of the company. Managers and employees were expecting the division to be closed down. It was not a happy place.

When Preston came into SBD, he saw something no else did—an operation that could be transformed into a market leader and a huge revenue generator. His insight was that furniture companies competed by offering customers a bewildering array of options—thousands of fabrics, colors, and desk, chair, and partition styles—but that was not what customers at the cheaper end of the furniture market wanted. Primarily they just wanted good-quality, reliable furniture quickly. Because of the extreme customization, average shipping time in the industry was more than three months from the first sales contact. Preston thought that if they significantly reduced the lag time, they could develop a significant competitive advantage.

First, Preston had to enroll the managers and employees in his vision. He began holding weekly meetings with all department managers and worked on building partnership with them. They decided to eliminate all but a few popular furniture options from their catalog and offer those in only the most basic colors. As a group, they identified the most significant bottleneck at their manufacturing plant and threw their collective effort and resources at it until it was no longer a bottleneck. Then they went after the next bottleneck, and so on.

As the division's shipping times improved, SBD began to get the attention of distributors. The managers realized that distributors were, in some ways, more important than actual customers as determinants of revenue. They discovered that because the furniture industry was notorious for missed and incomplete shipments, distributors who installed the office furniture typically promised delivery dates much further in the future, warehoused the furniture until they had all the right components and parts, and then installed it for the customer. Preston's team could see that if SBD reduced this burden on distributors—guaranteed on-time delivery and 100 percent correct shipment and offered to ship it directly to the customer—they would significantly reduce the distributor's expenses and improve their business. And the distributors in turn would bring a lot more business to SBD.

Preston's belief in the people and the business was infectious. At first, he hit a wall of resignation and cynicism, but as results began to produce more results, a positive spiral of continuous improvement took hold, and things got better and better, faster and faster. He saw the positive potential not only in the business but in the people around him. He didn't tell them what to do; instead, he asked them to make commitments and then held them to those commitments. If people didn't think something was possible, they talked and talked until they could agree on what would have to happen to make it possible—and then did it. He instituted a system that gave everyone in the plant a significant stake in the division's success, creating a strong incentive for partnership. Within eighteen months, they were guaranteeing delivery within one week or the furniture would be free. SBD was growing at 25 percent a year, with higher profit margins than any other division in the company, in an industry with no growth at all.

What happens when we let go of a deficit mind-set and develop an appreciative mind-set? We start to see our organizations primarily as people and human relationships with the limitless capacity and potential to achieve whatever the imagination can conceive of. Social systems are not like biological systems. Human systems are sense-making systems, so the comparison breaks down when we start to talk about learning and innovation. In the past fifty years, however, we have trained managers to think of organizations as biological systems, as complicated sequences of cause and effect influenced by their environments: if you do A, B, and C in environment D, then E will follow. But there are no simple or complicated ABC formulas that always work, because we each create our own experience, and people co-create the social systems they live in. Although social scientists have been trying to discover the laws of human nature since the nineteenth century, about the best they've come up with is the dictum that "a behavior rewarded tends to be repeated."[2] And notice it only "tends," because rewarded behavior isn't always repeated.

Organizations are based on intersubjective truths, not objective truths. Are we good or bad? Are we successful or unsuccessful? Are we in conflict? The answers to these and a thousand other questions are intersubjective truths. We can collect objective data to try and help us figure out the objective truth, but the results of the research become true in an intersubjective sense only when the people involved believe the results are true.

When it comes to business, the key limitations to growth and profitability are almost always the limitations in our thinking. People in the furniture industry thought that three-month delivery times were reasonable—everyone else was doing it, so it must be true. It was only when the employees at SBD began to believe that they could make 100 percent reliable deliveries in a week that they began moving in the direction that ultimately turned the furniture business on its head. Breakthroughs in business results almost always require people to change their limiting beliefs, and they need an appreciative mind-set to do so.

This kind of breakthrough in business models is not that common, but you can create breakthroughs in your partnerships all the time by focusing on what you want more of and seeing the path to getting it. For most of us, that happens in one-to-one relationships. Instead of paying attention to what is annoying, difficult, or bad in those you want partnership with, focus on what you do want and begin with the assumption that it is already there, just waiting to be brought into being. Let me give you an example.

Jerry, a manager who was trying to develop his Appreciative Self, found himself stumped over a "problem person" who worked for him. Bernice had been in her job before he arrived and was protected by her union. Jerry thought she was obnoxious and intimidating, with a minimal work ethic, and believed that she poisoned the whole atmosphere in the office. His attempts to give Bernice corrective feedback had met with sullen silence and no change in her attitude. He could not think of what he wanted more of from Bernice and tried out different ideas with me: "I want her to be nicer." "What's nicer?" I asked. He described what she would stop doing if she were nicer. "I want her to just do her job." "Does she do her job now?" I asked. He thought for a moment. "Actually, she really knows her job, but she just doesn't care. That's it—I want her to care more." "What would it look like if she cared more?" But all he could come up with were things she would stop doing if she cared more. "You're going to have to work harder at figuring out what it is you want to see in her," I said.

Jerry was still trying to figure this out when, a few days later, he was in a meeting with his regional manager and his staff, including Bernice. His manager was describing a new service that they would begin to offer customers and his belief that they needed to transfer someone from another office with expertise to provide the service. Jerry said, "We don't need someone else. Bernice knows more about that than anyone we could transfer. Don't you, Bernice?" Bernice did not change her sullen expression but nodded her head, and the regional manager said, "OK, we'll start out with Bernice, but if you feel you need more support on this, let me know," and the meeting concluded.

An hour later, Bernice came back into Jerry's office with a list of ideas for how to launch the new service. Jerry was stunned; she had never taken the initiative on anything before. But at that moment, because he was working on developing an appreciative mind-set, he started to see the part of Bernice that wanted to be recognized as the best at something, that wanted to make a valued contribution, and he began paying attention to and building on that part of her.

Two weeks later when I saw Jerry, he was buoyant at the change in Bernice. "She still uses coarse language and makes fun of me, but I have to say that she has really turned around in terms of her work, and other people are noticing it, too. She actually stayed late at the office last week! No one can remember her ever doing that before."

Since we co-create the world through our actions, it turns out that our biases have a much more profound impact than merely clouding our perceptions. It is not just that someone who wears rose-colored glasses sees a rose-colored world. Research in many areas of human existence consistently shows that prophecies are self-fulfilling, that what we believe will happen is more likely to happen because of our beliefs.[3] One of the most striking examples is the research initiated by Robert Rosenthal, whose studies led to the concept that came to be known as the Pygmalion effect. Dozens of researchers have conducted hundreds of studies with children and adults and found the same effect. If you tell a teacher that a randomly selected group of people is the best at something in the course, by the end of the course those people are the best! It doesn't matter whether you are teaching reading to children or marksmanship to army recruits, the results are the same. The teacher expects randomly chosen student A to be the best, and by the end of the course, based on objective tests of achievement, he is. How does this happen? Potential explanations have been proposed, but none has been proved.

When this phenomenon occurs in healing, it is called the "placebo effect." This is what happens when you give sick people something they think is medicine—about 30 percent will get better simply because they believe they will. The reality of self-fulfilling prophecy is so accepted in medicine that tests of new drugs must contain placebos and be administered by people who don't know which is the placebo and which is real. And the new drug is not considered effective unless there are more cures among the people who took it than among the people who took the placebo. How about that! A significant number of people will get better if they think they are going to get better! Subjective truths can have an impact on what appear to be objective realities.

We Get More of Whatever We Pay Attention To

An ancient piece of wisdom says that whatever we pay attention to increases. It's as though simply paying attention to something invests it with more energy. The Appreciative Self chooses to pay attention to things she can value, care about, be happy with, and want more of. She recognizes that inquiry into intersubjective truth can be either a looking at the past, where we try to uncover the agreements we've had, or a looking to the future, where we try to uncover the agreements we want to have. The appreciative mind-set is more interested in the latter kind of truth.

This means, first of all, being clear about what you want more of. Sometimes that is easy, and sometimes it isn't. Like Jerry in the story above, people often begin by knowing what they want less of, especially from other people. "I want her to stop gossiping," "I want him to stop interrupting me when I talk," "I want them to stop filing nuisance grievances." OK, but what do you want more of? You cannot use the skills of the Appreciative Self to stop something, at least not directly. Appreciation is used to amplify things, to create intersubjective reality by increasing the amount or frequency of something you want more of.

Second, it means assuming the best in people even when you don't have much evidence for it. This works because just about everyone you will encounter in your work life wants to live up to the normal everyday human virtues of doing good, being fair, being courageous, treating others well, being competent, making a contribution, and so on. It's pretty safe to assume that a desire to have those qualities lies latent even when the qualities themselves are not evident. If you see them, you call them out. When I see a person as courageous, he is motivated to act more courageously than when I expect him to act fearfully and cautiously. So if I can hold on to a positive image of what the person wants to be, of the qualities he wants to live up to, I am more likely to get those from him.

Steve was a highly intelligent professional with a lot of passion for the work he did, and Patrice needed to be in partnership with him to get her work done well. Steve upset just about everyone he worked with; people found him overbearing and pushy. He always seemed to be telling them they weren't doing things the right way. Other managers in the organization who worked with Steve often had negative reactions to him. They felt he lectured them (on and on) and often thought he was telling them how they ought to manage. Among themselves they complained about his know-it-all attitude. Patrice had a lot of company in assuming negative qualities and motivations in Steve, but she wanted to make it better, so she screwed up her courage and tried to talk with him about it. That didn't help much, as Steve vacillated between being defensive and becoming forlorn and confused. He promised to do better, but the only change was that he seemed to avoid her.

Then Patrice had a conversation with Steve's boss, Louise. Louise had figured out that Steve was actually well-intentioned and wanted most of all to be seen as helpful. All the negative impacts Steve had on others occurred when he was trying to be helpful—actions that appeared know-it-all, controlling, and criticizing were actually coming from a sincere desire to help others be successful. Because of that, Steve just couldn't understand the feedback he had been getting from Patrice, but once she understood his positive intent, she was bothered much less by his manner and focused more on the contributions he was making to their joint success. She was able to explain what she needed from him that would be even more helpful, and he was glad to do it. After a while, he didn't seem annoying to her at all.

Part of this kind of change, of course, comes from a change in awareness: Patrice's map about Steve changed, so her experience did as well. But part of it is also due to changes in the other person's behavior—and others notice it as well. That happens because we are co-constructing one another in our relationships, which means that my experience—what I think, feel, and want—is influenced by the people I'm around. And the differences in my experience lead me to act differently, to be different. For example, when I am around my students, who (at least pretend to) believe that what I say is intelligent and worth their attention, I feel and act quite differently than I do around my parents and siblings, who have quite a different opinion about me. In a sense, I am being co-constructed in each of those interactions, and I show up differently as a result. There had to be a part of Steve that knew he was annoying people, and part of his annoying behavior came from feeling defensive around them. The more people focused on the parts of Steve they didn't like, the more of that they got. When Patrice started focusing on the part of Steve that wanted to be seen as helpful and as a valued contributor, she got more of that. In a way, Steve was being co-constructed in each of these interactions and showed up differently as a result.

My point is that your beliefs about the people and teams you work with probably become reality. But having an appreciative mind-set is not about taking a Pollyannaish view of people. It's about having a map that acknowledges the power maps have to create relationships between people. Some of that undoubtedly comes from the co-construction of social reality. But part of it might also come from even murkier places where the subjective and intersubjective seem to affect objective realities.

Your Thoughts Do Affect Others

As I interact with you, what I think and feel and want about you affects what I do, and so I have a role in creating the you that shows up. That seems like a reasonable assumption, and it should explain the Pygmalion effect, but it doesn't. Researchers have conducted hundreds of studies trying to explain the differences in student outcomes by examining the interactions between students and teachers in minute detail and have not really produced anything convincing. Where does that leave us? Is it possible that my thoughts, independent of anything I say or do, influence you? If that's true, do my negative thoughts about people keep their negative behavior in place? If I had more appreciative thoughts, would these people change? I've come to believe that changing our mind-sets about the people we interact with is the most powerful way we have of influencing their behavior. This is what happened the first time I put this idea into practice.

My colleague and I were working with a group of thirty-five engineering managers and their direct reports at a five-day workshop, the kick-off for a long-term change effort. After the first three days, I was totally frustrated and becoming hostile toward the people we were working with. My partner agreed that they were reluctant, resistant, suspicious of our motives, argumentative, narrow-minded, and closed to our ideas and suggestions, but he was less emotionally affected than I was. He had worked with this client system longer and seemed to be taking it in stride. But I was fused and getting emotionally hooked by their behavior.

Toward the end of the third day, I found myself responding sarcastically to some of them. I realized that if I continued to do this, I would lose any chance of being effective with them, so I decided to try out some ideas I had been developing about how to alter my experience. The next morning, I got up an hour earlier than usual and put myself into a quiet, meditative mood. Then, one by one, I visualized what each of the thirty-five people looked like when they were five years old. As I got a clear visual picture, I imagined myself putting that person in my heart and felt the loving feelings I can have for any sweet five-year-old. When I felt the loving feeling, I went on to the next person until I had done this with each of them.

An hour later, when the fourth day of the workshop started, the atmosphere in the room was completely different from what it had been the previous three days. Right from the start, the group enthusiastically participated in the activities I suggested. They were open, interested, and completely receptive to our ideas. The day was a huge success and a turning point in our work with them. My partner and I were stunned by the change in their behavior. We had a hard time believing it was just from my morning exercise, but we could not find any other reason for the change. Interestingly, the participants we talked to about this later either had not noticed a difference or agreed there had been a difference but could not name what it was.

Can I explain the change in this social system by conventional notions of cause and effect? No. So this and a variety of other experiences have led me to question our commonly held assumptions about cause and effect, at least as they apply to people, and to conclude that we somehow affect one another with our unspoken thoughts and feelings. There are a number of simple experiments that demonstrate this. One of the simplest involves a group of people and two volunteers. I usually ask a strong man and a petite woman. The strong man sits with his back to the group so that he cannot see what I or the group is doing. He holds out one of his arms, parallel to the floor, and resists while the petite woman tries to force his arm down. Usually she can't. Then I ask the group to focus an emotion at the man, and on a board or flip chart that he can't see I write the word "hate." After five or ten seconds, I ask the woman to try to push his arm down again. She can do it easily. The group's negative emotion, directed at him, weakens his bioenergy system. I then ask the group to direct another feeling toward the man and write "love" on the board. After five or ten seconds, the woman once again tries to push his arm down, but it is now held solidly in place. I have done this with dozens of groups, and it never fails. In fact, some people have said they can sense the change in the emotions directed at them. If you try this yourself, it's important to make sure that you and the others have enough time to really feel the emotion you are directing at the subject. And be sure to end with love, as you don't want the poor person walking around with other people's hate in them.

I suggest that a person's thoughts and feelings have an effect on other people and that the thoughts and feelings of those in authority have an even bigger impact on the people who work for them. If you are a manager, you are probably having an effect on people who work for you simply by the way you think about them. Wait a minute, you may say. Doesn't this totally contradict what you were saying earlier about boundaries and keeping you and me separate? From my point of view, it is paradoxical but not contradictory. Both things are true: we each create our own experience, and the unspoken thoughts and feelings of others affect us. From the point of view of differentiation and learning, the most useful map to have is that I create the impact you have on me. From the point of view of creating partnership and a culture of clarity, the most useful map is that my idea of you affects the you that shows up. These are just two maps, not the truth—which none of us knows. They are paradoxical, but that doesn't make them any less useful. However people show up around you, you have a part in that. You can create a different experience, even of people that everyone finds difficult or annoying, by adopting an appreciative mind-set around them. Begin with the assumption that, in their world, whatever they are doing makes perfect sense and comes from a reasonable set of motivations.

The Three-Step Process

How does the appreciative mind-set get out of the normal, taken-for-granted deficit consciousness and focus on creating more of what it wants? I've found it useful to think of it as a three-step process.[4] The first step begins with noticing that you are focusing on what you don't want or don't like (in a person, interaction, or pattern of organizing) and making a conscious effort to step back from that and think about what you can like about the current situation. In the story about Steve and Patrice above, Patrice stepped back from her experience of being criticized and told what to do and noticed that she could value Steve's good ideas and desire to be helpful. The next step is getting clear about what you want more of—what would be ideal for this person or interaction. Normally, we try to figure out how to fix what we see as the problem. How are we going to avoid dealing with Steve? How do we get Steve to stop being so obnoxious? Neither of these approaches would be very effective, and they are deadly for sustaining partnerships. Instead, Patrice focused on what she wanted, thinking that it would be wonderful if Steve were more caring and considerate in his interactions with her and showed greater sensitivity to her thoughts and feelings. (Later in this chapter, I describe how to track and fan what you like in a person.) The third step in developing an appreciative mind-set is to consider how your construction of your own experience and actions could be contributing to the problem. Patrice might have realized that her exasperation and curt interactions with Steve might have been exacerbating his behavior and then chosen to act differently around him.

In the table on the next page, I have mapped out the process based on one of my work experiences. I was the coordinator of a team that met once a month to discuss common tasks and make decisions. One team member took a lot of time airing her issues and concerns about other groups and management. She would point out all the reasons why any particular decision was no good but did not offer constructive alternatives. Sometimes I wanted to leap across the table and strangle her.

After I used this three step process, our meetings improved considerably, and I was able to be in a real partnership with her. When you are stuck in a relationship in which you want or need partnership, and the other person is the "problem," the first thing you have to do is figure out what there is to value about who that person is and what he is doing. Often you can do that by separating his impact on you from his intent.

Align with Their Positive Intent

Much of what we do is the result of a series of mostly unconscious calculations in which we balance what we want, what others want, and how much we and they want it. For the most part, we seek to find ways to satisfy our needs without harming others and, if possible, helping them to satisfy their needs, too. These actions are guided by our maps, and if our maps are faulty, our outcomes will be bent, too. Sure, people sometimes have less than good intentions, and sometimes their disconnection leads them to do harmful things unconsciously. But I have found that even actions that repulse me are often motivated by intentions I find praiseworthy—it's the person's map for how to accomplish those outcomes that

Changing a Deficit Mind-Set to an Appreciative Mind-Set

Deficit Mind-Set	Appreciative Mind-Set
Step 1 **What I didn't like**	**What I do like**
She always points out what is wrong with things without ever having any useful alternatives. She just yaks on and on with her cynicism until I feel like shooting myself.	I notice the intelligence in what she is pointing out—she always has a good point. I also like the passion and caring behind her critiques.
Step 2 **Wondering how to fix the problem**	**Identifying what I want more of**
How am I going to get her to shut up so we can do something useful during our meetings and not watch the group's energy drain away?	I want her to provide constructive alternatives. I want to harness her passion for the benefit of the group.
Step 3 **Noticing what I'm doing that maintains the pattern**	**Taking responsibility for my experience**
I have not done anything to change the circumstances of her involvement. As I examine my real wants, I notice there is a part of me that wants others to get frustrated with her, too, and marginalize her. I realize I have unresolved anger towards some things she has said to me in the past.	Time to grow up here. I think I will meet with her before the team meeting to hear her concerns and then challenge her in a supportive way to bring actionable alternatives to the group. That way, I can take on her concerns beforehand so she doesn't have to talk about them during the meetings.

leads to actions I don't like. If I focus on understanding the map and the positive intentions, I open up a space where it's more possible to be in partnership.

Ferd, a supervisor in accounting, was an old-timer with a long memory and high standards who let people know when they made mistakes. Alana, an HR manager who supported him, happened to be there on unrelated business one day when she observed him berating a young, cowed employee. She was angered by the emotional abuse she witnessed and had a number of negative judgments about Ferd and his behavior. But she was also curious about what kind of experience led him to act that way. She followed him back to his office, knocked on the door, and asked if he had a minute. Ferd looked at Alana suspiciously, no doubt thinking that she was going to give him a lecture about his behavior, and motioned to a chair. Then she said, "I was watching you out there, and it occurred to me that you must really care about the quality of work coming out of your department." His expression changed. He took her measure and then said, "No, that's not it. I just want so much for them, the young ones, and they don't know how tough it really is. But after they work for me for a while, they get it, and they move on to better positions."

It turned out that Ferd had managed the department for a long, long time and believed he had been dead-ended early in his career because no one had pushed him. As he talked about how much he wanted for the "bright-eyed innocents" who came to him in entry-level jobs, he pulled from his files a list showing every person who had ever worked for him, and where that person now was in the company. He choked up a little as he looked over the list, as if each name were some precious creation of his that he had loved and nurtured, taking enormous pride in those who had advanced far. Alana left with a very different story about Ferd and much greater willingness and ability to be in partnership with him in the future.

I believe that if Alana had gone into that conversation focused on her negative judgments, wanting to change Ferd before understanding him, she would never have found out what was really behind his actions. He shared a tender, heartfelt side of himself with her, and people don't do that when they are being judged negatively by others. Ferd's theory of action—the best way to toughen up his apprentices—might not be yours or mine. But that is a different issue from thinking of him as a bad, troubled, or evil person.

When you ask people for interpersonal clarity, it is always much easier when they believe that you see their positive intentions. If you look for and see the positive intent behind actions that seem negative (e.g., manipulative, insensitive, malicious, incompetent), you have a greater ability to create clarity and partnership. Exposing the truth of their experience is not as threatening as it would be if you were focused on the negative impact. Focusing on the negative impact will close people down. When you demonstrate openness to seeing the good intentions behind behaviors that have a negative impact, you make yourself an ally to the other person. Imagine a conversation between Patrice and Steve after Steve has once again spoken in a way that implies Patrice doesn't understand the technology they are working on. But this time, Patrice is focusing on the positive intent behind his actions.

Patrice: *Steve, you really, really care about me and this project being successful, don't you?*

Steve: *Oh yeah, it's a really important project.*

Patrice: *And you said what you just said because you want to help me be as effective as I can, didn't you?*

Steve: *Oh yeah, exactly. I'm really behind you, but I guess it kind of came out wrong, didn't it?*

Patrice: *Well, I really value your knowledge, but when you talk that way, it kind of implies that I'm an idiot.*

Steve: *Oh, I'm so sorry. I don't think that at all. I'm just not sure how much you know about thermal reflux interoperability, and, you know, there are a lot of people around here who don't really understand it.*

Patrice: *I want you to be covering my blind sides. I just want you to figure out what they are before you assume I don't know what I'm talking about, OK?*

Steve: *Yeah, OK, that's fair. Well, let me ask you then, what stuff are you not so sure about?*

In this conversation, Patrice has created interpersonal clarity in the moment. It's not exactly a learning conversation, but it has many of the same attributes. She's described, in the here and now, the thoughts, feelings, and wants she has about what Steve has just said. Steve gets to describe his thoughts, feelings, and wants as well. By looking for the positive intent, Patrice is able to lead learning in a way that is quick, builds the relationship, and moves them to an important conversation about those areas in which she does depend on Steve's expertise. As I've said, the Appreciative Self sees the future unfolding in the present—sees the potential in people and processes and acts in ways that make those latent attributes manifest. If Patrice wanted to create a partnership with Steve in which he was caring and considerate toward her, seeing his positive intent is the first step. Next, she needs to find ways to amplify the considerate and caring parts of Steve. That takes us to the next two aspects of the Appreciative Self, tracking and fanning.

Find with Tracking

Creating more of what you want is a kind of change process, but it is quite different from what you read about in books on change management. I call it "amplification" and have used it to improve performance and increase profitability in companies.[5] The idea is that whatever you want more of already exists, even if only in small quantities, so you need to begin by uncovering where it is. Think of a hunter tracking game in the jungle. It takes constant attention, a light step, and the ability to see the clues hidden in the surrounding foliage. So tracking is, most profoundly, the ability to see what you want more of as already being there. Sometimes you just have to start with a leap of faith.

A team from Healthy World, a nongovernmental organization, had entered the small, war-torn African country to get permission from the ruler to begin inoculating children against diarrhea, one of the major causes of infant mortality. There were reports that government forces were killing women and children in outlying villages, and just before the audience with the ruler, someone had given the team a videotape of a recent massacre. The irony of inoculating children who might then be gunned down was not lost on the team, and Jack, the team leader, decided to try and do something about it.

When he met with the ruler, he explained the team's desire to inocu-late the children and asked for permission to do so, which he received. He then asked the ruler for help in opening the first clinic, to begin "saving the children of your country." The ruler agreed to do that. Then, in a risky move, Jack asked for a videotape recorder and played the tape of the ruler's troops massacring women and children. He said nothing more except to thank the ruler for giving his permission to "save the children of your country."

A few days later, when the outdoor clinic was set up and mothers were lined up with children to get the inoculations, the Healthy World staff put a syringe in the ruler's hands and invited him to give the injec-tions. As the long line of thankful mothers, joyful over the blessing they were receiving from the hand of their ruler, moved past, the Healthy World staff kept saying to him, "You are saving the children of your country. Now you really are becoming the father of your nation." The ruler so enjoyed himself that he decided to cancel all his engagements and spent the next few weeks traveling throughout the country with the clinic, personally inoculating children and being reminded over and over that he really was becoming the father of his nation. The mas-sacres stopped.

In this case, Jack and his staff looked for and found the part of this leader that cared about the people he ruled. It wasn't something that peo-ple would have instantly seen in this man. In a sense, they had to take a leap of faith and look hard for every sign of compassion in him with the appreciative mind-set that some part of him wanted to be and could be amplified into the "father of his nation."

It's easy to track something that already exists in abundance. One sen-ior manager I know personally tours his far-flung operations twice a year. He spends one or two days at each location while managers and employ-ees make presentations on the best improvements they've made in one of three areas: increased operating efficiency, customer satisfaction, and product improvement. His expectation is that the people who were per-sonally involved in the improvements will make the presentations. If he believes there's more potential in an idea or a group of people, he will give them more resources to keep doing whatever they are doing. In a sense, he has trained his managers to do his tracking for him, and his personal attention and methods of amplification ensure a steady stream of improvements for him to amplify.

It can be difficult, however, to track something when we don't see it there in the first place. This is the tough part of tracking and is what makes amplification processes more than just positive reinforcement. The Appreciative Self begins with the assumption that whatever we want more of already exists, if only in tiny quantities. We begin by believing in and looking for the best in people and organizations. We have to get over the belief that our experience is "the truth" and assume that we can have a different experience by changing our maps. Numerous managers who have learned this technique have discovered that when they start to look for something they didn't think was there, they begin to see it. The more attention they pay to it, the more of it they get. Let me tell you one more dramatic story about the impact the Appreciative Self can have on creating partnership.

Tim, the consultant, flew in for his usual monthly two-day plant visit, and as usual Fred, the operations manager, met him at the airport. Tim had been working at the plant for six months and was credited with helping to create a lot of positive change in work relationships, which was paying off in productivity and quality improvements. But Fred met Tim at the airport with a tale of doom and gloom. Two weeks ago, the replacement for the regional vice president, who was physically based at this plant, took up his new position. The new RVP, Eric, had a reputation throughout the company as ruthless, demanding, aggressive, manipulative, and very hard to work for. But as a plant manager in another region, he had gotten results in more than one operation, and that had led to this promotion. Tim's clear leadership style seemed the complete opposite of Eric's style, and Fred thought that Eric would quickly pull the plug on Tim's consultancy. As they drove back to the plant, Fred regaled Tim with stories of Eric's abusive behavior since his arrival. Things sounded very bad indeed. Tim decided to try to keep an open mind.

When Tim arrived at the plant, a number of people came up to him to talk about their despair over the changes that had occurred at the plant since Eric had arrived. At ten that morning, the usual management meeting took place, but the atmosphere was even worse than it had been when Tim first started working there. Sure enough, Eric was bossy, sarcastic, and demeaning. People were completely closed down, and no truth-telling was going on. Tim decided that he would not be able to do anything for them if he got caught up in their sense of helplessness and pessimism. Instead, he began tracking the part of Eric that wanted to be a wise, compassionate, and loved leader. He looked and looked, and he noticed at one point in the meeting that Eric offered some good ideas about how to deal with a personnel problem. During a break, Tim mentioned to Eric how wise and compassionate that idea was. Over the next two days, Tim was in Eric's presence a few more times, and each time he ignored everything else about Eric and just paid attention to the part of Eric that wanted to be loved as a leader. Whenever he saw Eric do something that had the slightest wisdom or compassion in it, he said something about it.

During lunch on the second day, Eric sent Tim a message saying that he wanted to see Tim before he left for the day. Everyone, including Tim, assumed that Tim was going to be given the pink slip and that would be the end of that. When Tim went to see Eric, however, something quite different happened. Eric almost broke down as he described to Tim his realization that he had gotten where he was by being ruthless, demanding, and aggressive, but those characteristics would not be effective at his current management level. This scared him, and he didn't know what to do. He asked Tim to help him, and the work went on from there.

It seems obvious to me, and I'm sure it is to you, that if Tim had paid attention to what he didn't like in Eric's behavior, he would have quickly been shown the door. Using an appreciative mind-set and tracking the best parts of Eric allowed the wise and compassionate parts of Eric to recognize an ally—someone who saw what others weren't seeing—and created enough trust that he was able to confide his doubts and fears to Tim. Let's face it, who are you going to turn to for help and advice? Someone who sees the worst in you or someone who sees the best in you? The Appreciative Self creates partnership by tracking the best in people and fanning it when he sees it.

Someone who is good at tracking is constantly looking for what she wants more of, without presupposing where she'll find it. When I teach appreciative leadership to people, they find that one of the hardest things is remaining alert to what they want to track. It's relatively easy to figure out what quality or attribute they want to see more of in another person—and just as easy for a week to go by before they remember they're supposed to be tracking it. The Aware Self is an important ally here. You could say that tracking is awareness with a purpose.

A friend and I attended a conference where the leaders of two dozen successful NGOs had been invited to talk with academics about processes of change across political and economic boundaries. We were excited about being able to witness some of the world's best trackers in action over the coming week. We were a little disappointed, however, at how little tracking we saw. But one image has always stayed with me, and it says a lot about the difference between the trackers and the rest. Everyone used to go to a large conference room between sessions to hear major speeches or discuss what was being learned at the conference. Most people walked in, found a seat, and sat down. But the really good trackers did not sit down. They constantly wandered about talking to anyone and everyone. You might call this "good networking," and it is, except the trackers weren't just collecting contacts; they were stalking larger game. Each of them was looking for more of something. I have since learned that I can often tell who the good trackers are just by noticing how much each person moves around in a crowd. Good tracking takes constant movement and awareness, looking for more and more of the thing being tracked, never assuming you know where you'll find it.

Increase with Fanning

I use the term *fanning* to suggest what happens when you fan a small fire and turn it into a roaring blaze. You are fanning when you look for ways to increase what you want more of. You could think of it as positive reinforcement, though fanning strategies are more inventive than that. There is some evidence that any kind of attention, even negative attention, tends to amplify the object of the attention. In many situations, attention is a kind of reinforcement.

At a company-sponsored leadership training course, I talked about amplification processes as one of a set of change-management options, and a woman approached me at the break to tell me she finally understood what she was doing. Right out of high school, she had begun working as a clerk at the customer service center of a large company and, after many years, had worked her way up to supervisor. The center, located in a major city, consistently ranked high on productivity and customer satisfaction (though she never understood why it got better ratings than others), and six months ago she had been promoted to manager of a small rural region with a dozen centers. She told me that she had an appointment with the president of the company the very next day and was supposed to tell him how she had been able to propel the region from an 83 percent customer satisfaction rating to 92 percent, something unheard of in the company. She said, "Thank God I took this course because I did not know what I was going to say to the man. But now I see it. I just pay attention to what people are doing well and ignore what I don't like. It's what I've always done."

In my early years as a researcher and consultant, when I did lots of interviews and gave managers anonymous feedback, I found a number of common complaints, no matter the kind of organization. One of the most common was the reaction to the question "What do people get rewarded for around here?" Workers and lower-level managers would almost invariably laugh or shake their heads and say something like "Rewards?! You don't get rewarded for anything around here. The only time you ever hear anything is when something's wrong. If you do a great job, well, that's what you're supposed to do, and no one pays any attention. But as soon as there's a problem, you sure hear about that!" No wonder that in such environments, the simple act of noticing the great job people do daily can lead to huge improvements in quality and productivity.

When people first learn about fanning, they tend to think of it as praise, but that's not really it. There is an element of praise in it, and praise, especially from leaders people look up to, can be extremely helpful in creating that strong sense of self required for self-differentiation.[6] But praise alone does little to amplify. Many companies have "employee of the month" programs, which are designed to use praise as a positive motivator. But such programs will just get swallowed up in the interpersonal mush if the person or committee doing the praising is not really operating from an appreciative mind-set. There are two problems here.

The first problem occurs when the praise is just the result of some impersonal mechanism (e.g., most widgets sold). If it is, it may be an incentive for some people, but it is not an amplification process. Praising programs that are poorly thought through sometimes has the opposite effect from that intended. I know of one company that tried to influence its managers to improve employee relations by having employees vote for the best supervisor of the month. Unfortunately, the supervisor who was widely seen as the most lax and ineffective won the first vote, and after that there was a race to the bottom as other supervisors tried to win votes by coddling the employees. This created friction between supervisors who were willing to indulge employees and those who believed that not doing so was in the company's best interests. The latter became more and more disenchanted and upset with employees, and partnership between supervisors and workers got worse instead of better.

The second problem with handing out awards for exceptional work is that they almost never describe what that exceptional work was. Untargeted praise doesn't amplify much. It might make people feel good for a little while, but they don't really know what they're being praised for. I've come to think it is much more effective for leaders to point out what they appreciate and want more of in a matter-of-fact way than to lavish unfocused praise on workers. Tracking and fanning are about looking for what you want more of and saying something positive about it whenever you see it. The more authority the person doing the tracking and fanning has, the greater the impact. It doesn't require a lot of finesse.

Walter, the CFO, ran the worldwide management meeting every two weeks with forty or so of the company's senior managers in attendance, either in person or by video hookup. While serving as a consultant to the executive team, I decided to attend a few meetings and see what was going on. It was the usual "death by PowerPoint" affair, so one day, before the meeting, I asked Walter what he actually wanted to accomplish in the meetings. He told me, "What I really want is for people to share their problems and help each other solve them." I coached him to pay attention during the next meeting, and whenever he saw that happening, to say something about it, praise it, and ask for more.

During a typical presentation on a department's budget and goals, Walter asked the presenter, "How did you solve that problem?" The presenter said, "Product Development lent us a couple of people for two months to clear out our backlog." At this, Walter responded with

"Great! That's just what I want to hear. People in different departments sharing resources to solve each other's problems. Let's all stand up and give Product Development a round of applause." And he leapt to his feet, clapping loudly, while the rest of the group looked at him as if he had just dropped in from Mars. The managers glanced around sheepishly while sort of standing up and applauding halfheartedly. I thought to myself, "Oh no, that's not what I meant—way too cheesy," and wondered how Walter could manage damage control.

But a few weeks later, I was stunned by the speed with which the focus of the meetings had begun to change. Managers were talking a great deal more about how they were collaborating to solve problems across boundaries. By the third or fourth meeting, every ten minutes or so a manager would describe how some other unit had made a contribution to his unit, and all the managers would instantly jump to their feet and applaud thunderously. In cases of really outstanding cooperation, they'd do the wave around the board table. It was fun and energizing.

Much more could be said about fanning from the perspectives of leadership and change, which I've written about elsewhere, but here I want to focus on your ability to create partnership and organizational learning. Simply put, if you focus on what you like, appreciate, and want more of, others are much more likely to be interested in partnering with you than if you constantly point out what you don't like, deprecate, and want less of. A recent study of influence networks found that, more than any other variable, having a positive attitude leads to more informal influence in organizations.[7]

There is an important caveat to how you go about fanning, and once again it is a reminder that fanning is not so much about praise. I became aware of this when I was teaching appreciative leadership to a group of managers who were asked to go out and try it on someone for a week. One woman came back and said, "Well, that sure didn't work. I decided to track and fan my son about passing more in hockey. I was in the stands at his game this weekend, yelling 'Way to go!' whenever he made a good pass, and at one point he told me to shut up!" When I heard that story, I burst out laughing. Of course any sixteen-year-old is going to want his mother to shut up if she's yelling "Way to go" all the time—it's embarrassing. But would he feel the same way if Wayne Gretzky were in the stands yelling

"Way to go"? I don't think so. And therein lies an important distinction between praise and fanning.

When I praise you, I set up a role relationship in which, implicitly, I am the one who knows (the expert, the authority) and you are the one who knows less (an apprentice or a follower of some sort). Teenage boys are trying to break the dependent bonds with their mothers, and because this woman's son did not hold his mother as having expertise in hockey, he did not hear her praise as a positive thing. Rather, he heard it as baby-ing. And something similar goes on in all relationships. If I see you as hav-ing a role that makes your praise legitimate (you're my boss, you have more expertise), then I will like your praise. If I don't see you in that role, I'm more likely to find your praise annoying or patronizing. That does not amplify anything.

One way out of this dilemma is to be a Descriptive Self and describe your experience, not your judgments. Praise comes from a judgment, and if I don't think you have the right to be making a judgment about me, however positive, I may not feel good about it. But describing your expe-rience allows you to identify what you like and want more of without judging me. So instead of saying "You were great," you could say "I felt good when . . ." When you talk about the impact the person had on you, about the quality or attribute you are tracking and fanning, you are much, much less likely to create a negative response in the other person.

What do you do when the people you need to be in partnership with are not living up to your needs or expectations? Coming down hard on them or escalating issues up the hierarchy might get you temporary relief, but that won't help you build relationships in which everyone is commit-ted to your joint success. Tracking and fanning what you want more of seems to work much better. Here is a somewhat long but instructive story of one manager's attempt to get into partnership with his entire interna-tional, 1,500-person software organization by using a fanning strategy.

Ali was a middle manager in a very flat organization. He was respon-sible for pilot testing the new release of some enterprise software. During the testing, he had to get as many people in the company as he could to use it at the same time in order to ensure it could stand up to hundreds of simultaneous users. Inside the company, this was known as a "blitz" and had happened six or so times in the company's history. Ali started the process by broadcasting the following e-mail to everyone in the company.

> **The Initial E-mail Request**
>
> As we enter the final stages before the release of SoftCo Enterprise 8.5, we need your help to ensure the stability and performance of this release. We will be staging two company-wide blitzes on version 8.5 on Wednesday, March 20th, and these are key milestones we need to hit before we can ship the product.
>
> We conduct blitzes to gather a variety of metrics around product performance, scalability and stability (see Monday's Web article for more details on blitzing). The main goals of tomorrow's blitz are:
>
> - to validate the scalability of the product (get as many real users as possible using the system at once); and
>
> - to provide an opportunity for everyone in the company to have a look at version 8.5 and see how it handles with heavy user loads
>
> We will be conducting the blitzes at 8:00AM Pacific Time and also at 4:00PM Pacific Time.
>
> - Morning blitzes will include North America and EMEA
>
> - Afternoon blitzes will include North America and Asia Pac
>
> I realize we're all busy with quarter-end, but it would be great if you could plan to spend 15–20 minutes actively exploring the system (we will provide a blitz script) at either of these times tomorrow. Thanks in advance for helping out.

Soon after the blitz, Ali approached me, concerned that there had been only about four hundred concurrent sessions. That was not nearly as much participation as he needed. He was going to have to organize another one and get more people involved, and he was wondering what to do about it. He didn't want to take his problems up the chain of command, but he thought it was his only option. How else could he get people's attention voluntarily? He thought of sending another e-mail begging employees to participate and warning of the dire consequences to the company if they didn't. Would that be better?

I suggested a fanning strategy. I told him, "Make sure you send a note to the people in charge of those departments that gave you fair to good participation in the last blitz, thank them for their help, tell them you didn't get enough users last time, and ask for their full support again on Monday. Also, send a note to all senior managers and let them know what the positive impact of the last blitz was, who really stepped up, why you need to do another one Monday, and what you want from them." Ali did that and organized another blitz that went reasonably well but still didn't get him to the numbers he wanted. By this time, he had read up on my amplification strategies and wrote another broadcast e-mail that went like this:

The Second Broadcast E-mail

WOW!

It was great to see that we had over 560 live connections in yesterday's blitz, which is almost a record. I want to especially thank Buddy Conway, Doug Gillespie, and Jane Woo for their strong leadership of their teams on this blitz. Of special note were 10 members of the team from LMO that stayed back (after 7PM) and blitzed, creating 110 concurrent sessions.

Ali went on to review what they learned from the blitz and why they needed to do another one. Then he issued the following challenge:

The challenge is to see which leaders in the company are able to get the largest % of their team members involved in the blitz. Rewards will be provided at the next site meeting. With human nature in mind, we wanted to provide a bit of an extra incentive to help encourage your teams. Nothing like having someone do something stupid. Yep, that's where I get to step up to the plate. If we get more than 650 concurrent connections, Ali (+ Sachi the wonder dog) are in the drink. Vancouver, winter, water temperature 35-40F on one of the slimiest beaches for an 800M swim.

So come on, I challenge the group to put me in the drink!

The Third Broadcast E-mail

I feel really overwhelmed with the level of participation in the blitz yesterday. 1,400 concurrent sessions is an amazing achievement that you and your teams should be really proud of. The company, in true SoftCo spirit, lived up to the challenge, and now it looks like it is time for Sachi and me to do a little swimming. It is a great feeling to know that we have grown the strengths of an enterprise software company without losing the flexibility and drive that makes SoftCo a unique place to work.

Ali then went on to describe in detail the great things people and groups did.

Ali was able to engage people he had never even met in a spirit of partnership by focusing on the best of what people did (not what they didn't do) and asking for more. He sought and found partnership without having to resort to power or other tactics that diminish partnership. Fanning is about finding ways to build positive spirals of partnership while dealing with what look like obstacles to getting more of what you want. One of the best acts of fanning I've ever seen happened a few decades ago when companies were trying to implement quality circles in manufacturing.

Janice, a young quality supervisor who had shown an interest in Japanese quality methods, was placed on special assignment to help implement quality circles. At the time, quality circles, made up of employees who meet in groups on company time to identify and solve problems in their areas, were a very new idea. Being a natural clear leader, Janice decided to work from strength and targeted the skilled trades area as a place to start. Employees there were accustomed to taking the initiative and solving problems. She found a couple of supervisors who supported the idea and began two quality circles using company-sponsored materials.

After about a month, she got wind from the supervisors that their general supervisor, Rob, was not at all supportive of the quality circles. He did not think it was a good idea to have employees meet on company time to do the work of supervisors. He figured the workers would just goof off or come up with demands that management would not be able to meet. He was worried that other employees would demand the same hour off and his efficiencies would go down. Janice's attempts to persuade him otherwise had no effect. Rob hadn't done anything yet because the supervisors were committed to the quality circles, but it looked like he was going to pull the plug.

Janice thought that Jim, the plant superintendent who was Rob's boss's boss, would be quite excited by the issues the quality circles were discussing. She put together the minutes from previous meetings and showed them to Jim. As she expected, Jim was excited by what he saw. The skilled tradesmen were talking about issues that were always causing problems for the department, and any solutions they came up with would really make a difference. Janice said, "What I'd really like you to do is go see Rob and tell him how much you like what the circles are doing. Ask him to keep up the good work. And it might be better if you didn't mention you heard about it from me." That's just what Jim did. And Rob became a supporter of quality circles.

Notice how different this is from more traditional power plays and the use of authority to deal with issues. Janice reported to the plant manager who supported quality circles and could have asked him to "get Rob in line." But that would only have made a more resentful adversary out of Rob and could have created problems in her work with other supervisors. As a change strategy, amplification doesn't create the negative repercussions that push methods and "burning platforms" do. Appreciative processes are more likely to create the strong social bonds, good feelings, and sense of camaraderie that real organizational learning requires.

Fanning strategies depend on the circumstances and situation and are limited only by your imagination. When applied to the process of organizational learning, the Appreciative Self accelerates the speed at which leaders can create a culture of clarity in any team or organization. You need to track interpersonal clarity and any actions that serve to increase clarity and diminish the mush. As a leader, that means welcoming expressions of resistance to your ideas and plans; praising people for expressing different mental maps on how to accomplish your goals; asking for more and clearer expressions of what people really observe, think, feel, and want; rewarding people for clearing out the mush among themselves; and holding a space open to explore the here and now when that is what is needed. As the clichés say, it takes courage to call a time-out in the middle of a fire, and sometimes you have to go slow to go fast. Clearly, this takes a good level of self-differentiation and telling people over and over that you want to know what they are experiencing but will not take responsibility for their experience. You want to know what they want but won't take responsibility for ensuring that they get it. What you want and are willing to give is partnership.

Exercises to Develop Your Appreciative Self

Exercise 19: Using the Gratitudes to Increase Your Appreciative Mind-Set

Sometimes it's hard to have an appreciative mind-set, especially when life just isn't that good. With all the stress and problems we face, we may lose any sense of appreciation. Depression, too, makes it very difficult to pay much attention to the best in ourselves and in others. One thing that has made a big difference in my ability to have an appreciative mind-Set is something I call "the gratitudes." It is simply spending a few minutes, once or twice a day, thinking about what I am grateful for. I invented this at a time when nothing in life seemed good to me.

At first, I would exhaust my list of gratitudes in about fifteen seconds! But I would try to sit out the five minutes I had allotted to the exercise, trying to think of other things and feeling almost guilty that I had so little I was grateful for. One effect of this routine was that I started to notice people who had it worse than me. I could at least be grateful that my life was better than theirs. Slowly I began to notice that I really did have a lot to be grateful for, and this spiraled into more and more gratitude, until one day, a few months later, I noticed that I was walking down the street with a smile on my face. I could easily fill up five minutes thinking about the things I was grateful for and realized that I didn't need to do the gratitudes anymore.

You can do the gratitudes out loud with your partner or just silently to yourself. You can just think about them or journal them. Doing the gratitudes always makes it easier to track what you want more of in others. If you are finding it hard to be appreciative, I strongly urge you to try it for a few weeks.

Another way to work with the gratitudes is to think of some person or situation that is bothering you. List all the things that bother you about that person or situation. Now make a list of how things could be worse. Once you are ready, tell your learning partner about this second list, starting each sentence with "I'm grateful that . . ." Once you have finished your list, continue to complete the sentence "I'm grateful that . . ." about any other positive things you can see about this person or situation. As your learning partner listens, if she has any other things for you to consider being grateful for, she should suggest them.

Exercise 20: **Three-Step Process**

Another exercise that will help you increase your appreciative mind-set is to identify a relationship that is not working as well as you'd like and go through the process outlined below.

From a Deficit Mind-Set to an Appreciative Mind-Set

	Deficit Mind-Set	Appreciative Mind-Set
Step 1	What don't you like?	What do you like?
Step 2	How are you thinking about this as a problem to fix?	Identify what you want more of.
Step 3	What are you doing that maintains the pattern?	How can you take responsibility for your experience?

Use your learning partner as a sounding board, particularly about what you might be doing to maintain the pattern.

Exercise 21: **Align with Their Positive Intent**

Think of someone you have negative judgments of and write down the behaviors that upset you. Underneath each behavior, list the stories you have made up to explain his behavior: your idea of the things he is thinking, feeling, or wanting that are behind the behavior that upsets you. Now try to come up with alternative explanations for his behavior that are reasonable, things you could imagine causing you or some other reasonable person to act the same way. The next time the person acts this way, interact with him based on this other set of assumptions and see what happens.

Exercise 22: **Tracking and Fanning**

Tracking and fanning go together, so although they are two separate skills, you really practice them together. To do this, think of some behavior you'd like more of from someone at home or at work. Remember, it can't be something you want less of disguised as something you want more of. With your partner, identify what, exactly, you'll see if and when you see more of it. Pick someone who is low-risk, so if this exercise blows up in your face, it will cause minimal damage.

Then simply be on the lookout for the behavior. When you see it, notice it, describe your positive experience, and ask for more. If it is a behavior you don't think you'll ever see without some prompting, tell the person what you want more of and then fan like heck as soon as you see it. For example, one of my students wanted his mother to get along better with her sons-in-law and daughters-in-law and decided that she needed to talk less and listen more at family dinners. He began by talking with her about her relationships with her in-laws, using the appreciative mind-set that she wanted good relationships, and discovered that indeed she did but didn't know how to get them. So he asked for what he wanted. He asked her, at the next family dinner, to talk less and listen more, to be curious about others and ask questions. At the next dinner, she did, he fanned, and the rest is history.

Review your progress with your partner at regular intervals. Together, think up some meta-fanning strategies.

Exercise 23: **Tracking an Attribute**

If it's an attribute or attitude you want more of, tracking is trickier. Then you have to see it yourself, behind the person's behavior. Remember the stories of the "father of his nation" and Eric, the leader who wanted to be wise and compassionate. These are examples of situations in which tracking is hardest. You need to assume that the attribute you want more of is indeed behind the actions you see.

If you find it difficult to track an attribute, start by choosing one attribute you want to see more of in people generally, something like generosity or thoughtfulness. Then, at work, in every interaction you have, assume that the attribute exists in everyone, even if just in little ways. Work at noticing when it might be present in other people's behavior. Don't worry about fanning it, just pay attention to it. You'll notice that you forget to track, sometimes rather quickly. Just start tracking again. See how long you can keep tracking for that attribute before you forget about doing it. Each day, try to increase the

---

Exercise 23: **Tracking an Attribute** cont'd

amount of time you spend tracking it until you can go for hours without losing track. When you start being able to see the attribute you are looking for in most people, review with your partner any differences you notice in your interactions with people.

Summary

Creating partnership and organizational learning is much easier when leaders are operating from an appreciative mind-set that pays attention to the strengths and capabilities in people and processes, when they see the potential that is wanting to grow and be expressed, when they track and fan what they want more of. It may actually be a necessary condition for creating a culture of clarity.

Being an Appreciative Self requires an appreciative mind-set, paying attention to the normal human virtues in everyone and the positive intent behind what appear to be weird or malicious actions. An appreciative mind-set requires a map that says that your beliefs have an impact on the world you inhabit and that you get more of whatever you pay attention to. The Appreciative Self is about attending to and noticing those things that call out the best in us as people—the kinds of things most of us value, hope for, and want in our work lives. An appreciative mind-set is focused not on identifying and fixing what we want less of but on tracking and fanning what we want more of.

You align with the positive intent of other people based on the assumption that they are all heroes of their own stories, that there is a reasonable explanation behind what appears to you to be malicious, incompetent, or insensitive behavior. When you give people the benefit of the doubt, you are almost never wrong.

One of the really neat things about the appreciative process as a method of leadership is that anyone can use it, regardless of his level of authority. You may have noticed that in a number of the examples in this chapter, the people using the appreciative process didn't have authority over those they were tracking and fanning. Anyone can use the appreciative process to influence other people, but, like anything else, power amplifies the effect. Using the appreciative process, a supervisor can influence a few people (including people with more authority). A CEO, however, can influence a whole organization.

Tracking involves seeing what you want more of as already there. You can't fan something you can't see. Sometimes it takes a leap of faith to believe that the positive qualities or attributes you want more of are already there. Sometimes tracking requires seeing the subtle clues and tiny instances that give you a place to start fanning. Tracking means that you do not take all the positive effort, skills, imagination, and motivation people bring to the job every day for granted. If you want to create a culture in which partnership flourishes, you need to be tracking people's willingness to tell the truth of their experience, clear out the mush, and learn from their collective experience.

Fanning is about turning the little flame of positive potential into a roaring fire. By simply paying attention to something, you tend to get more of it, but skillful application of praise goes a long way toward amplifying your efforts. Be careful not to overstep your relationship when you praise; praise is a judgment and is received positively only if the person thinks you have a right to express a judgment. Describing your positive experience, rather than your judgment, is the safest way to go about fanning others. The consummate Appreciative Self uses fanning to overcome obstacles to learning and performing, creating partners rather than adversaries while getting the job done.

The Learning Conversation in Depth

Each of the skill sets I've described up to this point has its own use. Being aware helps you be more choiceful about what you say and do. Being descriptive helps reduce the inaccurate stories people make up about you. Being curious helps you understand where others are coming from. Being appreciative helps you get more of what you want. Each of these is useful. But for creating successful partnerships at work, these skills deliver their biggest gift when they are combined in an organizational learning conversation. In chapter 2, I gave a couple of examples of learning conversations and described their purpose. In this chapter, I want to go into more depth about the process, how to do it, what gets in the way, and how to overcome those barriers.

Learning Conversations Versus Performance Management

When I teach clear leadership to managers, we always reach a point at which we have to get clear about the distinction between a learning conversation and a performance management conversation. A learning conversation is not about me helping you learn what you are doing wrong or need to do better. That's a performance management conversation, and it is important to have those with people who work for you and are not meeting your performance expectations. Some learning needs to take place during a performance management conversation. As a manager, the first thing you need to learn during a performance management conversation (and it may take more than one to figure this out) is the basis of the person's lack of performance. It is almost always one of four things:

- The person doesn't know what's expected of her. It's a goal or role clarity problem.

- The person doesn't know how to do what's expected of him. It is a competency or knowledge problem.

- The person doesn't want to do what's expected of her. It's a motivation problem.

- The person doesn't have the information, tools, or resources to do what's expected of him. It's an infrastructure problem.

It's most useful to look at these in this order. First, if people don't know what's expected of them, how can they possibly provide it? And how did it get to the point that they don't know? Now that is something you could have a learning conversation about. Second, if they don't have the skills or knowledge to do the job, the rest is moot. What are you willing to do to get these people up to speed? Are you better off finding a more suitable job for them and finding others who are competent? If you have a motivation problem, that's a whole other kettle of fish. You can work at trying to help them get motivated, by providing more incentives, for example, but in the end you need to be clear about the kind of performance you expect and the consequences for lack of performance. Be sure you are willing and able to enact those consequences or your credibility and authority will be diminished. As for the fourth problem, it's rare to find an organization where people feel they have enough information, tools, time, or money, so it's important that you understand what the constraints really are and decide for yourself how to respond to the perceptions of others.

You don't go into a learning conversation to deal with a performance management issue. You do it to get out of the mush and create interpersonal clarity. Sometimes you may decide you need to have a learning conversation before you have a performance management conversation, to make sure you really understand what is going on in your patterns of interaction. Or you may decide you need one after a performance management conversation. But performance management conversations happen only with people whose performance you are responsible for, while learning conversations can happen with anyone you want or need to be in partnership with. Typically, you ask for a learning conversation when you are feeling dissatisfied with the interactions, maybe because you find the interactions unproductive or because you don't feel good during or after the interactions. Or perhaps a person says something that causes you to make up negative stories about what is going on in his head, or seems to say one thing but then does another. It could be that a person is doing things that you think are detrimental to the success of the project, or seems to be upset, and you don't know why. Learning conversations cut through the mush and get the partnerships back on track.

You probably have a story about how the other person is the cause of the problem, but for a successful learning conversation you need to believe that this is just your story and be open to the likelihood that his story will be quite different. The proper attitude going into a learning conversation is a spirit of inquiry. How am I creating this experience for myself? What is my part in this problem pattern? If you can hold that attitude, then you will find that discussing the things most people tend to avoid talking about—the things that cause relationships to break down—will almost always work out well. Rather than making things worse, learning conversations make things better.

The Learning Conversation Process

In a learning conversation, one person describes his experience, using the experience cube to help him describe all his observations, thoughts and mental maps, feelings and emotions, and wants, goals, and desires along with all the stories he is making up. The other person is curious until she is clear about his experience. She uses the experience cube to track what she is finding out and to notice what she still doesn't know. She asks questions so that she will be able to fully understand his experience. She helps him explore and deepen his awareness of his own experience. Before moving on, she demonstrates that she does understand his experience by summarizing it back to him so that he can tell her that she's got it. Then they switch roles. They go back and forth until they are completely clear, as shown in the table on the following pages.

Steps in an Organizational Learning Conversation

Step	Initiator	Other Person
1	Check that you are willing to learn about yourself in this conversation. Check that the other person is willing to explore this issue with you at this time in this place. Ask him to have a learning conversation with you.	Tell the truth about your readiness to learn about yourself, the initiator, and your relationship. Set another time and place if you need to.
2	Use the experience cube to describe your experience of the problem pattern. Talk about what you want now. Check to ensure the other person understands you. Once you feel that you've finished, describe your here-and-now experience.	Actively listen and seek clarity about the other person's experience and maps. Use the experience cube to guide your listening and help her deepen her awareness of her experience. Check to see if she is finished when you think you fully understand her and summarize back her experience until she feels fully heard.
3	Actively listen and seek clarity about the other person's experience and maps. Use the experience cube to guide your listening and help him deepen his awareness of his experience. Check to see if he is finished when you think you fully understand him and summarize back his experience until he feels fully heard.	Describe your here-and-now experience, the impact of what you have just heard. Use the experience cube to describe your experience of the problem pattern and respond to what you just heard. Own what was true about the other person's experience of you. Check to make sure she understands you. Once you feel that you've finished, describe your here-and-now experience.
4	Describe your here-and-now experience, the impact of what you have just heard. Use the experience cube to describe your experience of the problem	Actively listen and seek clarity about the other person's experience and maps. Use the experience cube to guide your listening and help her deepen her aware-

4	pattern and respond to what you just heard. Own what was true about the other person's experience of you. Check to make sure he understands you. Once you feel that you've finished, describe your here-and-now experience.	ness of her experience. Check to make sure that she is finished once you think you fully understand her and summarize back her experience until she feels fully heard.
5	Continue this conversation until you are each clear about the other person's thoughts, feelings, wants, and any relevant maps.	
6	State what you have learned about your part in the problem pattern.	
7	Describe what you are willing to do differently in the future. If you don't know, proceed to problem solving.	

At the end of a successful learning conversation, both people are able to describe their part in creating the problem pattern. And as I've said before, 80 percent of the time, that in itself will eliminate the problem. What about the other 20 percent? They discover what the real problem is, and in work relationships, that is almost always one of four things:

- They don't agree on goals (the purpose or objectives of this partnership).
- They don't agree on roles (who is responsible for what).
- They don't agree on procedures (how they'll go about accomplishing their goals).
- They have a resourcing problem (they lack the information, tools, time, or money to accomplish their goals).

Once you know the real problem, you can use conventional conflict-management and problem-solving processes to address it. There are lots of them and they are useful, but not as long as you are in the mush.

Another way to describe the learning conversation process is shown in the figure below. You use the skills of the Aware Self, the Descriptive Self, and the Curious Self, in that sequence, switching skill sets back and forth, until you've developed interpersonal clarity about the issue.

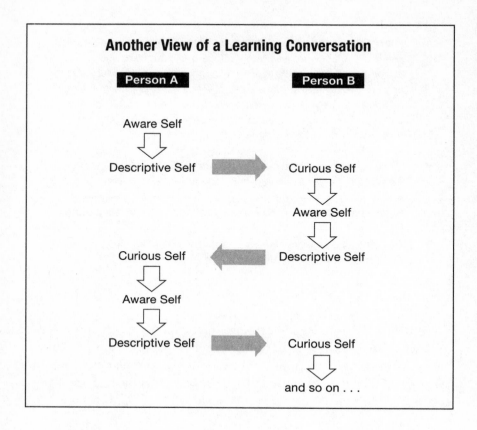

In addition, all of the skills and processes I've described in this book can be tinged with appreciation. Bringing an appreciative mind-set to organizational learning is about seeing the best in ourselves, others, and our organizations even when we are trying to change problem patterns. As I described in chapter 7, compassion, a state of being most aligned with an appreciative mind-set, helps us get past shame-based defenses in ourselves and others so that we can uncover subjective truth. As an Aware Self, you are aided by holding an appreciative mind-set even toward the negative parts of yourself. Embracing your humanity and lack of perfection as part of the complexity of the human condition helps open you up to seeing your less-than-perfect thoughts, feelings, and wants. Appreciatively describing them and letting appreciation guide your curiosity make it easier for others to tell their truth. Organizational learning conversations are less threatening when at least one person is operating from the

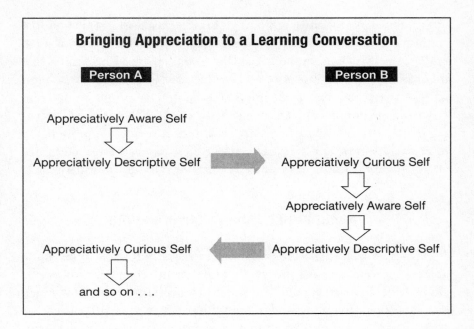

Bringing Appreciation to a Learning Conversation

Appreciative Self. A master at organizational learning conversations brings his Appreciative Self to the process as shown in the figure above.

The learning conversation process is just as applicable to understanding high-performance patterns as it is to investigating a problem pattern. When we use awareness, curiosity, and description to understand the best in our work relationships and organizations, we are leveraging clear leadership with a powerful form of inquiry—appreciative inquiry—that can lead to a virtuous cycle of improvement. In an appreciative inquiry, we ask people to tell us their stories of work and the organization at its very best. These stories can then displace all the negative stories existing in the interpersonal mush and change the organization's inner dialogue.

I and others have written extensively on appreciative inquiry elsewhere, and I don't want to cover that territory here.[1] Let's just say that those who operate from the Appreciative Self bring to the process of organizational learning an interest in what could be as they explore what is best in the experiences of other people.

But even when we're dealing with problem patterns, people who operate from an appreciative mind-set are much more able to get others engaged in exploring the truth of their experience. Most people find that getting to interpersonal clarity requires actions that are, at least at first, fairly scary. I'll talk more about that later in this chapter. The point is that the manager who operates from an Appreciative Self makes it much less scary. A boss who is paying attention to the best in the people around him creates an environment that is much friendlier to collaboration and learning from collective experience. There is less competency compulsion and less fear of being shamed. It may be impossible to create a real culture of clarity unless the leader has a strong commitment to the Appreciative Self.

Managing Learning Conversations

A learning conversation needs to be well managed, with a clear beginning and ending. Whether the process is formal or informal depends on the strength of the partnership, how much trust already exists, how much tension people are feeling, and so on. With partners who trust each other and constantly clear out the mush, it can be done rapidly and informally. A more formal and slower process is called for when people have not had much experience clearing out the mush with one another, when there is a lot of tension and emotion about the issues, and/or when there isn't a lot of trust. There are three essential elements in a successful learning conversation:

- Enter with the right attitude.
- Fully explore each person's experience.
- Describe each person's here-and-now experience before every transition.

Enter with the Right Attitude

With the right attitude, you understand that your purpose in having the learning conversation is to learn about your own part in creating the problem pattern. You need to believe that since you are a part of the system that is creating this problem pattern, you have a part in it. A learning conversation is an inquiry. We are learning something together. It is not about solving a problem or telling other people what you really think or asking for what you want. Any of those things might happen, but if you go into a learning conversation with that kind of agenda, you'll probably have the kinds of conversations that lead nowhere. Think of a learning conversation as an attempt to understand your part in the problem pattern. People who enter these conversations with that attitude will have a different kind of conversation that will lead somewhere. During a learning conversation, when you're being a Descriptive Self, your job is to fully explore your experience. Chances are that if they are doing a good job of staying open, you will uncover aspects of your experience that you weren't aware of before the conversation began. When you're being a Curious Self, your job is to fully explore their experience. If you do a good job of that, they will become aware of aspects of their experience that they weren't aware of.

In order to do this well, you have to be differentiated from your own experience. You have to be willing and able to hold out your experience and look at it dispassionately. It's like looking at something interesting you just picked up from the ground. You hold it in your hands and turn it over and around, exploring the different facets of it. There's nothing threatening about exposing and exploring your experience if you aren't identified with it. Remember, you have experience, but you are not your experience. If you aren't identified with your experience, you don't have to defend it or explain it or be ashamed of it. It just is what it is. Being around people who won't judge your experience or try to fix it for you helps a lot, but in the end you are the one creating your experience, and the way you treat it is up to you.

Fully Explore Each Person's Experience

In successful learning conversations, one person's experience is fully explored before the other person says anything to try and change it. Instead, the second person has to demonstrate that he fully understand the first person's experience, by summarizing it back, before he responds to anything he has just heard. This is particularly difficult to do when you are listening to the other person's less-than-perfect experience of you. When I'm in a learning conversation, I usually know within a minute or two what misperception the other person has of me. I'm thinking, "Oh, that's not what I meant" or "Oh, that's not what happened." My natural instinct is to want to stop her at that moment and explain what I really meant or what really happened. But that would short-circuit the learning conversation and lead to the same old same old. Instead, what I need to do is hold on to my response and keep a mental list of things I want to tell the other person. Before I respond to anything, I need to ask more questions and fully explore her experience. Before I tell her the truth of my experience, I have to demonstrate that I understand hers by summarizing it back. Once I've done that, then it's my turn to tell her about my experience, and chances are that she will be willing and able to hear how mine is different from hers.

Describe Each Person's Here-and-Now Experience Before Every Transition

Depending on how new the relationship is and how much tension there is in it, you can do one more thing to help make learning conversations successful. As I tell you about my experience, and you listen to it, I am probably making up a story about how my words are landing on you, especially if I'm not sure about our relationship because it's new or we are in conflict. In effect, new mush is being created even as we are trying to clear out old mush. So it can be very helpful to reduce the sense making that goes on in the learning conversation.

During a learning conversation, I am usually talking about the past—things you have done and said, or haven't done or said, and the thoughts, feelings, and wants I've had about them and how they are affecting me now. After you summarize back what you've heard and we're ready to transition to you being descriptive, it can be very helpful to have us both do a lap around the experience cube. After I've finished talking about my experience of the problem pattern and I think you get it, I describe what I'm observing, thinking, feeling, and wanting right now. Before you respond to what you've been hearing from me, you describe what you are experiencing right now, using your mental list. Then you talk about your experience of the things I've just talked about. This gives us a good way to keep clearing out the mush.

When you are leading a learning conversation with someone who doesn't know much about it or isn't skilled at it, you have to coach her through the process. When it's her turn to be descriptive, you need to ask her questions to help her fully explore and describe her experience. When she uses you-language, stop her and ask her who she is referring to. When she hurls a judgment at you, ask her what experience led her to the judgment. When it's her turn to be curious, coach her to not respond but to just listen. Stop frequently and ask her to summarize back what she's heard. Coach her to think about what questions she has about your experience and to ask them. The more comfortable and familiar you are with learning conversations, the easier this is to do. The less comfortable you are, the more you will need props like the first diagram in this chapter, to help both of you step through the process, or a third party who can serve as a coach.

Coaching Others Through Learning Conversations

If you are a manager who wants to build a culture of interpersonal clarity in your team, unit, or organization, you can help make that happen by coaching the people who work for you on having learning conversations with one another. If you believe that a culture of clarity is necessary for the successful completion of tasks in your department, then clarity is just as appropriate a requirement as any other work behavior. However, it's not very effective to ask people for things they don't know how to do, so you have to either coach them yourself or hire someone who can.

I advise managers who take the Clear Leadership course to coach others through learning conversations before attempting difficult conversations themselves. That's because there is no better way to get familiar and comfortable with the process than by helping two other people have a learning conversation, as long as you aren't emotionally involved. If you know that two people who work for you are in the mush with each other and it is interfering with their ability to collaborate, you have a perfect opportunity to practice and build your skills. Explain the nature and purpose of the learning conversation, set a time and place for them to meet, and facilitate the conversation. As a learning conversation coach, your job is to lay out and enforce the ground rules of the conversation. You decide whose turn it is to be descriptive and whose turn it is to be curious. You decide when it's time for one person stop describing and the other to start summarizing. Notice when it's time for each person to take a here-and-now lap around the experience cube. Help them get into their appreciative mind-sets and see the positive intent in the other. Try to empathize with both people and imagine what they must be experiencing. Notice what is not being said and ask questions to help both parties understand each other more.

You can have a learning conversation with people who haven't read the Clear Leadership book or completed the course, but it generally doesn't work to launch into one with someone who knows nothing about this kind of conversation. You first need to educate the other person about the assumptions behind a learning conversation, what you hope to accomplish, and the overall process. If people don't mind reading, you could give them chapter 2 of this book. If they don't want to read, you'll have to describe what a learning conversation is all about. See the box for a good basic list.

What People Need to Know Before a Learning Conversation

- Experience is composed of four elements: observations, thoughts, feelings, and wants. Whatever the interaction or event, each person's experience will in some way be different from everyone else's.

- We are compelled to make sense of the people in our lives who are important to us. When we don't have information about some element of their experience, we make up a story to fill in the gaps. When we are confused about the behavior of people we work with, instead of asking them about it we usually talk to third parties to try to make sense of them. As a result, our work relationships become filled with interpersonal mush and our interactions are based on stories we've made up that we haven't checked out.

- The nature of interpersonal mush is that, over time, the stories we make up become worse than the reality. As a result, interpersonal mush eventually destroys the ability to collaborate and be in partnership. Most of the conflicts and people problems at work are a result of the mush. In order to maintain healthy partnerships, people need to occasionally clear out the mush and attain interpersonal clarity. With interpersonal clarity, each person knows what his own experience is, what the other person's experience is, and the difference between those experiences.

- The learning conversation is the process for attaining interpersonal clarity. In a learning conversation, people take turns fully exploring one person's experience at a time. One person describes what she observes, thinks, feels, and wants, while the other person listens, ask questions, and summarizes back. It is essential that they don't respond or try to explain until it is their turn to have their experience explored. Only after the first person believes that the second person really understands her experience does the second person respond and describe his experience. While that is happening, the first person does not respond; she just asks questions and summarizes back what she's hearing. They do this back and forth until they are both completely clear.

What About Those Who Won't "Play"?

At this point you may be thinking "This learning conversation process is all well and good if the other person is competent, fair-minded, moderately differentiated, and reasonable. But what about my boss [or whoever looms in your mind as a source of pain at work]?" So let's talk about that.

The first question is, does this person want to be in partnership with you? Does he want to be in a relationship in which you both feel committed to the success of your joint project or process? If he doesn't, then, no, none of this will be of much use. But is it really true that he doesn't want to be in partnership? Have you asked, or is that just your story? What would it take to find out if he wants to be in partnership with you? Maybe *he* doesn't think it's possible. Would things change if he thought it were? Maybe you have been operating from competing positions, but underneath there are actually complementary interests.

If you find yourself in a conflict with another person with whom you need to be in partnership, you might find the perspectives and techniques developed at the Harvard Negotiation Project useful for uncovering interests that can be the basis of partnership.[2] You don't have to share goals, but you do need to share common or complementary interests to be in partnership. For example, if you are my supplier, we may not have common goals—you may want to sell to me at the highest price possible, and I may want to buy from you at the lowest price possible—but we can be in partnership if we focus on our common interests. These could be things like maintaining a cost of supply that makes it unlikely I will switch to one of your competitors, making me happy enough with your product and service that I will say good things to your potential customers, and saving you money and me patience by delivering only exactly what I need. So the first thing we need to establish is the basis of our partnership, a shared definition of success for the project or process we're engaged in. And that needs to be revisited from time to time, especially when the partnership seems to be going off the rails. In a learning conversation, it is useful to check on and recommit to the basis of the partnership.

The Boss and Others in the Hierarchy

When I am teaching clear leadership to managers, one of the first people they think of being Descriptive Selves with is their bosses, and they usually think it would be a bad idea. My first response to this idea is that you can't create learning conversations with people who are not learners. If you have a boss who gets anxious when people say things he doesn't want to hear, and doesn't respond well to hearing about the impact he is having on others, then it's probably not a good idea to be descriptive around him. Authority creates barriers to interpersonal clarity, and there may be nothing you can do about that. But that doesn't mean you can't create a culture of clarity underneath you. That is the place to focus—not on those above you, but on those below you in the hierarchy. Leaders have to go first because their authority creates barriers. So at first, I ask managers to not worry so much about how to create clarity with their bosses and focus instead on how they can create clarity with their peers and subordinates.

Later, however, I return to the matter of the boss. How is it that thousands of managers have come through the Clear Leadership course and only a handful have not wanted to create cultures of clarity and more effective partnerships with those who work for them, and yet so many people apparently have a boss who is different? Could it be that their stories about their bosses are not accurate? Could it be that the way they have tried to be descriptive with their bosses in the past has not been very skillful, or that the stories they have made up about their bosses' reactions are inaccurate? In my work with managers at all levels of organizational hierarchies, I've found the following pattern in the sense making: When people look upward in hierarchies, they tend to focus more on the role than on the person; when people look downward in hierarchies, they tend to focus more on the person than on the role.

So on the one hand, when people think of their boss, their experience is shaped by their maps of the person's role. They tend to think in terms of role relations. And because the boss has some power over their lives, they're cautious, as if there is some danger there. They'll say to themselves, "I'm just a lowly middle manager, why would the VP have any interest in partnering with me?" The experience they have while in that person's presence will be shaped by their general orientation to authority (trustworthy or not, caring or not, and so on). Many people's fear of being descriptive around their boss is not based on any actual event or is based on one "bad" experience they had although they didn't really know what was going on in their boss. And this tendency becomes even more pronounced the further up the hierarchy they go.

On the other hand, when people think of those who are lower in the hierarchy, they think in terms of a person, someone who doesn't have the same power over their lives as a boss does. This means they aren't naturally cautious about what they think and say. They might not realize the impact of talking to people as if they were just peers. For example, if they grouse about something, it can become a much bigger deal than just letting off steam. If they muse about how something could be changed, it can become a much bigger deal than just idle daydreaming. Those who rise up the corporate hierarchy often learn the hard way that they need to watch what they say and do very carefully so that they don't inadvertently start a snowball of mush that turns into an avalanche. Their apparent reticence, their careful choosing of words and gestures, then creates an even greater sense of caution among employees. For this reason, executives need to learn how to be even more descriptive of what is going on in their heads—letting people know that they are just trying out ideas when they are idly musing, that they are just letting off steam when they complain about something. And they particularly need to be descriptive and appreciative when someone is describing an unpleasant truth.

Understanding the dilemma and constraints of authority is helpful for developing partnership with your boss or anyone higher in the corporate hierarchy. Barry Oshry has developed a useful perspective for understanding patterns of sense making and interpersonal mush that occur among different levels in organizations.[3] Oshry explains that people's sense making is not entirely random. There are predictable patterns to how tops, middles, bottoms, and customers make sense of one another in ways that land them in the mush and destroy partnership. Understanding these patterns will help you be even more effective in using clear leadership skills to build partnership.

In building partnership with people who have more authority than you, the key things are to show them that you share their purpose and to keep it simple for them. Think of the people lower down in the hierarchy in your organization. Imagine if any of them, regardless of his role, came up to you and described in a one-minute pitch exactly the issues that are top of mind for you and explained that he was interested in accomplishing your purpose. Then he took the next minute to describe what he wanted to do to address those issues and what he needed from you. Wouldn't you be interested in partnering with him? Of course you would. And if you had that conversation with your boss, and you were able to take actions that increased the chances of success, don't you think your boss would be open to a learning conversation when your partnership started to go off the rails? Or maybe your boss really is hopelessly fused and/or disconnected.

Peers and Others

What about people you want to be in partnership with who don't have authority over you? You still need to establish the basis of the partnership, but that conversation probably doesn't feel as threatening. There may be people you work with who are not interested in being in partnership with you. Maybe they feel competitive with you. Maybe they're just mean-spirited. If you've taken the time to really check out your story and have concluded there's no chance, then my advice is to walk away. If you can work around them, do so. If you can't, then you will have to decide how much you are willing to fight to get through them and the tactics you are willing to use. It's your value decision. Personally, I can support dirty tactics if the ends are important enough and there's no other way through, but I'd try hard to find that other way first. This is not just altruistic. If you believe, as I do, that we co-construct the organizations we live in by our actions, then you should recognize that using power plays and manipulation to accomplish your aims creates a world of power plays and manipulation. It's not a one-time deal.

The map I've developed for dealing with adversaries without sacrificing integrity goes like this: I tell adversaries what I am trying to accomplish, how they are getting in the way, what I want them to do instead, and what I am prepared to do if they don't do what I ask. At least when I pull the power play, it won't be a surprise, and they will have had a chance to make it different. It's hardball, but I reason that by acting that way, I am still creating a world of integrity.

How about the people who say they want to be in partnership with you, and apparently do share the same purpose, but, you are convinced, can't have a learning conversation? People give lots of explanations for believing that a learning conversation wouldn't possibly work, and they fall along a continuum. At one end is the person who, when you raise concerns about her behavior, gets so angry and defensive that it's hard for you to stay engaged. At the other end is the type of person who becomes so anxious and apologetic that you can't really find out what his experience is. In some cases, you are triggering their reactivity, as described in chapter 7. You need to back off and think about how to dampen whatever is

Responding to Shame Defenses

Shame Reaction	Disarming Response— Taking Away the Threat
Withdrawal	Nonjudgmental invitation: expressing a sincere interest in their actual experience and promising not to judge it
Perfection	Permission to fail: being clear that you are in this conversation not to judge who they are or how well they did but just to understand the different points of view
Contempt	Acknowledgment of their worth: describing what you value about them and why you want to be in partnership with them
Power	Unsolicited respect: similar to acknowledging their worth but more from a position of deference
Anger	Agreement: describing how you can understand why they are angry and what makes you angry as well
Humor	Patience: telling them "I'm ready when you are" in a nonshaming way
Counterattack	Absorption: saying things like "You could be right" or "That may be true"

causing the reaction. What shame button are you hitting? How can you take the same issue but reframe it to confront for insight? How do they tend to defend against their shame? In the box is a set of ideas for how to respond to a shame defense and get people to engage in learning conversations.[4] Remember that shame comes from their negative self-judgments. They are trying to avoid the pain they feel about those things, so a disarming response will shift their focus away from the painful images.

The more difficult it is for you to have a learning conversation with someone, the slower and more formal the process needs to be. In these situations, a neutral facilitator or coach who guides the learning conversation can make a world of difference.

The longer the mush has gone on, and the more investment you have in the relationship, the scarier it can be to start the process of getting to interpersonal clarity. There is no question that it is much easier to create interpersonal clarity if you begin a relationship with the expectation that you will be clear with each other and clear out the mush when it shows up right at the start. For relationships with years of piled-up mush, however, the cleanup process is fraught with danger. First of all, there has probably been some fusion and disconnection in the relationship. You have implicitly signed up to manage each other's anxiety. If you decide to get clear, you first need to acknowledge that and agree that you won't hold each other responsible for your experience anymore. Second, just the process of acknowledging things you've thought and felt but not said can leave the other person feeling some betrayal and distrust. "Why didn't you ever tell me?" "How could you be feeling that all this time and I had no idea?" This is when a facilitator may be even more important, and it will probably take a number of conversations to get the partnership back on the rails.

It must be acknowledged, however, that a small percentage of the general population is simply not able to take part in learning conversations. One theory is that these people are so damaged that they have no self— they don't have an experience that is separate from yours. Instead, they are constantly monitoring the expectations of others so that they know what they should be thinking, feeling, and wanting. They can't become aware of their here-and-now experience and so are incapable of describing it. For whatever reason, there are people who are not able or willing to be in learning relationships. But they are truly few and far between.

What Stops You from Starting the Conversation?

Once people unravel and confront all their rationalizations for why it's not a good idea to engage in a learning conversation, they have to confront the main reason they don't think it would be a good idea—their own fears. From a totally rational point of view, what's so scary? I tell you my experience, you tell me yours, and we stop making up stories. What's the big deal? Yet when people think about telling the truth of their experience to others, they generally get anxious, and their expectation is that it will make things worse, not better.

I think the main reason we are afraid of having learning conversations is that we've had too many people respond by getting reactive when we tried to describe the truth of our experience. They told us that we were giving them a bad experience or judged our experience negatively. They showed little curiosity about our experience. Instead, they tried to change it or at least get us to stop talking about it.

For some people, the problem has been that they are not very skilled at being descriptive. They talk as if their truth is the truth, lay their judgments on others as though these are revealed wisdom, and respond to different experiences with arguments. But most of the managers who come through the Clear Leadership course are a lot more polished than that. They know how to be diplomatic, yet they still don't believe that leveling with people they want to be in partnership with will make things better. Why is that?

I've concluded that most of the learning conversations people tried to have, when they talked in the here and now and got real about their concerns and issues, were with people they were in intimate relationships with—parents, siblings, spouses, personal and romantic friends. And trying to gain interpersonal clarity is much more anxiety-provoking in intimate relationships than in work relationships. There's more fusion. Intimacy and separation anxiety are much more easily triggered. There are greater expectations that we will look after the other's experience, and those expectations are so deep and ingrained that family systems therapists don't think therapy is of much use in changing them. A manager in his early thirties who had just gotten married took the Clear Leadership course and was very excited about using the skills with his new wife. His wife, however, informed him she was not interested. That was how she talked with her girlfriends, she said, not with him. He was crushed. When I ran into him nine months later, they were no longer married.

I find it incredibly ironic that a relationship's capacity to withstand people describing their real here-and-now experience of each other appears to be inversely related to the degree of intimacy in the relationship. In other words, people who aren't close friends don't usually get reactive when they describe their experience of each other to each other.

It's much easier to just treat the other person's experience like something interesting they happened to notice. They can look at it and marvel at its complexity without getting bent out of shape. In intimate relationships, it's so much tougher to not take responsibility for the other person's experience, to not be invested in that person's experience, to not have your own experience depend on the other person's experience. But in nonintimate relationships it's a different thing. There is much less at stake.

Getting clear doesn't make things worse, because the stories we've made up about each other are worse than the reality. Most managers leave the Clear Leadership course hungry to build the kind of relationships they've created from a few hours of here-and-now interaction with their colleagues. If your fear of using clear leadership skills is based on bad experiences in intimate relationships, I urge you to try it out in your nonintimate relationships at work. What stops you are the negative stories you make up about how others will react to you telling the truth of your experience. But it's much more likely, especially if you make a point of understanding the other person's experience, that work will become a much better place, where you don't have to pretend to be someone you are not, where you have a sense of real connection and partnership.

When Is the Best Time to Have a Learning Conversation?

Evidence shows that people develop a lot of implicit expectations of one another after just a few hours of interaction. A new person comes to work in my department, and fairly quickly I have a story about who she is and how we'll work together. As long as she does what I expect, or doesn't do something I don't expect, everything is fine. But inevitably she'll do something that lands on me a little poorly. Maybe she passes me in the hall without saying hello. Maybe I notice that my pen is missing after she leaves my office. At that point, I'm feeling a little annoyed, but the feeling is so small that no one else would notice.

What do most of us do then? We ignore it and hope the feeling goes away. And sometimes it does. But more often that's the moment when the mush starts to creep in. It begins to build on itself, and it builds and builds until the possibility of partnership wanes or we have an intense learning conversation. Most of the learning conversations I've described in this book are of that nature. They took place way after the initial event that started people down the path of mush. How much easier it would have been if, when that first puzzling or slightly annoying event occurred, my co-worker and I just had the conversation. You see, "problems" usually come from an expectation we've created, a map we've made up about ourselves and another person. We didn't negotiate it, and it didn't come from some deep knowledge about the other person. So if I inquired into her experience early on, I'd learn what part of my map is faulty and needs some adjustment. I'd probably learn that whatever I was taking personally had nothing to do with me. It would be a simple conversation and an easy adjustment. But that's not what most of us do. Why not?

People come up with any number of reasons. I don't want to seem petty or needy, do I? It's such a small thing, why even bring it up? Won't my co-worker have an even more negative impression of me? I don't want to seem oversensitive. And so on. At some time during a Clear Leadership course, all participants are asked to engage in learning conversations with the people they've had this kind of experience with. When people are asked to indicate those with whom they've had such an experience, the anxiety is palpable. As the learning conversations take place, the anxiety turns to energy and a tremendous rush of excitement. People find that the conversations open up a whole set of opportunities for more connection with one another. They come out of those conversations not only feeling better about the initial incidents but having much greater rapport with the other people. It's always the high point in the course.

If you have a learning conversation with someone while the issues are small, it builds the partnership, so that you can handle the big issues when they arise. It creates the expectation that you will clear out the mush as it shows up and helps develop the skills and trust you need to do so. So the best time to have a learning conversation is when you first realize you are making up a story about a person you want to be in partnership with, while the issues are small and easy to handle.

Summary

An organizational learning conversation is an inquiry conducted by two or more people into their patterns of interaction for the purpose of clearing out the mush. When they do that, they learn how they are creating their own experience and can make different choices about how they want to be in partnership. I've adapted a perspective from Ron Short that goes something like this: It is difficult for me to change you, and it's difficult for me to change me, too. But I can change our pattern of interaction in a second if I change my map.

When you bring all the skills of the Aware, Descriptive, Curious, and Appreciative Selves to the learning conversation, you increase the chances that the conversation will be successful. You will have learned more about your own experience, helped other people uncover new things about their experience, and understood your part in the problem pattern. It's more likely that the process will have strengthened and renewed these partnerships. The key factors in a successful learning conversation are to enter with a spirit of inquiry, to fully explore and understand one person's experience before the other person responds, and to follow the experience cube in describing each person's here-and-now experience before every transition.

Conclusion

Learning to Sustain Collaborative Organizations

The requirements of a fast-paced, interconnected world are pushing us in myriad ways to rethink how we live and work together in groups, organizations, communities, and nations, and as a planet. Business has embraced this faster than public or governmental organizations, probably because competition has forced it to. In the postindustrial world, businesses are increasingly based on knowledge work, corporate valuations are based on human capital, and we are entering a period of extreme competition for talent as companies jostle over a limited pool of the people needed to support the growth of successful businesses. Leaders realize they need to create an organization that utilizes the diverse talents of its members and sustains their willingness to commit their energy to the organization's success. They realize that they need to create work structures that can learn and perform simultaneously, and they have responded with a vast array of experiments in flattening hierarchies, empowering workforces, and creating cross-functional and geographically dispersed teams. In the end, all these efforts are about creating the conditions for real collaboration and partnership, work systems in which all are voluntarily committed to the success of whatever project or process they are jointly engaged in.

In the past thirty years, we have also seen an explosion in technologies for creating partnership. These range from the hard information-technology processes like groupware and knowledge management to the

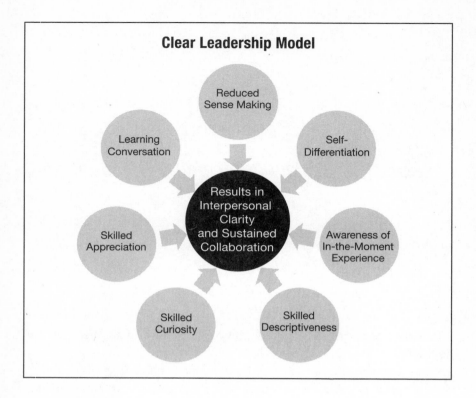

soft organization development processes like future search and appreciative inquiry. We are getting better and better at initiating collaboration
within and between groups, but we have had much less luck with sustaining it. Statistics on any type of partnership, from marriage to team-
based organizations, reveal a pretty poor track record.[1] This book is an
attempt to understand why that is and what can be done about it.

The fundamental premise of clear leadership is that interpersonal
mush causes many of these failures, especially between people who want
to be in partnership. I have tried to summarize the clear leadership model
in the figures in this chapter. The first figure shows the knowledge and
skills required, at a high level, to learn from our collective experience and
sustain partnership. The next figure describes in more detail the processes
that lead to interpersonal mush and failed partnerships. Because our
industrial-age organizational cultures teach us to use a mystery–mastery
approach to interpersonal encounters, we keep the realities of our experience and our sense making to ourselves. Instead of talking about what we

are observing, thinking, feeling, and wanting, our cultural assumptions teach us to keep these to ourselves (mystery) and to try and gain influence over others (mastery). From this older point of view, interpersonal competence and leadership are about being persuasive and getting others to agree with our perspectives and proposals. People who are able to maintain momentum in the face of repressed conflict, smooth things over, avoid creating awkwardness or embarrassment, maintain the veneer of harmony, and get people with different interests to compromise are seen as having good people skills. That works well enough in a command-and-control world, but in a world of collaboration, it doesn't—not in the long run.

Real partnership means giving everyone an equal voice—and that means everyone needs to have access to the same information and be part of the same choices. In a collaborative world, I can't decide for you what you need to know and what's better left unsaid. Conflicts cannot simply be ignored and repressed by the force of authority. Instead, what's required is an ability to get things out in the open and clear the air, to build real commitment to decisions, to develop synergistic teams, and to be able to openly discuss failures and successes and learn from everyone's experience. We need a different set of interpersonal skills that create collective inquiry so that we can learn from our experiences together and develop common understandings. The last figure summarizes the main themes from the book in the set of processes that result in interpersonal clarity and allow people who want to be in partnership, who want to build and work in collaborative organizations, to sustain them.

Through acknowledging that I create my own experience and being comfortable interacting right here, right now, I increase my ability to be aware of each element of my experience and the mental maps that are influencing my experience. By checking out my experience with others and staying aware of what I know versus what I'm making up, I reduce my inaccurate sense making. I work at creating clarity through telling people the truth of my experience while staying differentiated from my feelings and my wants—realizing that I have feelings and wants, but I am not my feelings and wants. I also stay curious about other people's experience, not to take responsibility for it but to ensure I understand it, can provide information they need to reduce their inaccurate sense making, and can stay in partnership. This requires that I maintain a level of self-differentiation in my interactions and not manage my anxiety through fusion or

The Normal Human Processes
That Make Collaboration Unsustainable

PROBLEMS OF AWARENESS	PROBLEMS OF SENSE MAKING	LACK OF DESCRIPTIVENESS
Thinking others cause your experience	Making up stories about others' experience without checking them out	Not telling people the truth about your experience
Not knowing what a lot of your experience is	Forgetting that the stories are stories and thinking they are the truth	Talking about judgments as if they were the truth
Being oriented to what should be rather than what is		Hiding your wants and feelings
Confusing your maps with the territory		

RESULTS IN

Inability to learn from collective experience	Interpersonal mush	Unsustainable collaboration and partnership

disconnection. And it all works so much better if I can sustain an appreciative approach to my interactions—focusing on what I want, expecting the best in others, and seeing the positive potentials that are waiting to emerge. As a result, I am able to create conversations that allow us to learn from our collective experience and keep clearing out the mush, ensuring that our partnership does not fail simply because of the stories we've made up to make sense of each other.

The Normal Human Processes
That Make Collaboration Unsustainable cont'd

LACK OF CURIOSITY	LACK OF SELF-DIFFERENTIATION	LACK OF APPRECIATION
Trying to change other people's experience instead of just understanding it

Not fully exploring the experience of others | Managing your anxiety through hiding your experience when you think it might upset others

Trying to change the experience of others or what they say about their experience

Talking about your experience as if others should be having a similar experience | Focusing on what isn't working and what you don't want

Assuming others have a negative intent

Ameliorating weakness |

RESULTS IN

Inability to learn from collective experience	Interpersonal mush	Unsustainable collaboration and partnership

Three Kinds of Inquiry

Clear leadership is about creating inquiry when our performance or relationships are not what we want them to be, and it's about leading learning in the midst of performing. A learning conversation is an inquiry. Three of the skill sets I've covered in this book—the Aware Self, the

The Clear Leadership Model in More Detail

AWARENESS OF IN-THE-MOMENT EXPERIENCE	REDUCED SENSE MAKING	SKILLED DESCRIPTIVENESS
Acknowledging that you create your own experience	Checking out your stories with others	Describing your experience without voicing judgments about others
Being comfortable interacting right here, right now	Getting clear about what you know versus what you make up	Being transparent but not overly intimate
Working at being aware of all four elements of your experience		Describing your feelings without expressing them
Identifying your mental maps and their impact on your experience		Describing what you want without making others responsible for giving it to you

RESULTS IN

Ability to learn from collective experience	Interpersonal clarity	Sustained collaboration and partnership

Curious Self, and the Appreciative Self—are forms of inquiry or ways of knowing. Given that so many different kinds of realities have an impact on social systems, we need more forms of inquiry than the ones science and technology have given us. Command-and-control forms of organizing tend to reinforce objective truth as the only kind of truth worth exploring. As we become ever more global and diverse in our social orga-

The Clear Leadership Model in More Detail cont'd

SKILLED CURIOSITY	SELF-DIFFERENTIATION	SKILLED APPRECIATION
Making it appealing for others to be descriptive	Not managing your anxiety through others	Focusing on what is working and what you want
Fully exploring the experience of others	Trying to be separate from and connected to others at the same time	Assuming others have a positive intent
Not trying to change their experience	Looking after your needs and the needs of the relationship	Building on strengths
	Talking about your experience and assuming others will be having a different one	

RESULTS IN

Ability to learn from collective experience	Interpersonal clarity	Sustained collaboration and partnership

nizations, real collaboration increasingly requires us to understand how to think about, explore, and validate other kinds of truth—subjective and intersubjective truth. I believe that self-awareness, curiosity, and appreciation form a basis for exploring all these different kinds of truths in organizations and society. In the figure below, I list some of the important differences between awareness, curiosity, and appreciation as methods of inquiry.

Differences Between Aware, Curious, and Appreciative Ways of Knowing			
	Aware Self	Curious Self	Appreciative Self
Is interested in	What's inside	What's outside	What could be
Form of consciousness	Reflection	Observation	Faith
Data collection process	Awareness of here-and-now experience	Asking questions and listening	Tracking
Interpreted through	Sensation	Logic and reason	Imagination
Type of truth uncovered	Subjective	Objective and intersubjective	Intersubjective

The Aware Self is interested in knowing what is going on inside him. He uses reflection on his here-and-now experience to arrive at subjective truth. He interprets the information he gets mostly through his body— through the sensations that tell him that he is correct or that he hasn't quite got to the truth yet. The Curious Self is interested in knowing what is going on outside herself, particularly in others. She uses observation and questions to collect information that she then subjects to logic and reason in order to arrive at a very different kind of truth. The Curious Self operates in the realm of objective and intersubjective truths. While the Aware and Curious Selves are interested in different forms of what is, the Appreciative Self is more interested in what could be. Rather than operating on the basis of hypothesis testing and doubt that is proper for issues of objective truth, appreciation operates on the basis of faith—faith in the human capacity to create any kind of social process that can be imagined and valued. Through looking for what he wants more of and interpreting what he sees through his imagination, the Appreciative Self uncovers and creates new intersubjective truths about the social realities he is interested in.

You can see why these three skills are required for leading learning in organizations. They represent a balanced approach to understanding and describing the truths of our organizational lives. Through these skills, we gain clarity, not just where the light is brightest, but in all facets of social reality.

Creating a Culture of Clarity

The Descriptive Self is about expression, and inquiry needs to be balanced with expression if it is to be of practical value. With these four skill sets in hand, through a balance of inquiry and expression, you can facilitate conversations that create new insights into people's experience and lead to lasting partnerships. These can be inquiries into problem patterns or into the best of what we know. I believe that real organizational learning, learning that changes the fundamental patterns of organizing, happens one conversation at a time. As people learn the skills and accept the legitimacy of having that kind of conversation, they can build an organizational culture that values interpersonal clarity and no longer tolerates interpersonal mush.

People's ability to create learning conversations depends on their skills and character. Whether they will be motivated to try also depends on the kind of culture that leaders create in their teams, departments, and organizations. A culture of clarity requires a set of shared assumptions. Real shared assumptions come not from plaques on the wall or training programs or motivational speakers but from the way leaders behave day in and day out. To create a culture of clarity, leaders have to express assumptions that are consistent with those shown in "The Clear Leadership Model in More Detail" table, and they must act in a way that is consistent with those assumptions. The assumptions, boiled down to their essence, are as follows:

- In every interaction, everyone is having a different experience. We all have a right to our own experience. Each person's experience has equal status, though when it comes to objective issues, some may be more valid.

- If we don't say what our experience is, others will make it up and treat that as if it's the truth. We need to be willing to tell ourselves and others what we are observing, thinking, feeling, and wanting. We have to be able to describe our feelings without expressing them and to tell others our wants without holding them responsible for satisfying those wants.

- We are going to make up stories about other people's experience. We can't stop that, but we can and should check out our stories before assuming they are true and acting on them.

- We create our own experience, and so we are creating the impact other people have on us. We need to stay self-differentiated and not hold other people responsible for our experience. We also need to stay connected and curious about other people's experience so we can clear out the mush before it becomes toxic.

- When we're having unsatisfactory interactions with someone we want to collaborate with, we need to have an organizational learning conversation in which we each take responsibility for uncovering the part we play in creating the problem.

The ability to create a culture of clarity depends on the leader's degree of differentiation in his work relationships. The more a leader's internal experience depends on what others are saying or doing, the harder it is to manage the anxiety of saying and hearing other people's truth. Fear and anxiety, particularly the avoidance of fear and anxiety, underlie a lot of the mediocrity in organizations. People who can create learning conversations are able to contain their own anxiety and act as a damper on others' anxiety. They do this not by repressing or being unconscious about their anxiety but by being less anxious, because they are not in a fused or disconnected state, and by being aware of their feelings without letting those feelings control them.

Life Commitments

After years of teaching this material, I'm convinced that most people can learn the skills and increase their self-differentiation and appreciative mind-set. But although each of the Selves is a set of skills, self-differentiation and appreciation require something deeper. These two are more like ways of being than skills—they require a commitment to living a certain way that people can only choose for themselves. In a sense, each is a life path. By choosing them, you exclude other paths, and that is always one of the toughest things about choosing a path.

If you choose to lead a self-differentiated life, you can't also choose a life in which you are responsible for other people's happiness, or in which you are an island and nothing touches you. You can't lead a life of indifference to your inner world, ignoring the forces of your unconscious mind. Choosing self-differentiation entails a desire to fully explore and understand yourself and the other people you choose to be connected to.

If you choose the path of appreciation, you can't also choose the path of scientific doubt. If you begin from a place of doubt, where other people's goodness, trustworthiness, and so on have to be proved before you acknowledge them, you won't be able to track well. Choosing appreciation requires a willingness to work on the basis of faith, not only believing that something is true even if you haven't already seen it but believing that your choices affect the social world you live in, that your way of thinking about other people affects what you find. If you try it, I think you will be amazed at the power of the appreciative mind-set and appreciative leadership for managing people and change. Without command and control, the old push-and-pummel methods of getting people to do what you want them to do (veiled threats, authority, punishments) are not viable. But leadership is still the art of creating followership—getting people to do what you think is best. Tracking and fanning are, as far as I've been able to discover, the most effective means of influencing attitudes and behavior in collaborative relationships. They work because they increase, not decrease as so many other change strategies do, people's willingness to be in partnership with you.

I am an idealist and I am hopeful. I am hopeful that we can develop business organizations that create wealth, serve their customers well, and are good for the planet and good for the people who work in them. I think the business environment increasingly selects those kinds of organizations for survival. I am sure that the new organizations we are creating will be less oppressive to the human spirit; they will be places where our collective efforts bring out the best in one another. I also believe that business is the greatest force for creating partnership and collaboration around the world, even in places where it now appears all but absent. What other form of human endeavor is so consistently able to reach across divides of race, religion, ethnicity, and language to create common interests and partnership? But I am also sure that the new, collaborative forms of organizing will have their shadow sides as well. It is one of the paradoxical realities of human relations that every new form of organizing contains within it the seeds of its own destruction, which is another way of saying that every solution, including this one, will eventually create new problems. It's one of the things that keeps life interesting!

Appendix

Research on the Impact of Clear Leadership in Organizations

How do you go about creating a culture of clarity? How well do these skills actually transfer back to the job? What changes will you see as a result of managers being trained in clear leadership? Here I want to share with you what my students, clients, and I have discovered to date about the impact of clear leadership skills on people, teams, and organizations and describe how to go about building a culture of clarity in your organization.

The Impact of Clear Leadership in Organizations

Given today's war for talent, researchers are studying why people take jobs and leave jobs, and it's become a cliché that people quit supervisors, not jobs. A lot of evidence has accumulated suggesting that people's experience of their work is strongly influenced by their boss. Considering the nature of experience, this isn't really surprising. In one of our early studies of clear leadership, we took that idea a step further and wondered if, at any workplace, there was a key manager who set the work climate for everyone. For example, if you work at a branch of a large bank, wouldn't your work climate be more influenced by the branch manager than by someone at the larger bank? And if you worked for a company with multiple departments all located in a large building, wouldn't your climate be more influenced by the manager of that department than by the president of the company? To find out, some students and I asked a random group of people if they could identify the manager who set the climate for their day-to-day work experience, and everybody could. In fact, most people could instantly name that person. Since level of trust consistently relates to people's ability to collaborate and sustain partnerships, we decided to study the impact on trust of behaviors we could link to clear leadership.[1] Using a questionnaire, we asked one hundred people to describe that key manager using a set of traits related to clear leadership skills and the manager's level of self-differentiation. We then matched their answers to questions we asked them about their degree of trust toward that manager and the overall climate of trust in the workplace. The questions are shown in the following table. We found high correlations between the manager's ability to maintain clear self-boundaries (a proxy for self-differentiation), his or her level of Curious Self, and the degree of trust and sense of partnership people felt for that manager. Those two variables alone accounted for 78 percent of the variance in how much people trusted that manager, and the Curious Self items had the strongest impact. That is an astoundingly strong result, but not that surprising from the perspective argued in this book. Most people expect a person's character and skills to affect the level of trust others place in that individual. Maybe even more interesting was the impact of this manager's behavior on the climate of trust in the workplace—how people rated their colleagues in terms of partnership. Here the key manager's self-boundaries, level of fusion, Curious Self, and Descriptive Self were all correlated with the level of partnership people described experiencing with their workmates. When we examined the interaction of these variables, we found that the strongest impact on the overall climate of trust was the key manager's self-boundaries and fusion. That accounted for 34 percent of the variance in the trust climate. Look at the fusion and trust climate questions. This study indicates that a manager who "wants to please everyone" reduces the level of collaboration among people in an organization. Without the clear leadership model, it might be hard to understand why that is so.

Items and Factor Loadings for Climate of Trust Study

Trust in Manager

Factor Loading	Question
.868	I can talk freely to this individual about difficulties I am having at work and know that he/she will want to listen.
.855	Most people, even those who aren't close friends of this individual, trust and respect him/her.
.833	If I shared my problems with this person, I know he/she would respond constructively and caringly
.826	We have a sharing relationship. We can both freely share our ideas, feelings, and hopes.

Climate of Trust

Factor Loading	Question
.846	I have full confidence in the skills of my workmates in my part of the organization.
.810	I can trust the people in this part of the organization to lend me a hand if I need it.
.791	Most of my workmates can be relied upon to do what they say they will do.
.774	If I got into difficulties at work, I know people in this part of my organization would try and help me out.

Clear Self-Boundaries

Factor Loading	Question
.793	This manager tends to be pretty stable under stress.
.785	This manager tends to remain pretty calm under stress.
−.686	This manager bases his/her decisions on perceptions rather than facts. (Reversed)
.651	This manager does not get upset over things he/she cannot change.
−.567	At times this manager's feelings get the best of him/her and he/she has trouble thinking. (Reversed)
.551	When this manager is having an argument with someone, he/she seems to separate his/her thoughts about the issue from his/her feelings about the person.

Items and Factor Loadings for Climate of Trust Study cont'd

Curious Self

Factor Loading	Question
.698	This manager seeks to understand me.
.616	This manager invites me to talk about our working relationship.
.593	This manager wants to know what others want.
.402	This manager is aware of how he/she impacts others.

Descriptive Self (Reversed)

Factor Loading	Question
.794	It's hard to know what this manager feels about anything.
.692	It's hard to know what this manager thinks about anything.
.606	It's hard to know what this manager wants about anything.

Fusion

Factor Loading	Question
.748	This manager has a hard time saying no.
.743	This manager is easily swayed by an emotional appeal.
.725	This manager wants to please everyone.
.688	This manager tends to get too close to people.

In another study, we interviewed twenty managers who had been through the Clear Leadership course along with their peers and asked how those managers had changed and how those changes had affected the workplace.[2] The first finding of note was that more than 90 percent of the managers said they had changed their behavior at work as a result of the course, and those claims were supported by their peers. This is an outstanding result when you consider that most researchers conclude that less than 10 percent of training transfers back to the workplace. Another study with a larger sample at another organization replicated this finding.[3] In both studies, these were the three most common changes: people realized when they were sense making and became much more active in checking out their stories, people used the experience cube to get clear about their own experience and other people's experience, and people felt much more empowered to speak up and talk about their experience with those they wanted to be in partnership with.

In the second study, we asked people to tell us how the Clear Leadership course had affected the organization but didn't give them any preset answers to choose from. Their responses are in the table on the next page. Interestingly, the most common response was "improved retention." Some managers felt that the people who worked for them were happier and that they had been able to initiate learning conversations with dissatisfied employees and clear up those dissatisfactions. Some described their conversations with employees who weren't going to get something they wanted and how very different that was when they were willing to be self-differentiated and clear—their employees had even thanked them for their clarity! Equally interesting was the number of people who stated that they had stayed with the organization as a result of the training program (we found a similar outcome in the first study). Some said they had been getting ready to leave the organization but changed their mind because of the philosophy espoused in the course and their desire to work in a culture of clarity. Many believed that reducing interpersonal mush was increasing the overall health and morale of the workplace.

Improved meetings were the most common source of gains in organizational efficiency and productivity. Some respondents pointed to more focused meetings and faster decisions, "but most explained that what made the difference was not having to return to the same issues time after time. Instead, individuals using the Clear Leadership skills were better able to discuss an issue, move it forward with an action plan, and provide ample opportunity for others to continue the discussion if they believed something did not yet make sense. Participants described this process as much more effective and as saving considerable time in the long run. The benefit of supporting or furthering organizational goals came up repeatedly in various forms. For some, it was a newfound commitment toward organizational outcomes. For others, it was a greater appreciation for their part in organizational functioning. Many also stated a greater appreciation for the importance of providing personnel with a big picture or context to help them make sense of their jobs and organizational decisions."[4] In the second study, 95 percent of the respondents said they had

Observed Benefits of the Clear Leadership Course

**Percentage of respondents who mentioned
this benefit without prompting**

Improved retention	38
Improved health of the workplace	32
Achieved organizational goals	30
Increased collaboration	27
Increased productivity	27
Increased efficiency	24
Improved customer service	24

Source: R. Grossling, "Evaluating Clear Leadership's Impact on Individual and Organizational Performance" (research report, Simon Fraser University, 2006).
Note: These percentages would undoubtedly have been higher if we had given people this list of benefits and asked them to rate them.

used the clear leadership skills to manage conflict at work. This is another amazing result and has led me to study the impact of clear leadership on conflict management in more depth.

Clear Leadership and Conflict Management

In another early study, we looked at the effect of the key manager on the climate of conflict people experienced at work, and again we found that ratings of a work group's ability to discuss problems and conflicts and manage differences productively were related to the key manager's levels of fusion and Curious Self.[5] The less fused and the more curious the key manager, the better the work group at dealing openly and productively with conflicts.

More recently I've become intrigued with an emerging approach to understanding and managing conflict. Contemporary views on conflict emphasize either lack of agreement on things like goals and roles or competing interests as the source of conflict. Such views emphasize searching for ways to reframe conflicts so that definitions of goals and roles are shared and/or each party can satisfy its interests. A new narrative approach, based on the kind of social-constructionist philosophy that underpins clear leadership, argues that conflict is a way of making sense of a difficult relationship. We each have our story of a conflict, and once we have defined a relationship as being in conflict, we act out the story.

The narrative position fits well with the clear leadership model. I propose that most of the conflicts people have in organizations are actually the results of stories they've created to make sense of unpleasant interactions. Even though the words "conflict management" don't appear in this book or in the Clear Leadership course, I was interested in learning whether managers change the way they think about and handle conflicts as a result of the course. From the results of interviewing thirty-six managers who had been through the course, it appears that a significant number of them do.[6]

In this study, we asked managers to describe how they had gone about dealing with a conflict at work since taking the course. We asked them to describe how they'd thought about it, what they had done, and what had happened. We reasoned that they could still be using the dominant, interest-based mental map of conflict (popularized by Ury and Fisher in *Getting to Yes*), they could have replaced it with a story-based map of conflict, or they could have combined these two maps in some way. We then analyzed the interview transcripts and found, to our delight and amazement, that not one of them was thinking of conflict in purely interest-based ways. Sixteen had a completely story-based mental map of conflict and how to manage it, and the other sixteen had combined an interest-based approach with a story-based approach in some way.

We looked at the patterns in the way people described the conflicts. The most common pattern (45 percent of participants) was that a conflict turned out to be a misunderstanding between people whose stories needed to be checked out. Another group (24 percent) had completely rethought the conflict and come to the conclusion that they didn't really have one. They had redefined it as either something they had made up or the product of an inaccurate mental map. Even those who described their conflict as revolving around competing interests of some kind believed that their stories of the conflict had to be checked out and cleared up before anything useful could happen. Almost everyone interviewed reported thinking that conflict was a good thing, with 30 percent saying their views of conflict had improved because of the course. Only two respondents ascribed negative judgments to conflict, and 41 percent said that they had helped others resolve conflict by offering guidance or helping them clarify their thoughts. Another 65 percent had actually

mediated or facilitated the resolution of conflict between other people
using clear leadership skills, while 32 percent had attempted to teach clear
leadership skills to people who were in conflict so that they could take
action to resolve the conflict.

These are amazing results. We know that collaborative work systems
need people who can and will discuss and work through their conflicts
and not rely on escalating issues up the chain of command. Why does a
story-based approach to conflict seem to make it so much easier for that
to happen, compared to the interest-based, win-win approach most managers are taught? I think your average middle manager in your average
organization doesn't see how an interest-based approach is likely to do
him much good. To get to a win-win resolution, he must find some way
to accommodate the other person's interests. But as a typical middle, he
doesn't experience himself as having much control over what he does or
the resources he has to do it. Most of his work life consists of trading off
competing priorities with limited resources. He's already being pulled in
one hundred different directions, and trying to engage other people in
win-win conflict resolution is just likely to make his inability to meet their
needs painfully apparent. So instead, he tries to avoid surfacing the conflict and works around it. But a story-based perspective on conflict is
entirely different. He has complete control over whatever stories he's
making up and can potentially change the stories other people have simply by talking about the stories. If he holds the point of view that conflict
is likely to be the result of stories he and the other party have both made
up, he can see how putting a little effort into it might actually resolve the
conflict. And our research shows that it does.

The stories I've been told about conflicts that have been resolved
through clear leadership skills are very heartening. Mostly these are about
conflicts with bosses and subordinates (as well as spouses and children),
but sometimes they are about much larger groups of people. One story in
particular stands out in my mind because it had such a dramatic impact
on the entire organization.

Anile and Carol were directors of their respective units in a community-
based health services organization. They looked after the care of seniors. One was responsible for the care of those living in seniors homes
and one for nonresident care. They each had hundreds of people
working in their units and serviced thousands of seniors in their com-

munity. There were many kinds of geriatric services that resident and nonresident seniors both needed. As a result there were many, many opportunities for managers and employees in both units to collaborate, but that was not happening. Instead, relations between the two units were defensive and competitive. A strong "us versus them" mentality was evident in meetings, memos, and reports. The problems between the two units were visible throughout the larger organization and came to a head when the executive began pushing them to reorganize departments in order to better integrate and coordinate their services for greater efficiency and innovation. Apparently, in meetings between the two groups, people voted in blocs for their side, and the level of tension and conflict escalated.

It was also apparent to people in the rest of the organization that Anile and Carol could not stand each other. They were able to maintain a level of civility in their interactions, but the tension between them was plain to others. Senior managers in the organization were debating what to do about the two, becoming convinced that something drastic needed to be done.

Around this time, Anile and Carol took the Clear Leadership course independently. Each knew, however, that the other had taken the course, and the story goes that during a meeting with senior managers about the need to reorganize their departments, they looked at each other and almost simultaneously said, "I think we need to have a learning conversation." They walked over to a coffee shop and began a conversation that lasted more than two hours in which they unraveled five years of interpersonal mush. It turns out their problems began when Carol strongly recommended that Anile be the organization's representative on a big state commission on elder care. Anile had been furious, thinking that Carol had done this to avoid getting stuck with the extra work. But Carol had wanted to be on the commission, believing it would be a career-enhancing assignment, but out of sense of self-sacrifice and team play she had suggested that Anile represent their organization.

After they cleared up the mush and forgave each other, and themselves, for all the years of conflict and missed opportunities, they started talking about what they wanted going forward and discovered they had many ideals and visions in common. Over the next weeks, they began working on some bold and innovative ideas for how to integrate their departments and produce enhanced and more efficient service for seniors. But it was the changes in interactions between others in the two departments that most caught everyone else's attention. Within months, the old spirit of defensiveness and conflict shifted to a new spirit of cooperation and colleagueship. This dramatic change led to significant improvements in senior care and productivity and to the eventual reorganization of senior care, which was considered a huge success throughout the organization.

One of my favorite clichés is that organizations mirror the pathologies of their leaders. When senior managers are fighting, conflict seems to cascade through their respective organizational units. Developing and sustaining collaborative work systems requires a real spirit of partnership among leaders, and that can be very difficult to sustain.

Creating Cultures of Clarity

Many consultants believe that executive teams are an oxymoron. The nature of executive work makes it extremely difficult for executives to think or act like a team. Barry Oshry has a good explanation.[7] Because of the complexity and relentless pace of executive work, executive teams naturally deal with it by dividing up the work. As people focus on their individual parts, they become more and more isolated from one another and begin to wonder what the other executives are doing. Predictably, they develop stories about themselves and the other people in which they see themselves as doing more work than anyone else. Team members start to feel that they aren't getting enough respect from other members, and trust begins to decline. Because they operate in very different parts of the organization and are working on very different portfolios, they naturally develop very different perspectives on where the organization needs to go. When conflicts emerge over these differences, people attribute them to personality problems, with little appreciation of interpersonal mush and the systemic dynamics that effect executive teams, and any sense of partnership among them falls apart.

Without real partnership at the top, it's hard to imagine how an organization could sustain partnership anywhere else. So the executive team is the logical place to start in creating a culture of clarity throughout an organization. If it's a new team, build the processes and structures that will ensure the mush keeps getting swept away and partnership is built. If it's an established team, it will no doubt need a major cleanup to reestablish the spirit of partnership it needs. People on the executive team who are not able or willing to use the skills of clear leadership must be replaced. That's a harsh statement, but it's not possible to create a culture of clarity with a senior manager who is extremely fused or disconnected and/or has little interest in building partnerships with others. It just takes one person who bullies and scares others to close down a whole group and the entire organization.

The rational way to build a culture of clarity in an organization is to start with the senior team, working on their clear leadership skills, and then waterfall through the organization, teaching the skills and doing cleanup in each successive manager's team. Unfortunately, it's not what usually happens. More often, the Clear Leadership course is offered to middle managers as a leadership development experience, and people are unsure of where the senior leadership stands on these principles. A couple of years later, the senior leadership takes the course, and implementation of policies and procedures that support partnership and clarity then accelerates. Frankly, I've been amazed that a training program could have that much impact. My education, previous experience, and the research led me to expect very little real change from a training course, but tangible changes in organizational behavior are evident in companies whose managers have taken the Clear Leadership course. I am now engaged in a study that seeks to scientifically establish the magnitude of those changes in affecting organizational performance.

Research I've done on the transfer of Clear Leadership training has shown me that changing how people lead is as much about intervening in organizational culture as it is about skill development.[8] Our actions as leaders are conditioned to some extent by the organizational culture we operate in. If you think of culture as a set of collectively held assumptions, then it seems obvious that most organizations will have a set of collectively held assumptions about how leaders ought to behave. If you want to change how leaders lead, you have to change those assumptions. But changing culture is a lot harder than just making a list of what you want the new assumptions to be. Research on attempts to install new organizational cultures based on values developed by a group of executives shows that such efforts not only typically fail but generally result in nasty unintended consequences. Take, for example, the current attempt to install democracy in Iraq.

When we studied transfer of the Clear Leadership training, we found that the biggest obstacle to people using the skills was the fear that others would think what they were doing was unacceptable in some way. They were afraid of being put down and, in particular, were afraid that the language of clear leadership would put off the uninitiated. In other words, they were afraid that using clear leadership skills would violate the organization's cultural norms. On the other hand, transfer of the Clear Leadership training was most strongly supported when people saw others successfully using the skills, had a boss who had taken the course, and were given the opportunity for peer coaching with those who had taken the course. The tipping point in any unit seems to depend on how strongly the key manager is operating as a clear leader and how many other managers have completed the course. When the organization reaches that point, it leads to predictable changes in how people interact with one another. People begin to refer to the experience cube and use it to increase clarity. When things start to go sideways in a meeting, the person leading the meeting suggests taking a here-and-now lap around the experience cube. In small groups, gossip and sense making about others are no longer tolerated. People are expected to check out their stories with others. Managers and subordinates work more explicitly on developing partnership relationships, getting clear on their commitments to joint projects and processes, and opening up channels of communication about their experiences of those projects.

Those who want to create a culture of clarity through Clear Leadership training need to get as many people as possible through the course as quickly as they can and support interventions in the organization's culture. How do we shift our assumptions about people, partnership, leadership, and the way we treat one another around here? How do we make it OK for everyone to be having a different experience? How do we make it OK to talk about and explore all the sense making that is going on? How do we get people to understand that when they tell others what they want, they should not expect to get it? How do we make learning a mark of leadership competence? There are many different ways to do this, but explaining them goes far beyond the boundaries of this book. I'll just close by saying that appreciative inquiry and performance amplification are our best technologies at the moment to support this kind of cultural change in conjunction with clear leadership training.

Notes

Introduction

1. I want to acknowledge my debt to Barry Oshry, president of Power & Systems, Inc., from whom I first heard this definition of partnership. He is the author of *Seeing Systems: Unlocking the Mysteries of Organizational Life,* 2nd ed. (San Francisco: Berrett-Koehler, 2007).

2. I learned this way of thinking about experience from Ron Short and John Runyon. See R. Short, *A Special Kind of Leadership: The Key to Learning Organizations* (Seattle: The Leadership Group, 1991).

3. Those familiar with critical theory will see the influence of Jurgen Habermas in this section. See, for example, Habermas, J., *The Theory of Communicative Action,* Volume 1 (Boston: Beacon, 1984).

Chapter 1

1. K. Weick, *Making Sense in Organizations* (Thousand Oaks, CA: Sage, 1995).

2. E. Jaques, *Requisite Organization* (Arlington, VA: Cason Hall & Co., 1989).

3. S. Taylor and J. Brown, "Illusions and Well-Being: A Social Psychological Perspective on Mental Health," *Psychological Bulletin* 103 (1988): 193–210.

4. D. Q. Mills, *Rebirth of the Corporation* (New York: Wiley, 1991).

Chapter 3

1. Here I am building on the work of Murray Bowen and Family Systems Therapy; see M. Bowen, *Family Therapy in Clinical Practice* (New York: Aronson, 1978). My way of thinking about fusion and differentiation is a little different from Bowen's. For example, Bowen described "fusion" as a characteristic of a person. I am more inclined to see it as a characteristic of an interaction, but I use his labels in order to acknowledge my intellectual debt to him.

Chapter 4

1. J. Harvey, *The Abilene Paradox and Other Meditations on Management* (San Francisco: Jossey-Bass, 1988).

Chapter 5

1. P. Senge, *The Fifth Discipline* (New York: Doubleday Business, 1994).
2. K. Weick, *The Social Psychology of Organizing* (Reading, MA: Addison-Wesley, 1969).
3. C. Argyris and D. Schön, *Theory in Practice* (San Francisco: Jossey-Bass, 1974).
4. Ibid.

Chapter 6

1. This "left column, right column" approach to displaying interactions was developed by Chris Argyris and Donald Schön to help people learn about their defensive reasoning.

Chapter 7

1. I became aware of this while reading Sam Culbert's book *Mind-Set Management: The Heart of Leadership* (New York: Oxford University Press, 1996), in which he calls this process "the artifact of mind insight."
2. G. Kaufman, *The Psychology of Shame* (New York: Springer, 1996).
3. Ibid.
4. My thinking about confrontation was influenced by Bill Torbert's "Interpersonal Competence," in *The Modern American College,* ed. W. Chickering (New York: Random House, 1981), 172–90.
5. For more on understanding and influencing personal maps, see Culbert, *Mind-Set Management.*

Chapter 8

1. D. L. Cooperrider and D. Whitney, "A Positive Revolution in Change: Appreciative Inquiry," in *Appreciative Inquiry: An Emerging Direction for Organization Development,* ed. D. L. Cooperrider, P. F. Sorensen, Jr., T. F. Yaeger, and D. Whitney (Champaign, IL: Stipes, 2001).
2. G. Homans, *Social Behavior* (New York: Harcourt, Brace & World, 1961).
3. D. Eden, *Pygmalion in Management* (San Francisco: Jossey-Bass, 1990).
4. This section has been influenced by the work of Jackie Kelm; see her *Appreciative Living* (Wake Forest, NC: Venet, 2005).
5. The idea of this change process has evolved over the years through collaboration with Tom Pitman. See G. R. Bushe and T. Pitman, "Appreciative Process: A Method for Transformational Change," *Organization Development Practitioner* 23, no. 3 (1991): 1–4; and G. R. Bushe and T. Pitman, "Performance Amplification: Building a Strength-Based Organization," *Appreciative Inquiry Practitioner* 7, no. 4 (2008).
6. I wrote about Kohut's insights into the development of the self through praise in the first edition of this book. Some of that material is also in G. R. Bushe, "Praise and Blessing: The Function of the Leader Archetype," *Appreciative Inquiry Practitioner* 5, no. 4 (2005): 41–43.
7. W. Baker, R. Cross, and M. Wooten, "Positive Organizational Network Analysis and Energizing Relationships," in *Positive Organizational Scholarship*, ed. K. S. Cameron, J. E. Dutton, and R. E. Quinn (San Francisco: Berrett-Koehler, 2003), 328–42.

Chapter 9

1. For more information on appreciative inquiry and links to additional resources, visit www.gervasebushe.ca.

2. R. Fisher, W. Ury, and B. Patton, *Getting to Yes* (New York: Penguin, 1991).
3. Oshry, *Seeing Systems: Unlocking the Mysteries of Organizational Life.*
4. I would like to acknowledge Heather Parks for suggesting this idea to me.

Conclusion

1. See, for example, F. Heller, E. Pusic, G. Strauss, and B. Wilpert, *Organizational Participation: Myth and Reality* (London: Oxford, 1998); and J. Weiss and J. Hughes, "Want Collaboration?" *Harvard Business Review* 83, no. 3 (2005): 93–102.

Appendix

1. N. Chan, "Effects of Differentiated Leadership on Trust in the Workplace" (MBA thesis, Simon Fraser University, 1999).
2. Y. Kanu, "Leadership Development Training Transfer: A Case Study Assessment of Exterior Post-Training Factors of a Year-Long Leadership Development Program" (MBA thesis, Simon Fraser University, 2003).
3. R. Grossling, "Evaluating Clear Leadership's Impact on Individual and Organizational Performance" (research report, Simon Fraser University, 2006).
4. Ibid., 8.
5. M. Radomski, "The Effect of Differentiated Leadership on Conflict Management Climate" (MBA thesis, Simon Fraser University, 2000).
6. G. R. Bushe and R. Grossling, "Engaging Conflict: The Impact of Clear Leadership Training on How People Think About Conflict and Its Management" (research report, Simon Fraser University, 2006).
7. Oshry, *Seeing Systems: Unlocking the Mysteries of Organizational Life.*
8. Y. Gilpin-Jackson and G. R. Bushe, "Leadership Development Training Transfer: A Case Study of Post-Training Determinants," *Journal of Management Development* 26, no. 10 (2007): 980–1004.

Glossary

Appreciative Self: A model of the skills that support bringing out the best in one's partners and partnerships

Aware Self: A model of the skills that support one in knowing his or her in-the-moment experience

Clear leadership: A model of the skills required to lead organizational learning while working to clear out interpersonal mush and sustain collaboration

Culture of clarity: A social system in which people hold a set of assumptions and expectations that make it normal to have learning conversations and seek interpersonal clarity

Curious Self: A model of the skills that support uncovering other people's experience

Descriptive Self: A model of the skills that support making one's experience known to others in a way that enhances partnership

Disconnection: A description of an interaction in which one is not thinking about what experience others might be having, and not noticing that he or she is not aware of that

Experience cube: A model of experience that proposes experience is composed of four elements, and that someone who is totally aware would know, in any moment, what he or she is observing, thinking, feeling, and wanting; instead, people are unaware of a good deal of their experience

Fusion: A description of an interaction in which one is holding others responsible for his or her experience, and/or holding himself or herself responsible for others' experience, without thinking about it

Interpersonal clarity: A description of an interaction in which each person is aware of what his or her own experience is, what the other person's experience is, and the difference between the two

Interpersonal mush: A description of an interaction between two or more people that is based on stories they have made up about one another and have not checked out

Learning conversation: A technique for achieving interpersonal clarity and organizational learning

Organizational learning: An inquiry by two or more people into their patterns of organizing (how they work together) that produces new knowledge and leads to a change in their patterns of interaction

Reactivity: A state, usually driven by unconscious anxiety, in which a person is no longer curious about another's experience and tries to either change it or avoid hearing about it

Self-differentiation: The ability to be separate from and connected to others simultaneously

Sense making: Filling in the gaps about what one knows of another person's observations, thoughts, feelings, and wants so that what that person says and does makes sense

References

Argyris, C., and D. Schön. *Theory in Practice.* San Francisco: Jossey-Bass, 1974.

Baker, W., R. Cross, and M. Wooten. "Positive Organizational Network Analysis and Energizing Relationships." In *Positive Organizational Scholarship,* ed. K. S. Cameron, J. E. Dutton, and R. E. Quinn. San Francisco: Berrett-Koehler, 2003, 328–42.

Bowen, M. *Family Therapy in Clinical Practice.* New York: Aronson, 1978.

Bushe, G. R. "Praise and Blessing: The Function of the Leader Archetype," *Appreciative Inquiry Practitioner* 5, no. 4 (2005): 41–43.

Bushe, G. R., and R. Grossling. "Engaging Conflict: The Impact of Clear Leadership Training on How People Think About Conflict and Its Management." Research report, Simon Fraser University, 2006.

Bushe, G. R., and T. Pitman. "Appreciative Process: A Method for Transformational Change," *Organization Development Practitioner* 23, no. 3 (1991): 1–4.

Bushe, G. R., and T. Pitman. "Performance Amplification: Building a Strength-Based Organization," *Appreciative Inquiry Practitioner* 7, no. 4 (2008).

Chan, N. "Effects of Differentiated Leadership on Trust in the Workplace." MBA thesis, Simon Fraser University, 1999.

Cooperrider, D. L., and D. Whitney. "A Positive Revolution in Change: Appreciative Inquiry." In *Appreciative Inquiry: An Emerging Direction for Organization Development,* ed. D. L. Cooperrider, P. F. Sorensen, Jr., T. F. Yaeger, and D. Whitney. Champaign, IL: Stipes, 2001.

Culbert, S. *Mind-Set Management: The Heart of Leadership.* New York: Oxford University Press, 1996.

Eden, D. *Pygmalion in Management.* San Francisco: Jossey-Bass, 1990.

Fisher, R., W. Ury, and B. Patton. *Getting to Yes.* New York: Penguin, 1991.

Gilpin-Jackson, Y., and G. R. Bushe. "Leadership Development Training Transfer: A Case Study of Post-Training Determinants," *Journal of Management Development* 26, no. 10 (2007): 980–1004.

Grossling, R. "Evaluating Clear Leadership's Impact on Individual and Organizational Performance." Research report, Simon Fraser University, 2006.

Habermas, J. *The Theory of Communicative Action,* vol. 1. Boston: Beacon, 1984.

Harvey, J. *The Abilene Paradox and Other Meditations on Management.* San Francisco: Jossey-Bass, 1988.

Heller, F., E. Pusic, G. Strauss, and B. Wilpert. *Organizational Participation: Myth and Reality.* London: Oxford, 1998.

Homans, G. *Social Behavior.* New York: Harcourt, Brace & World, 1961.

Jaques, E. *Requisite Organization.* Arlington, VA: Cason Hall & Co., 1989.

Kanyu, Y. "Leadership Development Training Transfer: A Case Study Assessment of Exterior Post-Training Factors of a Year-Long Leadership Development Program." MBA thesis, Simon Fraser University, 2003.

Kaufman, G. *The Psychology of Shame.* New York: Springer, 1996.

Kelm, J. *Appreciative Living.* Wake Forest, NC: Venet, 2005.

Mills, D. Q. *Rebirth of the Corporation.* New York: Wiley, 1991.

Oshry, B. *Seeing Systems: Unlocking the Mysteries of Organizational Life,* 2nd ed. San Francisco: Berrett-Koehler, 2007.

Radomski, M. "The Effect of Differentiated Leadership on Conflict Management Climate." MBA thesis, Simon Fraser University, 2000.

Senge, P. *The Fifth Discipline.* New York: Doubleday Business, 1994.

Short, R. *A Special Kind of Leadership: The Key to Learning Organizations.* Seattle: The Leadership Group, 1991.

Taylor, S., and J. Brown. "Illusions and Well-Being: A Social Psychological Perspective on Mental Health," *Psychological Bulletin* 103 (1988): 193–210.

Torbert, B. "Interpersonal Competence." In *The Modern American College,* ed. W. Chickering. New York: Random House, 1981, 172–90.

Weick, K. *The Social Psychology of Organizing.* Reading, MA: Addison-Wesley, 1969.

Weick, K. *Making Sense in Organizations.* Thousand Oaks, CA: Sage, 1995.

Weiss, J., and J. Hughes. "Want Collaboration?" *Harvard Business Review* 83, no. 3 (2005): 93–102.

Index

active listening, 190–193
acts of differentiated leadership, 81–82
advice giving, 173
amplification, 218–220, 222
anger, 185, 253
anxiety: authority effects on, 72; avoidance of, 114; awareness of, 115; embarrassment, 114–115; interpersonal clarity and, 115; intimacy, 63–64, 75, 101; managing of, 67; separation, 63–64, 67, 75, 105, 255; types of, 63–64; unconscious, 115–116
appreciative inquiry, 243
appreciative mind-set: and attention, 208–211; benefits of, 205–206, 265; breakthroughs created by, 206; cultivation of, 203–214; deficit mind-set changed to, 215; description of, 202, 242; gratitudes used to increase, 231; life commitment to, 268–270; requirements for, 234; three-step process used by, 213–214, 232
Appreciative Self: aligning with positive intent, 214–218, 232, 234; Aware Self and, 266; characteristics of, 266; culture of clarity, 201; Curious Self and, 266; description of, 12; exercises for developing, 231–234; fanning, 222–231, 233, 235; focus of, 201–202; models and techniques for developing, 202; organizational learning affected by, 230; partnership creation affected by, 220–221; summary of, 234–235; tracking, 218–222, 224, 233–235
appreciative thoughts, 211
Argyris, Chris, 130, 133
asking questions, 149–151
attention, 208–211, 222
attitude, 244–245
authority: advantages and disadvantages of, 73; bias against, 73; fusion affected by, 72–73; hierarchy vs., 13, 26; learning conversations and, 251; mental maps and, 132; partnerships with people who have, 251; power from, 26–27
awareness: of anxiety, 115; choicefulness and, 142; clear language effects on, 119–123, 142; description of, 94; "fill in the cube" exercise, 110–119; journalizing for increasing, 141; mental

Bringing Clear Learning
to Your Organization

Using the models and concepts in this book, Clear Learning Ltd. creates unique, highly experiential management development programs that measurably improve participants' ability to lead people, organizations, and change.

Clear Learning courseware is particularly valuable for leaders who are building performing and learning cultures and who want to harness collaboration and the spirit of partnership while holding people to high standards and nurturing their desire to excel.

Clear Learning releases only courseware that meets stringent standards. All our courses exceed expectations in providing:

- New ideas that immediately make sense and give participants deeper insight into themselves, others, and situations
- Simple skills that can be applied at work and immediately produce an improvement in performance
- A learning process that has high engagement, high impact, and a high level of persistence

With nearly one hundred certified trainers around the world, Clear Learning provides courses on Clear Leadership; Appreciative Leadership and Change; Power, Systems, and Partnership; and Sustaining Partnership. Competent trainers can be licensed to teach these courses as well.

For more information on clear leadership–related courses,
visit **www.clearlearning.ca.**

Gervase Bushe is also available to provide highly rated talks on Clear Leadership, Appreciative Leadership, Appreciative Inquiry, and Partnership and Collaboration.

For more information on presentations by Gervase Bushe,
visit **www.gervasebushe.ca.**